D1140405

Trinity & All Sai....
ACCREDITED BY THE UNIVERSITY OF LEEDS

LIS LIBRARY
This book is due for return on or before the last date
stamped below

T.A.S.C. LIBRARY LEEDS

209553 7

Understanding the economy

an introduction to macroeconomics

fourth edition

Andrew Dunnett

Longman
London and New York

BRN
111292

209553

Addison Wesley Longman Limited
Edinburgh Gate
Harlow
Essex CM20 2JE
United Kingdom
and Associated Companies throughout the world

Published in the United States of America
by Addison Wesley Longman, New York

330.941 DUN

© Addison Wesley Longman Ltd 1998

The right of Andrew Dunnett to be identified
as author of this Work has been asserted by
him in accordance with the Copyright,
Designs and Patents Act 1988.

All rights reserved. No part of this publication may be
reproduced, stored in a retrieval system, or transmitted
in any form or by any means, electronic, mechanical,
photocopying, recording or otherwise, without either
the prior written permission of the publisher or a
licence permitting restricted copying in the United Kingdom
issued by the Copyright Licensing Agency Ltd,
90 Tottenham Court Road, London W1P 9HE.

First edition published 1982
Second edition published 1987
Third edition published 1992
Fourth edition published 1998

ISBN 0 582 32507 2

British Library Cataloguing-in-Publication Data

A catalogue record for this book is available from the
British Library

Library of Congress Cataloging-in-Publication Data

Set by 32 in 10/12pt Baskerville
Produced by Addison Wesley Longman Singapore Pte Ltd
Printed in Singapore

Contents

CHAPTER 7
The balance of payments and the determination of the exchange rate 111

CHAPTER 8
Exchange rates, competitiveness and trade flows 132

CHAPTER 9
The International Monetary System 144

CHAPTER 10
International aspects of inflation 159

The philosophy of the fourth edition of *Understanding the Economy* is the same as that for previous editions – namely to 'present theory relevant to policy in the real world.' Inevitably, however, over time there are changes in what one needs to focus on. The bitterness of the theoretical debate between the monetarists and the Keynesians which so characterised the 1980s has given way to a more prosaic and more pragmatic approach to economic policy. Labour is in power – until the year 2002 at least – but it will continue with the centrist or right-of-centre policies which characterised the final years of the previous administration.

The fourth edition of this book has undergone some fundamental restructuring, though much of the content of previous editions has been retained. The emphasis on the open nature of the UK economy – stressed so heavily in previous editions – is now so widely accepted that there is no longer any need to force the point by discussing this at the beginning of the book. I have therefore been able to place the chapters on the exchange rate and the balance of payments in a more coherent way later in the book. Whether this makes the order of presentation more logical or not is questionable, but it certainly makes it more conventional. There are a number of other structural changes in the new edition but much remains the same. In a similar way, structural changes are alleged to have taken place in the UK economy itself – and there have been significant changes – but much remains the same. In particular, the average growth rate – the primary yardstick by which the performance of the economy is judged – is much the same now as it was in the 1980s.

In other ways, however, the UK economy in 1997 is very different from what it was a few years ago. The rate of inflation is low. Unemployment is comparatively low and seems to respond more quickly to the economic cycles than it did previously (though one suspects that at least part of this is to do with the way in which it is measured). The current account of the balance of payments is almost in balance (strangely). There is a large PSBR which hampers any attempt to increase spending on public services (nothing new here). The Chancellor, Gordon Brown, has given control of interest rates – the most important instrument of short-term macroeconomic management – to a committee. And the attention of policy-makers throughout Europe is distracted by the requirements of the Maastricht convergence criteria.

In revising this book my objective has been primarily to clarify and simplify those sections which lacked those qualities in the previous edition. Thus small but important changes have been made to presentation. In addition, there are a number of new devices which are designed to make the book more accessible to the reader – to make it more 'user-friendly'. Key terms are highlighted and repeated at the end of each chapter with page references; there are chapter previews and chapter summaries; and the review questions at the end of each chapter now contain comprehensive answers at the end of the book.

Extracts from prefaces to previous editions

This book is directed towards first-year students doing economics either as a single discipline or as part of a broader social science or business studies degree; at those students taking professional examinations (for example, in accountancy); and at students of A-level economics. My experience with students such as these over several years made me increasingly aware that no suitable text existed. The problem with existing texts is that they are either too long-winded and weighty so that students miss the wood for the trees or too lightweight and descriptive with no strong analytical foundation. This book differs first in approach. It is non-mathematical since experience has taught me that the effort involved in understanding the mathematics often stands in the way of an appreciation of the *economic* analysis. However, I take issue with those of my colleagues who equate the use of mathematical techniques with analytical rigour. The two never have been equivalent and I believe that this text is highly analytical, rather than descriptive, even though the mathematical techniques it uses are of the most rudimentary kind.

Secondly, the methodological approach of this book differs from that of existing texts, which tend to be naively empiricist, assuming that we can either prove or disprove a particular theory simply by looking at the data. Moreover, these texts tend to be complacent, in as much as they give the impression that economists understand the way the economy works – whereas, in fact, we do not. I have tried to integrate within this text a more sophisticated methodological position which should allow students to realise that economic theories are no more than *theories*. I have also tried to give the reader an appreciation of how these theories and ideas came to be developed, so that they can place them in their historical and political perspective.

Though I have pointed out the shortcomings of empiricism, I have, however, tried to encourage students to confront their theories and prejudices with empirical data and to this end the book contains a fair amount of statistical material – enough, I hope, to whet readers' appetites to seek out more for themselves.

The over-riding consideration in deciding upon the form that this book should take was the desire to provide a framework within which to analyse important contemporary policy issues. Whether I have been successful in this endeavour is something which readers must judge for themselves.

1 Income and spending

Preview

The model of the circular flow of income is introduced in this chapter. The concepts introduced are fundamental axioms which all economists would agree on. However, if these ideas are extended they then constitute a particular paradigm – a particular interpretation – of the way the economy works.

1.1 A simple model of the macroeconomy

The purpose of this chapter is to present the reader with a number of models of the workings of the economy. For illustrative purposes, we shall first choose to talk about a desert island economy – one which is not subject to any outside influences. Suppose that there are just three people living on this island – doubtless the sole survivors from the shipwreck which left them stranded on this remote shore – and suppose further that each of these three individuals specialises in producing that in which they are most skilled. Individual A specialises in producing food, B specialises in making clothes and C specialises in making and repairing the crude dwellings in which they live. None of these three individuals is therefore self-sufficient, since each requires food, clothing and shelter to live, but by specialising and exchanging their surpluses, each of them is able to enjoy higher levels of consumption of food, clothing and shelter than if each person produced everything for themselves. This island economy therefore possesses some of the features of a real world economy – people on the island act as individual economic units and there is **specialisation** and **exchange**. There is one important feature which we have not mentioned,

1

however. In the real world, exchange takes place by means of transactions involving the use of an acceptable **medium of exchange**, usually money. In the absence of any such medium of exchange, the alternative is to engage in **barter** transactions, that is, to swap goods for goods rather than goods for money. Suppose we make the rather unlikely assumption that on our desert island there is an acceptable medium of exchange and that therefore the inhabitants decide to engage in monetary transactions rather than in barter. Assume that the medium of exchange they choose is coins, no doubt salvaged from the shipwreck, and that the value of coins they managed to salvage totals £10. This therefore represents the money supply in our desert-island economy.

Suppose we further assume that the following chain of events takes place over a given period of time, say one month. Individual A, who initially owns the £10, uses it to buy clothes from B. B, in turn, uses his income of £10 to pay C to repair his hut, and C, in turn, spends his income in buying food which A has produced. These transactions are illustrated diagrammatically in Fig. 1.1. We could therefore say that, in the month in question, total expenditure in our island economy was £30. This is equal to the combined income of the three individuals and it is also equal to the value of the goods and services produced in the economy. Thus we could say: **total expenditure = total income = value of total output of goods and services.**

What is true for our desert island economy is not necessarily true for the real world economy, but the equality between expenditure, income and output which we have identified should be regarded by the reader at this stage as something which is generally true.

It is important to note that total expenditure at £30 per month is financed by a money supply of only £10. The relationship between the **flow of expenditure** and the **stock of money** is given by the **velocity of circulation of money**. In our example this velocity is three times per month, that is, each pound changes hands three times in every month. In a year, therefore, money can be expected to change hands $3 \times 12 = 36$ times, and we would therefore say that the velocity of circulation is thirty-six times per year.

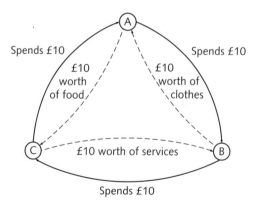

Figure 1.1 The circular flow of income

If the events of this one month are repeated throughout the rest of the year, total expenditure will be $12 \times £30$ or £360 per year and this will be equal to total income and the annual value of output (or **total product** as it is usually known). If we consider our three individuals as comprising the whole of the national economy then we can say that: **national expenditure** = **national income** = **national product** = £360 per year.

Per capita income is therefore £120 per year, but this unfortunately tells us nothing about the standard of living of our three individuals. That is, we cannot say from this information how much food, clothing and shelter the inhabitants are able to consume. We know the **value** of total output but we do not know what **volume** (what quantity) of goods and services this represents. To emphasise this point, consider what would happen on our desert island if the stock of money were doubled to £20. If we assume that the velocity of circulation remained unchanged at 36 times per year, then the value of national product would be £720 per year. This may represent a *real* increase in the value of goods and services produced and sold, or it may simply reflect a fall in the value of money, such that the purchasing power of each pound is only half what it was previously. Thus we should be careful to distinguish between increases in the **real value** of national output and increases in the **money value** of national output.

In many ways our desert island economy is not a particularly realistic model of a real economy. It has no contact with other islands, so there is no foreign trade. There is also no government on the island so there is no such thing as taxation or public spending. A more subtle point, however, is that the standard of living of the inhabitants may well be much higher than our estimates of national product would have us believe. That is because, if a statistician were preparing national income accounts for our island, he would include only those goods and services which were the subject of money transactions. He would thus exclude all the food which A produced and consumed himself, all the clothes which B produced and consumed himself, and the value of all the work which C did on his own shelter. If all of the individuals on the island were self-sufficient and did not indulge in money trade with their fellows, then conventional methods of measuring national output would value it at zero. This failure to take account of **home production** (that is, the production of goods for one's own consumption) also occurs in real economies, but it is likely to be a more serious shortcoming in the national accounts of our desert island.

1.2 A model of production and consumption

Our second model of the macroeconomy contains not three individuals but two *sectors*, a household sector (H) and a firm sector (F). In order to simplify matters initially, we will make the following assumptions:

(i) The economy is **closed**, that is, there are no imports or exports in our model.
(ii) Households spend all their income. They spend it, of course, on the output of the firm sector.

(iii) The firm sector is able to sell all that it produces. That is, firms do not build up stocks or run down stocks.

(iv) The firm sector is ultimately owned by the household sector, because all the paid-up share capital of firms is held by households.

The model, which is illustrated in Fig. 1.2, has a consumption side to it and a production side. The right-hand side illustrates consumption and here we have assumed that the flow of expenditure by households on purchasing the goods and services produced by the firm sector is, say, £100 million per year. Thus there is a flow of spending represented by the solid line and a corresponding flow of goods and services represented by the dotted line. This much is familiar to us from the previous example of the desert island.

The left-hand side of Fig. 1.2 illustrates the production aspect of the model. In our example, the value of goods and services produced and sold by the firm sector is £100 million per year. To produce this, firms must hire factors of production – labour, capital, land and so on – the value of which is also £100 million. This is because of assumption (iv) that we made, that the income of the firm sector (£100 million per year) is all distributed in the form of wages, rent, interest and profit. Wages and salaries are payment for labour services. Rent is a payment to the owners of land. Interest payments are a return to loan capital and profits represent the return to risk capital. It is because of the inclusion of risk capital as a factor of production that we can conclude that the firm sector uses factor inputs valued at £100 million to produce output valued at £100 million. At the end of the day it is

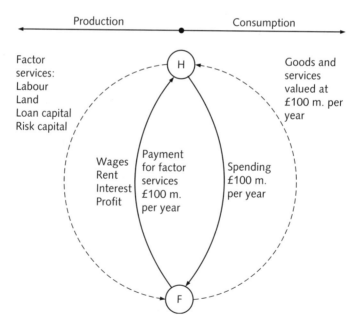

Figure 1.2 A model of consumption and production

left with nothing (that is, we assume that the firm does not retain any profits, it distributes them all to shareholders).

In our desert island economy, we noted that total spending, total income and the value of total output were all equal. Here, too, we see that total spending, total income and the value of goods and services produced are all £100 million per year. This model illustrates the way in which spending flows around the economy in a circular fashion from households to firms as payment for goods and services and back again to households as payment for factor services. No matter where we measure this flow, the size of the flow will be the same.

1.3 Equilibrium in the circular flow of income

Provided the four assumptions that we made in section 1.2 are satisfied, the **circular flow of income** will settle down at a particular level and stay there indefinitely. As long as nothing happens to disturb it, the circular flow of income will remain in a state of **equilibrium** – a state of balance – which in our example is at a level of £100 million per year.

This follows naturally from the assumptions we made. Households spend all their income (£100 million) on buying goods and services produced by the firm sector. Thus the value of goods and services which the firm sector produces and sells is also £100 million per year. To produce this output, firms hire £100 million worth of factor services and the income of the household sector is thus £100 million per year, which they in turn spend on buying goods and services and so on. This will continue indefinitely unless something happens to disturb the equilibrium.

What could happen to alter the size of the circular flow of income? Consider the first assumption that we made in section 1.2, that there are no imports or exports in our model. Suppose we now relax this assumption. If households spend part of their income, say £10 million, on buying imported goods, then expenditure on domestically produced goods would fall to £90 million. Firms find their sales have fallen to £90 million, and since there is no point in producing goods which cannot be sold, they will cut production to £90 million worth per year. Because less is being produced firms require fewer factors of production than they did previously – in fact they will only need £90 million worth of factors to produce £90 million worth of goods. Thus household income falls to £90 million. Figure 1.3 illustrates this.

Provided households do not buy any more imports, their expenditure on domestically produced goods and services in the next time period will be £90 million. Thus firms will continue to produce £90 million worth of output and hire £90 million worth of factors to do so. In short, the size of the circular flow of income will settle down at a new lower level of £90 million per year. This has occurred because expenditure has **leaked out** of the domestic economy. As a result output and income also fall. The level of employment will also be affected by this fall in output. Because they are producing fewer goods, firms will need less labour than they did previously. Therefore, the level of employment falls and, other things being equal, unemployment rises.

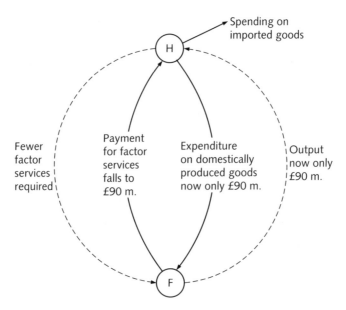

Spending on imported goods

H

Fewer factor services required

Payment for factor services falls to £90 m.

Expenditure on domestically produced goods now only £90 m.

Output now only £90 m.

F

Figure 1.3 The effect of a leakage

We have seen how spending on imports represents a **leakage** from the circular flow. By a similar argument, exports increase the overall level of spending in the economy and raise output, incomes and employment. Suppose firms receive additional export orders of £20 million. They will therefore raise their output from £90 million per year to £110 million per year. This means they have to hire more factors, and factor incomes therefore increase to £110 million. In the next time period, firms will be able to sell £110 million worth of goods to domestic customers, even though no more export sales are achieved. Thus the size of the circular flow of income increases to £110 million and stays there, as a result of the **injection** of additional spending into the economy in the form of export demand.

Spending can be injected into the economy, or can leak out of the economy in other ways. If people save part of their income, rather than spend it, then domestic expenditure will be reduced and, other things being equal, output will fall, leading to a fall in income and employment. Thus saving too represents a leakage from the circular flow. Firms too can save by not distributing all their profits. Therefore, undistributed corporate profits also represent a leakage of spending from the circular flow.

Finally, the government influences the size of the circular flow of income by its expenditure and taxation policies. If it increases income tax, for example, then households' disposable income, or take-home pay, will fall and this causes them to reduce their spending. Thus an increase in the amount of income tax taken by the government represents a leakage or **withdrawal** of spending from the circular flow in the same way as increased saving or expenditure on imported goods.

The same will be true for all other forms of taxation. An increase in corporation tax on companies' profits, for example, will reduce the amount of profits that firms can distribute to their shareholders, whose income will therefore fall.

Government expenditure, on the other hand, represents an injection into the circular flow. Increased expenditure on defence, road building, pensions, unemployment benefit or student grants all have the same effect in terms of our model. They inject additional spending into the circular flow which raises incomes, output, and employment. Additional defence spending, for example, results in increased sales for factories making tanks, stealth bombers, riot shields, army boots and so on. These factories will increase their output and in doing so may take on more labour.

1.4 The model of the circular flow – axiom or paradigm?

One important question should be raised at this stage. Do the models we have presented so far constitute **axioms** or **paradigms**? That is, do they represent sets of ideas about the way in which the economy operates, which are self-evidently true and on which everyone therefore agrees (axioms) or do they represent the views of a particular school of thought, views which are disputed by other schools (paradigms)?

The model of section 1.1 is undoubtedly axiomatic since the ideas which it sets forth are true by definition. Although the ideas of sections 1.2 and 1.3 appear to be simply a logical extension of these ideas, we have in fact introduced what amounts to a particular *interpretation* of the way the macroeconomy works, an interpretation which would be more readily accepted by some economists than by others. This interpretation is what we could call the **Keynesian paradigm**, the key element of which is the *emphasis on the level of demand* as being the factor which determines output and employment. Not all economists would be happy with the importance accorded to the level of demand in this model, preferring to concentrate more on the so-called **supply side** influences on output and employment in the economy. We shall return to this point in subsequent chapters.

Summary

Spending flows around the economy in a circular fashion. In a closed economy, spending, income and the value of output are all equal. The level of expenditure is influenced by the volume of injections and withdrawals. In the model that we have presented an increase in expenditure leads to an increase in incomes, in output and (possibly) to an increase in employment. As we shall see later this will not always be the case, of course. In an economy which is already operating at full capacity, a further increase in demand cannot result in an increase in output and this is a point which subsequent chapters explore.

Key terms

The following key terms have been introduced in this chapter. They are listed here in the order in which they first appear and the page number where they appear is also given. You will find these key terms in **bold** in the text. Each chapter contains a list of key terms and you may find these particularly useful for revision purposes.

Review questions

1.1 State whether the following are injections into the circular flow of income or withdrawals from it:
    (a) spending on imported goods;
    (b) saving part of one's income;
    (c) government spending on defence;
    (d) an increase in taxation;
    (e) an increase in export sales;
    (f) building a Channel Tunnel.
       Does it make any difference to your answer if the Channel Tunnel is financed by the Government as opposed to private companies?

1.2 Does an increase in aggregate demand (total spending) always lead to an increase in output? If not, why not?

1.3 Other things being equal, what effect will a cut in taxes have on the level of unemployment?

1.4 If people buy Fiat cars (assembled in Italy) rather than Rover cars, what effect will this have on the British economy?

1.5 State what effect the following will have on aggregate demand in the British economy, other things being equal (state increase/decrease/no change) and explain why. Also state what the effect will be on output.
    (a) a cut in income tax;
    (b) a Japanese electronics company builds a factory in Wales;
    (c) companies offering consumer credit lower their interest rates;

(d) central government spending on higher education is cut;

(e) retirement pensions are increased;

(f) a military force is sent to recapture the Falklands;

(g) increased expenditure on policing inner-city areas.

1.6 What will be the likely effect on the Florida economy of a hurricane hitting the Florida coast?

1.7 In the UK in 1985 total income was about £350 bn. In 1995 it was about £700 bn. Which of the following statements are correct:

(a) people were twice as well off in 1995 as they had been ten years earlier;

(b) the increase in living standards is of the order of 100 per cent;

(c) it is impossible to say by how much living standards rose if one only has this information;

(d) on average and other things being equal we can say that people were spending twice as much as ten years previously.

1.8 Suppose that everyone became more risk-averse and as a result decided to increase the insurance cover on their belongings. *Ceteris paribus*, would this increased expenditure on insurance constitute an increase in GNP (a measure of the value of output)?

If the same money were spent on gambling would this also be part of GNP?

Is the same true if the same money were spent on illegal black-market drugs?

Inflation: a preview

Preview

Inflation can be caused by demand factors or by cost factors. In practice the two tend to interact and reinforce one another. This chapter also explains how changes in the price level are measured by a price index such as the Retail Price Index.

2.1 Inflation, deflation and reflation

Consider these three words – inflation, deflation and reflation. Which is the odd one out? The answer is: the odd one out is inflation, which refers to prices. The other two, deflation and reflation, refer to the level of demand in the economy.

In Chapter 1 we noted that, at least in a closed economy, income, output and spending were all equal. Furthermore we showed that an increase in spending would result in an increase in income and output. Output was determined by the level of spending – which is sometimes expressed by saying simply that **output is demand determined**. While this is true by definition we also noted that an increase in demand might result in an increase in output in *real* terms or that it might simply result in an increase in the *money value* of output – that is, the effect of the increase in demand might be to cause prices to go up but the physical quantity of goods and services produced and sold might not change. This possibility – an increase in prices – is of course what we call **inflation** and is a phenomenon that is familiar to everyone.

One 'explanation' of the cause of inflation is related to the level of demand in the economy, and it is here that the terms **deflation** and **reflation** come in. Any policy which results in a fall in the level of demand can be described as a deflationary policy; and anything which leads to a rise in demand as a reflationary policy. It is possible that a reflationary policy may also be inflationary, in the sense that it may cause prices to rise, but this is not necessarily the case, as we shall see.

In this chapter we look at how economists explain the causes of inflation. We also look at the difficulties of measuring the rate at which prices are rising.

Finally, ask yourself this. If the words *deflation* and *reflation* are opposites, what word is the opposite to *inflation*? The answer of course is that there is no single word in English – or in any other language for that matter – which means the opposite to inflation. While the Eskimos have thirteen different words to describe various kinds of snow, because they need them, we do not need a word which means 'a fall in the price level' because it happens so rarely. As one economist is said to have remarked: 'The price system only works one way. Up.'

2.2 An analogy with microeconomics

We begin our exploration of the nature of the inflationary process by looking at what causes prices to rise in the market for an individual good or service. Consider the market for *widgets* (a hypothetical commodity much loved of economists, and used by them long before the name was applied to the little gadget that you find inside cans of draught beer). If widgets are not subject to price control then the market price of widgets – the equilibrium price – will be determined by demand and supply. The equilibrium price of widgets will rise if either the demand curve for widgets shifts to the right or the supply curve shifts to the left (or both).

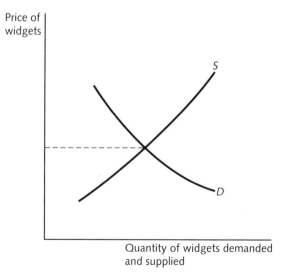

Figure 2.1 How the price of widgets is determined

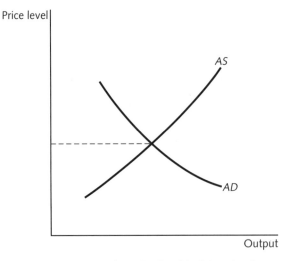

Figure 2.2 How the price level is determined

Now consider widgets to be a **composite commodity** – the bundle of goods and services which the average household buys each month (the same average household in fact that is used to compile the index of retail prices). We can then re-label the vertical axis in Fig. 2.1 as the **Retail Price Index** or the **price level**. Movements up the vertical axis therefore represent an increase in the average price level. By analogy, therefore, rises in the price level can be caused by shifts in the **aggregate demand schedule** – which is the equivalent of the demand curve and is labelled AD in Fig. 2.2 – or by shifts in the **aggregate supply schedule** (the equivalent of the supply curve, labelled AS). That is, inflation can be caused by demand factors or supply factors.

2.3 Shifts in aggregate supply

Consider for a moment the supply schedule. In microeconomics, the supply curve shows the maximum amount that suppliers are willing to supply at any particular price. Apart from price itself, the main determinant of this is the cost of supplying any particular amount, since revenue and cost together determine the profitability of any particular sale.

The lower the profitability of any sale, the less willing will sellers be to make that sale. An increase in production costs will, other things being equal, decrease profitability. Thus an increase in the costs of production will lead to a leftward shift of the supply curve, and to an increase in equilibrium price.

Similarly, in macroeconomics, inflation can be regarded as being **cost induced** when it results from a leftward shift of our (notional) aggregate supply schedule, reflecting an increase in production costs. This is illustrated in Fig. 2.3.

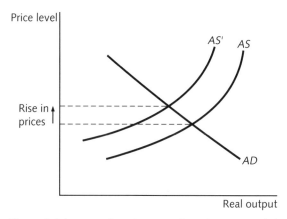

Figure 2.3 Increased costs cause the AS curve to shift

What sort of cost increases could be responsible for a shift in the supply schedule such as that shown in Fig. 2.3? In the context of the domestic economy, the cost increases could take the form of increased wage costs brought about by a situation in which groups of workers bid up wages – so-called **wage-push inflation**. In an international context these cost increases could be autonomous increases in the cost of essential raw materials brought about through producers' cartels flexing their economic and political muscle (the rise in the price of OPEC oil in the 1970s being the most obvious example of this). Alternatively, the increase in costs may be attributable to natural causes, such as late frosts ruining the coffee bean harvest.

Before proceeding with our analysis we should note two important features about Fig. 2.3. First, what we are measuring on the horizontal axis is our widget-based, composite commodity, **real output**. The output of the economy, consisting as it does of millions of different goods and services, has perforce to be measured in terms of the money value of those goods and services – that is, the market price at which they change hands. The problem with this is that the real value of money is falling. Money is a **yardstick** which we use to measure the value of things but this yardstick is continually shrinking. If to measure the length of an object we used a yardstick which was continuously shrinking we could never get an objective measure of the length.

If, however, we knew that our yardstick was shrinking by, say, 4 per cent a year we would know that a measurement taken in 1998 could be compared with one taken in 1997 by multiplying the 1998 figure by 100/104. Similarly, if we knew that the value of money was shrinking by 4 per cent per year we could multiply the money value of output in 1998 by 100/104 before comparing it with the value of output in 1997. This is known, rather confusingly, as **deflating** the **money value of output** in order to arrive at the **real value** of output. Only if we did this could we assess the extent to which real output had changed. (Note that this is a different meaning of the word 'deflating'.)

The second point to note in Fig. 2.3 is that the slope of the supply schedule becomes steeper as real output increases – using our elasticity concept we could say

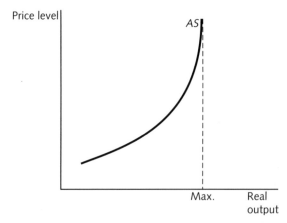

Figure 2.4 The maximum attainable level of real output

that the supply curve becomes more inelastic – that is, less responsive to changes in price. The economic rationale for this is as follows. At any particular point in time the state of technology can be taken as fixed and the factor endowments (labour, capital and land) can also be assumed to be fixed. As output increases, more and more of these factors will be drawn into the production process until eventually there will be no idle factors of production – no **spare capacity** – in the economy. At that point in time, with all the factors fully employed, the economy will be producing as much as it is capable of producing with the given state of technology. Real output cannot be increased beyond this level. We should therefore amend our figure to that shown in Fig. 2.4

2.4 Shifts in aggregate demand

We have just seen that increases in costs can cause inflation. This, however, is only half the picture because the pressure of demand is also important. Just as the price of widgets can rise as a result of a shift in the demand for widgets, so an increase in the aggregate price level can be caused by an increase in aggregate demand. Imagine for a moment that widgets are an essential raw material used in production (widgets have this happy knack of being anything the author deems them to be) and that the supply of widgets is fixed. If the demand for widgets increases (because new uses are discovered for them or because people are buying more of the finished product which widgets help create), then the price of widgets will rise because buyers are competing against each other to secure larger proportions of the fixed supply. Similarly, if we now redefine widgets to be our composite commodity, an increase in the price of this composite commodity – that is, a rise in the price level – can be caused by an increase in aggregate demand. In other words buyers are competing for the available supply and are thus driving up prices.

Before we go on to discuss the factors which affect demand, a further complexity should be noted. Inflation caused initially by demand pressure can be viewed, paradoxically, as cost-push inflation if the focus of our analysis switches from the world economy to the national economy. Consider our example of widgets as an essential raw material used in production. A rise in the world price of widgets can be caused by the establishment of a producer cartel, or it can be caused by an increase in the worldwide demand for widgets. From the focus of the national economy, however, the effect is the same – a rise in the price of imported widgets which increases the production cost of all goods with some widget content. In terms of the national economy, this would be termed **cost inflation**, even though the rise in the price of widgets could have been triggered off by an increase in the worldwide demand for them, and hence, at the international level, the roots of the inflation lay in demand pressure.

2.5 Demand versus cost inflation

By this stage the reader may well be wondering why we have taken such pains to make the analytical distinction between cost-induced and demand-induced inflation. Is it possible to distinguish the two in the real world? Is it possible to have pure cost-push inflation – that is, cost-induced inflation which is not accompanied by an increase in aggregate demand?

To shed some light on these questions, consider the following example of a hypothetical economy in which just three commodities are traded – shirts, bread and haircuts.

The prices at which they are sold are p_S, p_B and p_H and the amount bought (and therefore the amount sold) x_S, x_B and x_H respectively. $p_S x_S$ is thus total spending on shirts, and total expenditure in the economy (aggregate demand) is thus equal to expenditure on shirts plus expenditure on bread plus expenditure on haircuts:

that is, aggregate demand $= p_S x_S + p_B x_B + p_H x_H$ [2.1]

Now this equation is true by definition (thus strictly speaking it should be termed an **identity**). Therefore, the right-hand side must *always* equal the left-hand side. Bearing this is mind, consider what would happen if, as a result of militant action on the part of the Shirtworkers Union, wage rates rose in that industry. Note that here we are considering wage increases which result not from *demand* pressure in the labour market but from **autonomous** increases in wage costs, that is, increases in wages which are independent of the state of demand in the labour market. Will this spark off pure cost-push inflation?

There are several possible outcomes. The increased wages could all be offset by increases in labour productivity, such that *wage costs* did not rise. Or the increase in wage costs could all be paid out of profits, so that profits fell but shirt prices did not rise. If we assume that neither of these two things happens, however, then the result will be that shirt prices start to rise.

Suppose that the government senses this and, in an effort to control inflation, it introduces policies which increase the amount of tax revenue taken out of the system. It therefore succeeds in keeping the level of total spending at its pre-existing level. In other words the left-hand side of equation 2.1 (aggregate demand) is held fixed. But the right-hand side of equation 2.1 must be equal to the left-hand side, the fixed level of aggregate demand. In such a situation an increase in the price of shirts can only result in one of the following scenarios – or a combination of all three. Either:

(a) x_S, the amount of shirts purchased, falls by exactly the same amount as the price rose, thus leaving $p_S x_S$ (total expenditure on shirts) unchanged.
   or
(b) x_S does not fall, but x_B and x_H (spending on other commodities) do fall
   or
(c) p_B and p_H fall.

Consider each of these in turn.

(a) This is the scenario where the shirtworkers are 'pricing themselves out of the market'. Demand for their product falls in direct proportion to the increase in its price (that is, the price elasticity of demand $= 1$). The demand for shirt workers' labour will, therefore, fall as the demand for the product which they produce falls. This, we could tentatively say, would lead to unemployment among shirt workers.
(b) In this scenario the demand in other sectors of the economy falls, creating depressed labour markets and possibly unemployment in those sectors. The shirt workers have benefited at the expense of workers in other industries. They have 'grabbed a larger share of the national cake' for themselves.
(c) In this scenario there is a change in relative prices, shirts becoming more expensive relative to other commodities. The overall price level has remained unchanged, however.

The most likely outcome of the shirt workers' action is some combination of (a) and (b). This represents a fall in the volume of production, accompanied by a rise in unemployment.

We could, therefore, describe this as a *deflationary* situation (note that this is yet another interpretation of the word deflation, which here means a fall in output). Paradoxically, however, what we have here is both a fall in output and employment (deflation) coupled with a rise in the price level (inflation). Thus by restricting aggregate demand in a situation in which autonomous cost increases are occurring, the government has produced the worst possible outcome.

That is why many post-war governments have – at least until 1979 – preferred to act in an **accommodating** fashion, allowing the level of aggregate demand to rise so that the same volume of goods can be bought at the new higher prices. By allowing demand to rise they prevent the fall in sales – and therefore the fall in output and employment – that would otherwise have occurred. If the government acts in this accommodating fashion it is evidence that, even though it may be capable of restricting demand, it is unwilling to do so, preferring the evil of inflation to what it regards as the greater social evil of unemployment.

However, such a policy may encourage inflation in the longer term, because the shirt workers by their action appear to have gained increases in wages without suffering any fall in employment. This will have a demonstration effect on workers in other industries. Thus, the bread makers and the hairdressers will also push for wage increases which, if granted, will result in increases in the price of bread and haircuts. Inflation, therefore, proceeds and, as it does so, people develop **expectations** that the government will continue to act in an accommodating fashion by allowing demand to rise. Thus cost inflation and demand inflation reinforce one another.

2.6 Measuring the rate of inflation

Suppose that we continue to consider an economy in which only three goods are traded – shirts, bread and haircuts – and that over a particular twelve-month period the price of shirts rises by 10 per cent, the price of bread rises by 10 per cent and the price of haircuts by 20 per cent. What is the overall rate of inflation for the period? Clearly, it would be incorrect simply to average the inflation rates (to give a figure of 15 per cent) or to give equal weight to each commodity (to give a figure of 12.3 per cent). What we need is a set of **weights** which reflect the importance of each item in people's overall spending. The weights we use will be the proportion of the average household's expenditure devoted to each commodity. These are shown in Table 2.1.

Thus, the rate of inflation works out to be:

$$(10\% \times 0.3) + (10\% \times 0.5) + (20\% \times 0.2) = 12\%$$

Table 2.1 Weights for a hypothetical 3-good economy

	Increase in prices over 12-month period (%)	Weights Proportion of the average household's spending devoted to each commodity
Shirts	10	0.3
Bread	10	0.5
Haircuts	20	0.2
		——
		1.0

Table 2.2 All items index – parts per thousands (weights used in 1997)

Food	**136**	**Fuel and light**	**6**
Bread	6	Coal and solid fuels	1
Cereals	4	Electricity	21
Biscuits and cakes	9	Gas	17
Beef	4	Oil and other fuels	2
Home-killed lamb	1		
Imported lamb	1	**Household goods**	**72**
Pork	2	Furniture	20
Bacon	3	Furnishings	13
Poultry	6	Electrical appliances	9
Other meat	9	Other household equipment	7
Fresh fish	2	Household consumables	15
Processed fish	2	Pet care	8
Butter	1		
Oils and fats	2	**Household services**	**52**
Cheese	5	Postage	2
Eggs	2	Telephones, telemessages etc.	15
Fresh milk	8	Domestic services	10
Milk products	4	Fees and subscriptions	25
Tea	2		
Coffee and other hot drinks	2	**Clothing and footwear**	**56**
Soft drinks	10	Men's outerwear	11
Sugar and preserves	2	Women's outerwear	18
Sweets and chocolates	13	Children's outerwear	7
Unprocessed potatoes	1	Other clothing	10
Processed potatoes	4	Footwear	10
Fresh vegetables	7		
Processed vegetables	3	**Personal goods and services**	**40**
Fresh fruit	6	Personal articles	11
Processed fruit	1	Chemists' goods	19
Other foods	14	Personal services	10
Catering	**49**	**Motoring expenditure**	**128**
Restaurant meals	24	Purchase of motor vehicles	47
Canteen meals	7	Maintenance of vehicles	21
Take-aways and snacks	18	Petrol and oil	39
		Vehicle tax and insurance	21
Alcoholic drinks	**80**		
Beer (in pubs)	38	**Fares and other travel costs**	**20**
Beer (off-licence sales)	12	Rail fares	4
Wines and spirits (pubs)	11	Bus and coach fares	5
Wines and spirits (off-licence)	19	Other travel costs	11
Tobacco	**34**	**Leisure goods**	**47**
Cigarettes	31	Audio-visual equipment	10
Other tobacco	3	Records, tapes and CDs	6
		Toys, photographic, sports goods	11
Housing	**186**	Books and newspapers	13
Rent	47	Gardening product	7
Mortgage interest payments	39		
Depreciation	29	**Leisure services**	**59**
Council tax/ and rates	30	TV licences and rentals	10
Water and other charges	11	Entertainment/recreation	19
Repairs and maintenance	10	Foreign holidays	23
DIY materials	12	UK holidays	7
Insurance and ground rent	8		

Source: Office for National Statistics in *Business Monitor*, MM23.

This is the principle on which price indexes are worked out in practice. In Britain, the best known of these indexes is the General Index of Retail Prices, commonly called the Retail Price Index (RPI), The weights used in this index are based on an annual sample survey of spending habits, the Family Expenditure Survey.

Table 2.2 shows the weights used in 1997. Note that these weights relate to the average household. Low income households will tend to spend a larger proportion of their income on 'essentials' like food and a smaller proportion on 'luxuries' like restaurant meals.

It is particularly important to note that the RPI is not an index of essentials or of basic requirements needed to live. If this were the intention then certain 'luxury' items, like alcohol, tobacco and hairdressing, would be excluded from the index but this would involve the statistician in the impossible task of deciding what is 'essential' and what is a 'luxury' good. Rather, the index seeks to cover all those goods and services purchased by the typical household.

Summary

An increase in the price of an individual commodity can be caused by demand factors or by supply (cost) factors. Similarly in the macroeconomy the price level can rise as a result of demand factors ('demand-pull inflation') or cost factors ('cost-push inflation'). However, autonomous increases in wage costs – that is those which do not result from demand pressure in the labour market – are often accompanied by accommodating increases in aggregate demand, and this allows the price level to continue to move upwards. If demand were to be held in check then inflation could be checked, but the cost of this would be the higher unemployment that would result.

Key terms

Review questions

2.1 Which of the following could *ceteris paribus* be responsible for causing an increase in the price of houses in Ealing, a suburb of West London. Carefully explain the nature of the causal mechanism in each case, stating whether the mechanism is of the demand-pull or cost-push type.
(a) A cut in tax relief on mortgage interest payments;
(b) An increase in the cost of bricks;
(c) A fall in house prices in Acton (which borders Ealing);
(d) An increase in the money supply;
(e) An increase in wages paid to BBC employees, many of whom live in Ealing.

2.2 Which of the following statements are correct?
(a) An increase in Value Added Tax (VAT) is deflationary because it reduces aggregate demand.
(b) An increase in VAT is inflationary because it increases prices.
(c) An increase in VAT is reflationary because it increases aggregate demand.
(d) An increase in VAT is reflationary because it reduces aggregate demand.

2.3 Which of the following statements are correct?
(a) Cost increases invariably lead to price increases.
(b) An increase in wages will definitely give rise to cost-push inflationary forces.
(c) An increase in wages will *ceteris paribus* increase aggregate demand.
(d) A reflationary policy need not be inflationary.

2.4 In 1974 oil prices rose rapidly. In 1986 they fell. Were cost-push or demand-pull factors responsible for these movements?

2.5 'In Erehwon inflation was 30 per cent in 1996 and in that year an incomes policy was introduced with the result that a year later inflation had fallen to 15 per cent.' What is wrong with this statement?

2.6 In Bogravia people buy only imported wine, cheese (which is home produced) and theatre tickets. The proportion of income spent on these three items is as follows:
wine: 30 per cent
cheese: 60 per cent
theatre tickets: 10 per cent.
Between January 1996 and January 1997 the price of imports rose by 30 per cent, cheese by 45 per cent and theatre tickets by 10 per cent. What was the rate of inflation over the 12-month period?
(a) 35% (b) 37% (c) 15% (d) 47%.

3 The Keynesian model

Preview

This chapter presents the basic features of the Keynesian model, with its emphasis on injections and withdrawals as determinants of aggregate demand. The Keynesian analysis of savings and the multiplier are discussed. The nature of investment spending is examined, as are the determinants of investment. Finally the chapter looks at the way that the national accounts are constructed.

3.1 The Keynesian model in perspective

The epithet *Keynesian* is one which can be applied to much of our contemporary understanding about the way the macroeconomy works. John Maynard Keynes is acknowledged as the single most important influence on the body of theorising which we call macroeconomics. Prior to Keynes even the term macroeconomics itself would not have been in common usage. Rather, economists distinguished between the **Theory of Value**, which we now call microeconomics, and **monetary economics**, thus emphasising their view that in the study of the economy as a whole it was the stock of money which was of preeminent importance. Keynes' contribution was to demonstrate that, although the stock of money was important, it was the *flow of spending* which was even more important.

In the Keynesian model it is the flow of spending – or the level of aggregate demand – which is responsible for determining the values of most of the other variables in the macroeconomic system. As we saw in Chapter 2 it will have an influence on the rate of inflation. But it will also influence the level of output, the level of employment, and hence of unemployment, the level of investment, of savings, the rate of growth, spending on imports – in short, most of the other variables in the economy. Thus aggregate demand can rightly be said to be the single most important variable in the macroeconomic system.

In this chapter we take a detailed look at various aspects of what would normally be called the **Keynesian model**, beginning with a look at demand inflation.

3.2 Demand inflation

Although Keynes' classic work, *The General Theory of Employment, Interest and Money* (1936), also incorporates a cost-push analysis of inflation, it is with the demand-pull explanation of inflation that Keynesians are mostly associated. Consider what happens as the level of aggregate demand rises in an economy which is currently suffering a recession. Individual firms will find that the demand for their product is increasing. Future sales prospects look brighter and the firm decides to step up its production, as it now feels confident that it can sell more than previously. In order to produce more it may need to take on more labour, or to pay its existing workers to work overtime. It may feel so confident about future sales prospects that it decides to increase its productive capacity by installing extra machines.

The spending which each individual firm is undertaking in paying men to work overtime, employing additional labour, and buying new machinery, has a reinforcing effect on aggregate demand, which rises still further. The further increase in aggregate demand confirms the optimistic expectations of future sales prospects, and more expansion of production and employment is undertaken.

There will come a time, however, when the response of the economy to increases in aggregate demand starts to become sluggish. Firms will want to increase production, but they will encounter difficulties in hiring the extra labour that they need. To overcome this they may offer higher wage rates in an attempt to attract workers from other firms and other industries. These rival firms are forced to retaliate by paying higher wages in order to retain their existing workforce. Additional difficulties may be encountered. Firms wanting to expand production by installing new machines may find that there is now a long waiting-list for new capital equipment. The capital goods industries will be facing similar problems to the firms they supply, with rising wage costs eroding profitability. However, with full order books and customers waiting for delivery, firms can afford to increase prices without affecting sales, and this they do as a means of restoring profitability. Thus, prices in the economy start to rise.

In this view, then, the level of demand in the economy determines the volume of production and investment. It determines the level of employment (and unemployment) and, when the economy is operating at full capacity, it determines the rate of inflation.

3.3 The determinants of aggregate demand – injections and withdrawals

What then determines the level of this crucial variable, the level of aggregate demand? There are a number of conflicting opinions among economists about this. In this chapter we put forward the explanation offered by the Keynesian paradigm, and in Chapter 4 we consider the explanation offered by the monetarist school. It should be apparent, however, that most economists would profess to have some sympathies with both groups, so that the versions we shall present of 'Keynesian' and 'monetarist' ideas should be seen as 'ideal types'.

We saw in section 1.3 that crucial to the Keynesian view of the workings of the macroeconomy is the concept of macroeconomic equilibrium. Spending is assumed to flow around the economy in a circular fashion – from households to firms as payment for goods and services, and back again to households as payment for the factor services (labour, capital, etc.) which were used in production. The economy was said to be in equilibrium when the volume of the circular flow settled down at some particular level and stayed there. Equilibrium was maintained as long as the spending which leaked out of the system in the form of savings, spending on imports and tax payments, was matched by an exactly equal volume of injections – investment, government spending and export sales.

In symbols we could write that the condition for equilibrium is: $J = W$, that is, injections should be equal to withdrawals or: $S + M + T = I + X + G$, that is, savings, spending on imports and tax payments should be equal to new investment, export receipts and government spending.

When people spend their income on buying domestically produced goods they are creating income for the firms who make those goods. The firms use that income to pay their workforce, their suppliers, and their shareholders, who thus receive income, which they in turn spend. Now consider what would happen if, instead of spending all their income on domestically produced goods, they spent part of it on imports. This spending does not create income for domestic firms, who therefore suffer a fall in income. Payments to their shareholders, their workforce, and their suppliers will therefore be reduced. Since these groups will have suffered a fall income, they in turn will reduce their spending, and so on. In theory this process would continue and a new equilibrium would be reached at a lower level of national income since, in each successive spending-round, the size of the fall in spending will become less and less.

Suppose on average people spend 80p out of their last £1 of income. Let us suppose that income drops by £1 as a result of the initiating rise in imports. Consumption therefore falls by 80p, and this means domestic incomes will be reduced by 80p. In the next round, consumption will fall by 64p (80 per cent of 80p), implying a similar fall in domestic incomes. In the following round consumption falls again, as does income, but this time by 51.2p (80 per cent of 64p), and so on. This process continues through successive rounds until the fall in consumption and income becomes infinitely small, at which point the level of income will have reached its new equilibrium.

The overall drop in national income (that is, the change in the equilibrium level) which is brought about by the initial withdrawal will, however, be larger than the size of the initial withdrawal. This is the so-called **multiplier effect**. A change in the volume of injections or withdrawals will produce a larger change in aggregate demand once the changes have fully worked through the system.

In the Keynesian model, the impact on aggregate demand of an increase in withdrawals is the same whether this withdrawal takes the form of a rise in savings, an increase in spending on imported goods or an increase in taxes. Thus spending on imports is just one particular type of leakage from the system, and is analytically indistinguishable from other types of leakage. Similarly, in the simple Keynesian model an injection of additional investment will have the same effect as additional government spending or indeed of export demand. Each of the three forms of injection will have a similar impact in terms of raising the equilibrium level of income.

3.4 The manipulation of aggregate demand: the budget

The level of aggregate demand in the economy can be manipulated by the government. If it increases income tax this will reduce people's **disposable income** (or 'take-home' pay) and therefore reduce their ability to spend. This will lead to a fall in spending. On the other hand, if the government increases its spending (say, on education or roads or pensions) then this will increase incomes (of teachers, road-builders and pensioners) and therefore lead to an increase in spending.

The overall level of government spending relative to its revenue from taxation is known as its **budget stance**.

If government spending exceeds government tax revenue, this is said to be a **budget deficit**. There is thus a net addition to aggregate demand since the government takes out of the economy (in the form of taxation) less than it puts back (in the form of government spending). Such a budget is sometimes described as reflationary, which simply means that it adds to aggregate demand.

When government spending equals total tax revenue, this is said to be a **balanced budget**, and when tax revenues exceed government spending the budget is in **surplus**. A budget surplus is described as deflationary in the sense that it reduces aggregate demand.

3.5 A methodological note: an alternative view of the macroeconomy

We noted at the beginning of this chapter the extent to which Keynesian ideas transformed the way we view the workings of the macroeconomy. The concept of injections and withdrawals, of equilibrium in the circular flow, of the multiplier – all these ideas we owe to Keynes.

A word of warning, however. One should guard against the temptation of regarding Keynes as some sort of Messiah sent to show men – and particularly the pre-Keynesian or classical economists – the error of their ways. Although Keynes is often presented in this light, there is a two-fold danger in so doing. First, it encourages us to believe that the classical economists were fools and thus prevents us from trying to understand their view of the world. Second, it encourages the belief that Keynesian economics is correct, whilst the economics which preceded it was incorrect. That is, it leads us to accept uncritically that the Keynesian view of the world is, in some sense, 'true'. This is a very dangerous epistemological position.

What Keynes did was to present a way of analysing the workings of the macroeconomy. He provided a *theory* about the way the economy worked. Since his death in 1946, this has proved to be an enormously useful way of looking at the economy, and of controlling it. But this success should not obscure from us the fact that the economy will forever remain to us a **black box**, the workings of which we can never see. The black box sends out signals – prices are rising, unemployment is falling and so on – but we can never really know what causes these things to happen. All we can do is to construct **models** whose purpose is to simulate the behaviour of the real economy. The suitability of the models will be judged by the extent to which they appear to be able to simulate accurately what has happened in the real world, and what will happen in the future. If the simulations are realistic then we can say that the real world must be like our model. The **causal relationships** which we cannot see but which exist within the black box must be like the causal relationships of our theory.

In order to illustrate more clearly the point that Keynesian theory is nothing more than a *theory* about the way the world works, and in order to put Keynes' ideas into some sort of perspective, it is useful to investigate briefly some aspects of the classical system which the Keynesian revolution overthrew.

3.6 The classical view

For the **classical economists** – those that predated Keynes – the analysis of the macroeconomy relied heavily on what we now call demand and supply analysis.

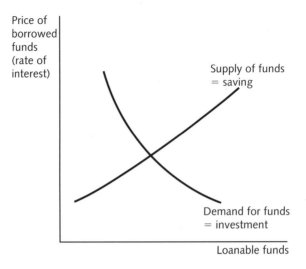

Figure 3.1 The market for loanable funds

This is clearly seen in the way in which they explained the behaviour of savings, investment and the rate of interest.

The rate of interest is the price of borrowed funds. For the classical economists it was natural to argue that this price would be determined by the interaction of the supply of these funds and the demand for them. The supply of loanable funds must come from income not consumed, that is, from savings. Similarly, the demand for funds comes from persons and businesses wishing to undertake investment in some project. In the classical system, the flow of savings is always matched by an exactly equal flow of investment, and this equality is assured by movements in the interest rate. Therefore, provided the government balances its budget (government spending = government tax revenuess) and that some mechanism ensures that the flow of imports is matched by an approximately equal flow of exports, then there can never be a situation in which there is a net withdrawal of spending from the circular flow or a net injection of spending into the circular flow. The spending which leaks out of the economy in the form of savings is always injected back into the economy in the form of an exactly equal volume of investment.

In our discussion of the Keynesian system, we saw how an increase in savings (a leakage of spending) will lead to a fall in aggregate demand. In the classical system, this does not happen because an increase in the volume of savings will cause interest rates to fall and thus encourage extra investment.

In Fig. 3.2, the increase in savings is shown by a shift in the savings function, reflecting a change in attitudes towards saving. This causes a movement along the investment schedule, as interest rates drop.

This analysis of the workings of the macroeconomy has a kind of faultless logic. Keynes attacked it, however, not because it was logically inconsistent, but because it

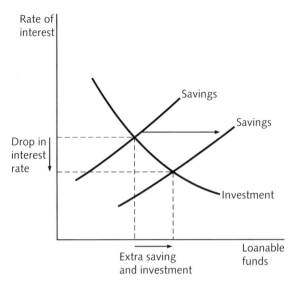

Figure 3.2 Increased savings cause interest rates to fall

was unrealistic. Savings behaviour, he argued, will not be much influenced by the rate of interest, and the decision to invest will depend upon other factors in addition to the rate of interest.

3.7 The Keynesian view – the behaviour of savings and investment

Savings are the residual element of income which is left over when consumption plans are satisfied. As such, the decision to save and the decision to consume were, for Keynes, two aspects of the same thing. Thus, if we have a satisfactory explanation of consumption behaviour, we also have an explanation of savings behaviour. This is what Keynes provided in his famous **consumption function** hypothesis. The consumption function is one of the cornerstones of the Keynesian system which has proved a fertile area for much subsequent work, both theoretical and empirical. For Keynes, the basic determinant of consumption (and thus of savings) was current income, and he specified the form of the relationship between the two. We look at this in more detail in section 3.13.

    Investment is undertaken by firms in the expectation that this expenditure will yield a rate of return in excess of the cost of the funds (that is, the market rate of interest). Thus, the level of investment spending is affected by interest rates, but it also depends upon future sales prospects. If entrepreneurs are optimistic about the future, they will invest now in order to increase their manufacturing capacity so that they can produce a larger volume of output which, they believe, they will be able to sell in the future. If they are apprehensive about future sales prospects they may defer the decision to invest, preferring not to risk the consequences of a decision which results in surplus productive capacity. We discuss the nature of investment spending in more detail in section 3.8.

It is important to note that the decision to save and the decision to invest are in the hands of different individuals. Saving is done by private individuals, whereas investment is undertaken by firms. There is no mechanism which ensures equality between the amount of saving which individuals plan to do and the amount of investment which firms plan to undertake.

If individuals decide to save more this releases resources from consumption. These resources may be taken up and used by firms to add to the stock of capital goods (that is, used for investment purposes). In this case, both savings and investment increase.

But what if investment does not increase, following a rise in savings? In this case aggregate demand will fall and the resources released from producing consumer goods will lie idle, causing the economy to go into recession. Clearly, then, the levels of savings and investment are vital elements in determining the overall level of activity in the economy, and we devote the next two sections (3.8 and 3.9) to a detailed examination of the determinants of these two variables.

3.8 The nature of investment

Up to now we have been using the term 'investment' without explaining exactly what is meant by it. There are in fact several different meanings of the word 'investment' and the rather cavalier attitude regarding the usage of the word – even among economists – is no doubt partly responsible for the confusion surrounding it.

Both consumption and investment are components of aggregate demand. They are both spending, which creates income for someone else. The distinction between consumption spending and investment spending is in practice not very clear cut, owing a good deal to accounting conventions rather than to any analytical distinctions. Nevertheless, the convention is to treat them as though they were different types of spending.

To understand the meaning of the concept of investment in macroeconomics, it is helpful to think of a closed economy (that is, one in which there are no imports or exports) and in which there is no government sector (that is, there is no government spending or taxation). In such an economy, we say there are just two sectors – the household sector and the firm sector. Although most individuals participate in both sectors, the two sectors are *analytically* distinct. The household sector consumes goods and services produced by the firm sector. Households derive their income by selling factor services to firms, and the firms pay the households in the form of wages and salaries, interest, dividends and rent. The households themselves are the ultimate owners of all the factors of production (labour, capital and land) because the firms themselves are ultimately owned by households. The firms merely buy in factors of production (raw materials, labour services, capital services and so on) and convert these inputs into an output which is valued more highly then the inputs (assuming the firm makes a profit). The excess of total revenues over total costs – the firm's profit – then accrues to the owners of the firm, the household sector.

The value of the total output of such an economy – or **national product** – can be calculated by the sum of the **values added** by each firm. This avoids the double-counting which would otherwise occur when firms buy factors of production from other firms. From the point of view of the economy as a whole, the contribution to total output made by an individual firm is equal to the value of its sales less the cost of factors of production bought in from other firms – in other words, its value added. The sum of all the values added is equal to the value of national product.

Now, the goods and services produced in an economy in a given year must be either consumed during that year or else they must be added to the stock of physical assets. Thus we can write that the value of national product (Y) must be equal to the sum of consumption expenditure (C) plus investment expenditure (I) where the term 'investment expenditure' should be taken to mean an addition to the stock of capital goods. Thus:

$$Y = C + I \qquad [3.1]$$

It is in this restricted sense that the term 'investment' should be interpreted in macroeconomics. Investment is any act of expenditure which adds to the **capital stock** of the economy. If an individual purchases shares, or antiques, or a country cottage, this does *not* constitute investment from a macroeconomic point of view. It merely represents a change of ownership. The stock of capital possessed by society remains unchanged.

Moreover, investment stands in direct contrast to consumption. Investment represents **forgone consumption**. The act of investment is one in which the purchaser abstains from *current* consumption in order to increase the economy's productive potential, and hence the possibilities for *future* consumption.

3.9 Fixed capital formation and inventory investment

Up to now we have been talking about investment as an addition to the stock of capital, and this **fixed capital formation** does, in fact, make up the vast bulk of investment expenditures. However, a small part of what is classified as investment expenditure takes the form of **inventory investment** – the building up of stocks of finished goods or raw materials. This may be a voluntary act or it may be the unintended consequence of an unexpected fall in sales, which then leaves the producer with more unsold goods than he or she planned to hold.

That this should be treated as investment can be seen when we recall our earlier statement that all the goods and services produced in an economy in a given year must be either consumed during that year or added to the stock of capital goods in the economy. We can now see that this statement is not entirely correct. It is true that all the goods and services produced in a given year must be either consumed or they must add to the stock of fixed capital but there is a third possibility – that they remain unsold. This third category represents inventory investment. From a macroeconomic viewpoint, it makes no difference whether the increase in stocks is of raw materials bought in from other firms, or work-in-progress, or finished goods. In every case it represents output of the firm sector which has *not yet been consumed* or added to the stock of fixed capital.

3.10 Gross and net investment

When we look at fixed capital formation we have to be careful to distinguish between **gross investment** and **net investment**. Part of the capital stock is used up in the process of production, simply because the machines used to produce that output will wear out, in the same way that a car wears out with use. Investment purchasing may serve simply to replace the capital used up in the process of production. Such expenditure would then be termed **replacement investment** and it does not increase the size of the capital stock. The capital stock will only increase if gross investment (that is, total investment) exceeds the amount required to replace the capital used up. That is, the size of the capital stock only increases if there is a positive amount of *net investment*, in addition to *replacement investment*.

3.11 The treatment of investment in the national accounts

This then is the concept of investment in macroeconomics. In practice, however, in the national accounts, the classification of expenditure into the investment category and other categories may be somewhat arbitrary.

First, because of the way in which the national accounts are prepared, investment is only capable of being undertaken by the firm sector. Thus, if a firm purchases a new car for one of its sales force, or a new computer, this is regarded as investment expenditure. If a private individual purchases the same items, this is regarded as consumption expenditure. The underlying motive for these purchases is the same in both cases – the acquisition of a capital asset which will yield a stream of useful services throughout the life of that asset. The only difference between the two cases is that, in the former, the acquisition of these assets is supposed to increase the economy's capacity to produce marketable goods and services, whereas in the latter case, even though the individual's capacity for self-gratification may be increased by the acquisition of these assets, the individual is not able to sell the increased satisfaction that he or she derives.

The distinction between the firm sector and the household sector is, of course, blurred when one considers the self-employed. Here individuals may choose, for tax reasons, to change their status from that of a private individual to that of a company, and thus any acquisition of capital assets they undertake which are relevant to their livelihood would be reclassified accordingly.

Nothing that has been said should be construed as implying that there is no clear analytical distinction between investment expenditure and consumption. Such an analytical distinction does exist, but it is difficult to apply in practice. Much expenditure, of course, could be construed as both consumption and investment. Perhaps the best example of this is expenditure on education, particularly higher education. It is enjoyed for its own sake, and thus represents consumption, but it also raises the earning power of the educated individual. Since the individual has to forgo earnings and thus consumption while acquiring education, we can thus legitimately talk about the individual *investing* in education. The role of educational spending as investment has been recognised for many years by economists and numerous studies have attempted to calculate the **rate of return** from it. Some studies have shown that this rate of return is substantial and this was used to justify the proposals to charge tuition fees for students at university, announced by the Government in 1997. However, it is worth noting that some recent studies have claimed that the rate of return, in terms of augmented future earnings, is rather low.

3.12 The determinants of investment

Having spent some time discussing the nature of investment, we now turn to an analysis of investment behaviour, taken here to mean expenditure on fixed capital formation.

A feature possessed by most items of capital equipment is that they have a purchase price in excess of the value of the output they can produce in any one year. Suppose, for example, that a machine whose purchase price is £3000 can produce goods valued at £1000 in each year of its life. If this is generally true for all machines in the economy, we say that the **capital-output ratio** is 3:1.

Now consider a situation in which a firm is currently employing all its productive capacity to meet the demand for its product. Suppose further that on the basis of forecasts the company anticipates an increase in the demand for their product next year which will enable them to sell an additional £1000 worth of output. In order to meet this demand, they will have to invest £3000 this year. This, of course, is in addition to any investment expenditure they would have to undertake to replace capital used up in the process of production – that is, the £3000 represents *net investment*. We can therefore say that net investment this year will be three times the anticipated rise in sales next year.

Now, the question remains: on what does the firm base its expectations of future sales prospects? The simplest explanation is to say that the company will base their forecasts on what has happened in the most recent past – if sales this year have been rising, they will anticipate a similar rise next year.

Thus, we formulate what is known as the simple **accelerator model** of investment behaviour:

$$I_t = \alpha(Y_t - Y_{t-1}) = \alpha\Delta Y_t \qquad\qquad [3.2]$$

where I_t stands for net investment this year, $(Y_t - Y_{t-1})$ stands for the growth in sales this year (that is, the difference between the level of sales this year and the level last year), and α stands for the accelerator coefficient, in this case 3. (Δ is the Greek letter delta which is used to mean 'change in'.)

Keynes based his analysis of the determinants of aggregate investment around an accelerator model such as this. The key factor to note is that the model suggests that investment spending will be very *volatile*, since small changes in output (Y) produce much larger changes in net investment (I).

It is easy to see from equation [3.2] that if there is no growth in output ($\Delta Y = 0$) then net investment will also be zero. Furthermore, if the economy experiences a downturn, so that output this year is less than output last year (that is, ΔY is negative), then net investment will be negative. What this means is that gross investment will be insufficient to replace the capital used up in the process of production. In other words, the capital stock will be run down.

In practice, accelerator models are only moderately successful in predicting investment behaviour. As Keynes acknowledged, investment will also be affected by the rate of interest and, by extending our example, we can see how the cost of funds will affect the profitability of an investment project and hence determine whether or not it is undertaken.

Suppose the machine in our example has a life of four years, after which time it is scrapped. The total value of its output, it would appear, is £4000 and, since this exceeds the purchase price of £3000, the investment yields a profit of £1000 and therefore must be worth undertaking. This argument is incorrect, however, since if the £3000 had been deposited in a bank for four years it would have earned interest over this period. The real profitability of the project should therefore take account of the interest cost of the funds tied up in the project.

To appraise the profitability of the project properly we should calculate its **Net Present Value (NPV)**. Let us simplify the real world somewhat and assume that the time profile of the investment is like that shown in Fig. 3.3.

The initial cost of the investment accrues at the beginning of year one. The revenues which the investment generates will, in practice, accrue continuously

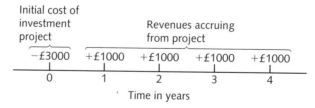

Figure 3.3 The Net Present Value of an investment project

throughout the next four years, but for simplicity we assume that they occur in four discrete lumps, the first at the end of year one and the last at the end of year four.

Because these revenues occur in the future they have to be **discounted**, that is, they should be valued less highly than if they had occurred earlier. Take, for example, the revenue of £1000 accruing at the end of year one. If the revenue had been received at the beginning of year one instead of at the end, then it could have been reinvested (by lending it to a bank, for example) and by the end of the twelve-month period the compound interest it would have earned would have increased its value to: £1000 × (1 + r), where r is the rate of interest that such funds could typically earn in a bank or some other low-risk alternative.

Therefore, the **present value** of £1000 accruing in twelve months' time

must be: $\dfrac{£1000}{1 + r}$

This is intuitively obvious, since $\dfrac{£1000}{1 + r}$ invested in a bank for twelve months will be worth:

$\dfrac{£1000}{1 + r} \times (1 + r) = £1000$ in twelve months' time.

Similarly, the present value of the £1000 which accrues at the end of year two must be:

$$\frac{£1000}{(1 + r)(1 + r)} = \frac{£1000}{(1 + r)^2}$$

since the value of this sum of money if invested for two years would be:

$$\frac{£1000}{(1 + r)(1 + r)} \times (1 + r)(1 + r) = £1000$$

Thus we can write that the present value of the future stream of revenues from the project is equal to:

$$\frac{£1000}{1 + r} + \frac{£1000}{(1 + r)^2} + \frac{£1000}{(1 + r)^3} + \frac{£1000}{(1 + r)^4}$$

A few minutes' work with a calculator will confirm that when r = 12 per cent this is approximately equal to £3037, so that the NPV is £37 (that is, the discounted stream of future revenues minus the initial capital cost). However, when r rises to 13 per cent the NPV falls to minus £25.

Any investment project which has a positive NPV will be worth undertaking since, in effect, it gives the firm a greater return than it could obtain by simply lending its money to the bank. But the NPV depends upon the rate used to discount future revenues and this rate is equal to the market rate of interest. As the market rate of interest rises, therefore, the NPV of a project will fall, and if it falls so much that it becomes negative the project will no longer be profitable and will be shelved. Thus, a rise in the rate of interest will reduce the amount of investment in the economy.

We can restate this conclusion in a slightly different way. It is easy to see that, in our example, there must be some rate of discount, somewhere between 12 and 13 per cent, that makes the NPV exactly equal to zero. This rate of discount is called the **Internal Rate of Return (IRR)** of the project. Now, as long as the *internal* rate of return exceeds the *external* rate of return (the cost of funds in the market generally), the investment will be worth undertaking. On the other hand, if the IRR is less than the market rate of interest, the investment will not be undertaken.

At any point in time there will be some marginal investment projects whose IRR just exceeds the market rate of interest. As the market rate of interest rises, these projects will become unprofitable and will be shelved. Thus, aggregate investment in fixed capital formation falls as interest rates rise.

3.13 Savings behaviour – the consumption function

For Keynes, as we saw, the basic determinant of consumption (and thus also of the level of savings) was current income. Consumption spending, he argued, would rise as income rose. His hypothesis was that, for most individuals consumption spending rises as income rises, though in general the rise in consumption is not as great as the rise in income. In other words, people tend to save part of their increased income. A particularly simple form of functional relationship which is consistent with these assumptions is:

$$C = a + bY \qquad\qquad [3.3]$$

where C is consumption spending, Y is income, and a and b are the parameters of the equation. To be consistent with Keynes' assumptions, a should be a positive number and b should be a positive fraction.

Although the assumptions Keynes made seem naive (particularly the assumption that people save part of their increased income!) a simple model of consumption behaviour of this form provides a starting point for the more sophisticated models of consumer behaviour which have developed out of it. Moreover, and most importantly, it provides the basis for the analysis of the multiplier, explained in the next section

3.14 The multiplier

In the consumption function equation, b is the **marginal propensity to consume (mpc)**. It measures the proportion of any increased income which is consumed.

The remaining fraction $(1-b)$ is saved, hence $(1-b)$ is known as the **marginal propensity to save** (**mps**).

To illustrate this, consider a simple numerical example where: $a = 100$ and $b = 0.8$.

If $Y = 600$ then:

$$C = 100 + 0.8(600) = 580$$

Now if income rises to 700 then:

$$C = 100 + 0.8(700) = 660$$

Thus spending rises by 80 when income rises by 100, implying an mpc of 0.8. Saving increases by $100 - 80 = 20$ as a result of the increase in income of 100, implying an mps of 0.2. Since the mps $= 1 - b = 1 - 0.8$, this is seen to be correct.

The mpc is a crucial parameter in the Keynesian system since it is one of the determinants of the value of the **multiplier**. The multiplier, which we introduced in section 3.3, measures the impact on aggregate demand of any change in the volume of injections or withdrawals.

Consider a closed economy where the mpc is equal to 0.8. What will be the effect in such an economy of a rise in the volume of injections of, say, £100? The immediate effect is, of course, to increase incomes by £100, which will cause an increase in spending of $0.8 \times £100 = £80$. In the next round, with incomes up a further £80, spending will rise by a further £64 and so on. Figure 3.4 illustrates the position after ten rounds. The total increase in income after ten rounds is equal to about £447. If we carried on for a very large number of successive rounds, the total increase in income would, in fact, be equal to £500. The size of the multiplier effect in this case would be equal to the ratio of the change in equilibrium income (£500) to the initiating change in the volume of injections (£100). That is, the value of the multiplier would be 5.

Clearly, however, it would take a large number of successive rounds for the full multiplier effect to work itself out. For the moment, however, it will be convenient to imagine that these successive spending rounds take place instantaneously. This will enable us to compare the original equilibrium position (that is, before the initiating rise in injections) with the final equilibrium position (that is, after the full multiplier effect has worked itself out). This is known, incidentally, as **comparative statics** analysis, since we are comparing two static equilibria without concerning ourselves with the **dynamic** problem of how long it takes the economy to move from one equilibrium position to another.

Provided we are prepared to work within the comparative statics framework, we can prove the above result quite simply. In a closed economy with no government sector, total spending is equal to the sum of consumption and investment expenditures

$$E = C + I \tag{3.4}$$

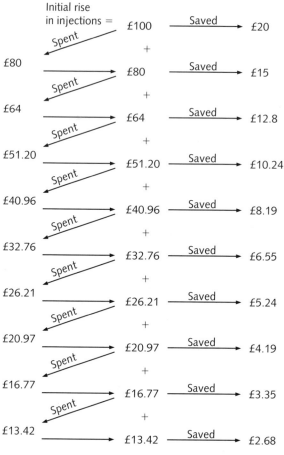

Figure 3.4 The multiplier effect

Our consumption function, as before, is:

$$C = a + bY$$

[3.3 repeated]

The initiating change in investment will be denoted by ΔI. Together with the original level of investment, I_0, this gives total investment:

$$I = I_0 + \Delta I$$

Now if we assume that the economy adjusts instantaneously to its new equilibrium position, which is the same thing as saying that it is always in equilibrium, we can write:

$$Y \overset{e}{=} E$$

[3.5]

and thus:

$$Y \overset{e}{=} E = a + bY + I_o + \Delta I$$

We can then proceed to simplify this equation as follows:

$$Y \overset{e}{=} a + bY + I_o + \Delta I$$

$$Y - bY \overset{e}{=} a + I_o + \Delta I$$

$$Y(1 - b) \overset{e}{=} a + I_o + \Delta I$$

$$Y \overset{e}{=} \frac{a}{1 - b} + \frac{1}{1 - b} I_o + \frac{1}{1 - b} \Delta I \qquad [3.6]$$

Thus we see from equation [3.6] that an increase in investment, ΔI, will cause an increase in equilibrium income which is $1/1 - b$ times as great. That is $1/1 - b$ is the multiplier.

Clearly, in this very restricted model the value of the multiplier is completely determined by the value of the marginal propensity to consume, b. If $b = 0.8$ then:

$$\text{multiplier} = \frac{1}{1 - 0.8} = 5$$

which proves the result we saw earlier.

Before concluding this section, we should re-state two caveats lest the reader is misled into thinking that the real world can be analysed in such simple terms.

The first is that we have been dealing here with a closed economy, with no government sector, and in such a model there is only one type of leakage, namely, savings. In the real world, spending leaks out of the system in other forms, principally in the form of spending on imported goods and in taxation. The value of the multiplier will be affected by these additional leakages.

The second problem is that we have been using comparative statics analysis which has enabled us to predict the economy's long run response to a rise in injections *once all the changes have worked their way through the economy*. We have assumed that this process takes place instantaneously and have therefore ignored problems concerning the economy's speed of response.

3.15 National income accounting

By this stage, readers will have acquired sufficient understanding of macroeconomic concepts to tackle the problems of national income accounting. There are two basic problems involved in accounting, namely, *what* to measure and *how* to measure it. Unfortunately, because of the difficulties involved in the question of how to measure things, the much more important question of what to measure is sometimes ignored. Worse still, the two questions are often confused, as the following will show.

The principal source of national income statistics in the United Kingdom is the **Blue Book** published annually in August. Although the official title of this publication is now simply *UK National Accounts* it was until comparatively recently – 1984 in fact – known officially as *National Income and Expenditure*. This was a particularly misleading title, as is the phrase 'national income accounting', since we are not primarily interested in national income or in national expenditure at all. Rather, we are interested in national *product*. The confusion is compounded because there are three separate methods of estimating national product – the income method, the expenditure method and the output method. It should be made quite clear, however, that national product estimated by the expenditure method is not the same thing as national expenditure, although superficially they do appear to be the same.

The situation is complicated even further by the fact that the national accounts are constructed in such a way that they appear to show that in every year:

national income = national expenditure

though, as we shall see, this is never true unless the balance of payments (excluding official financing) is exactly zero, which it never is. The supposed equality has no more significance than the fact that at the bottom of a company's balance sheet debits exactly equal credits, that is to say, no significance at all.

Under the very restrictive assumptions of the desert island model in Chapter 1, output, income and expenditure were all equal. Since such assumptions do not hold in the real world, the three measures will not, however, be equal and national accounts statisticians may attempt to estimate all three measures separately. In practice, however, it is usually sufficient to consider just two – on the one hand, income and output and, on the other, expenditure. In terms of the demand and supply analysis we introduced in Chapter 2, we have a dichotomy as follows:

	Aggregate demand	*Aggregate supply*
Other names	Total expenditure Total absorption	Total output Total product
National accounts nomenclature	National expenditure	National product National income
Symbol	E	Y

As we have said, in general, expenditure will not be equal to income/output though the accounts appear to show that they are. The relationship between the two is as follows:

$$C + I + G = E \qquad\qquad [3.7]$$

Total expenditure is equal to the sum of consumers' spending, investment spending and government spending. Note that all three categories of expenditure include spending on imported goods. This, therefore, gives us no indication of the *output* of the economy since much of the spending could be on imports, produced outside the country. Moreover, this measure fails to include all of the output which is exported. To arrive at a measure for output, therefore, we have to subtract from the above all of the spending which goes on imported goods and add on the value of goods exported. Thus

$$C + I + G + (X - M) = Y \qquad\qquad [3.8]$$

where Y stands for income and output and $(X - M)$ is net exports. Income and output are identical because the value of goods produced and sold must be equal to the income received from selling those goods. This explains why it is correct to use the terms national income and national product synonymously. It is not correct, however, to use the terms national expenditure and national product synonymously, that is, to assume that: $E = Y$.

This was an equilibrium condition, which we imposed on our model in section 3.13 to find the equilibrium level of national income – that is, the level of national income at which expenditure and income would be equal.

3.16 The accounts

Table 3.1 presents the basic accounts for 1990 and 1996.

Table 3.1 Gross National Product by category of expenditure 1990 and 1996 (£bn)

Line no.		1990	1996
1	Consumers' expenditure	347.5	473.5
2	General government final consumption	112.9	155.7
3	Gross domestic fixed capital formation	107.6	114.6
4	Value of physical increase in stocks and work-in-progress (inventory investment)	−1.8	2.9
5	Total domestic expenditure at market prices	566.2	746.8
6	*plus* exports of goods and services	133.1	217.1
7	*less* imports of goods and services	−148.3	−222.6
8	Gross domestic product at market prices	551.1	742.3
9	Net property income from abroad	1.3	9.6
10	Gross National Product at market prices	552.4	751.9
	Factor cost adjustment		
11	*less* taxes on expenditure *plus* subsidies	−72.2	−99.4
12	Gross National Product at factor cost	480.1	652.6
13	*less* capital consumption	−61.3	−77.3
14	Net national product at factor cost ('National income')	418.9	575.2

Source: UK National Accounts 1997, Table 1.2.

Up to line 8 the accounts correspond more or less to equation [3.8] above. Note that two types of investment are distinguished – fixed capital formation (line 3) and inventory investment (line 4)(see section 3.9). In 1990 inventory investment was negative, indicating a running down of stocks, which tends to occur in recessions. Note also that in these accounts line 2 includes only current spending by government, its capital spending being included in line 3.

Gross Domestic Product (GDP) (line 8) represents the value of all the goods and services produced domestically. Part of the income resulting from this production is sent abroad, to foreign shareholders and so on, but British residents also receive income from abroad by virtue of the shares which they hold in foreign companies. The net flow resulting from this, shown as **Net Property Income from abroad** (line 9) is added to GDP to give **Gross National Product (GNP)**. Net Property Income from abroad was a small positive amount in 1990 and a somewhat larger positive amount in 1996.

There then follows a **factor cost adjustment**. Up to this point in the accounts we have valued output at the prices which purchasers actually pay – 'market prices'. This overstates the true value of those goods and services, however, since market prices will be affected by sales taxes (VAT, excise duty, etc.) and by subsidies. Moreover, the income actually received by the producers of this output will exclude the sales tax, which is passed on directly to the government, but will include the subsidies. Hence, we subtract sales taxes and add back subsidies (subsidies are only a small amount) to arrive at our figure for **GNP at factor cost** (line 12).

Finally, we make an allowance for that part of the capital stock used up in the process of production (line 13). This figure, which is rather confusingly called **capital consumption** is a sort of depreciation allowance. It is only a very rough estimate since it is impossible to measure the amount of capital used up. Having done this we arrive (line 14) at our measure of **Net National Product** (**NNP**) which is sometimes called **National Income**.

3.17 Current price and constant price estimates

One can calculate from the last line of Table 3.1 that National Income was about 38 per cent larger in 1996 than it was in 1990 (£575 billion compared with £418 billion). This does not mean, of course, that people became 38 per cent better off in *real* terms since most of the increase was due to the fall in the value of the monetary yardstick by which income is measured. That is, most of the increase was due to inflation. These figures are known as **current price estimates** which means that the 1990 figures are measured in 1990 prices, the 1996 figures in 1996 prices and so on.

Figures which are adjusted for the fall in the value of money are known as **constant price estimates**. These are derived by applying an appropriate **price deflator** to the current price estimates. The compilation of such price deflators or price indexes was discussed in section 2.6. Table 3.2 gives a set of constant price

Table 3.2 Gross National Product by category of expenditure at 1990 prices (£ billion at 1990 prices)

Line no.		1990	1996
1	Consumers' expenditure	347.5	376.6
2	General government final consumption	112.9	122.4
3	Gross domestic fixed capital formation	107.6	104.1
4	Value of physical increase in stocks and work-in-progress (inventory investment)	−1.8	2.6
5	Total domestic expenditure at market prices	566.2	605.8
6	*plus* exports of goods and services	133.1	179.8
7	*less* imports of goods and services	−148.3	−184.7
8	Gross Domestic Product at market prices	551.1	601.7
9	Net property income from abroad	1.3	8.0
10	Gross National Product at market prices	552.4	609.7
	Factor cost adjustment		
11	*less* taxes on expenditure *plus* subsidies	−72.2	−77.1
12	Gross National Product at factor cost	480.1	532.5
13	*less* capital consumption	−61.3	−68.2
14	Net national product at factor cost ('National income')	418.9	464.3

Source: UK National Accounts 1997, Table 1.3.

estimates. The line numbers in Table 3.2 correspond to those in Table 3.1. Notice of course that the first column in both tables is the same, since both are measured in 1990 prices.

By looking at Table 3.2 we can see that in *real* terms the increase in National Income was only about 11 per cent (from £418 billion to £464 billion). This contrasts with the 38 per cent increase in **money National Income** (from £418 billion to £575 billion) that we observed in the earlier table.

Whether constant price or current price figures should be used in any particular application depends entirely on what those figures are intended to show. Current price figures cannot show meaningful changes in the value of variables over time since any real increase is swamped by the effect of inflation. Hence constant price estimates should be used to measure, for example, the growth in consumer spending between 1990 and 1996. If, however, one wished to know the change in the *proportion of GNP* devoted to consumption between two periods then current price estimates should be used in preference to constant price estimates.

3.18 The accuracy of the estimates

It should be emphasised that the figures we are dealing with are *estimates* of the magnitudes we are trying to measure. As such, the figures are subject to a

Table 3.3 Successive estimates of GNP at factor cost for 1991 (£ million)

As recorded in *UK National Accounts* 1992	497 329
As recorded in *UK National Accounts* 1993	495 144
As recorded in *UK National Accounts* 1994	495 683
As recorded in *UK National Accounts* 1995	495 326
As recorded in *UK National Accounts* 1996	496 403

Source: UK National Accounts 1992-96, Table 1.1.

margin of error, the overall size of which is difficult to assess. First, we know that the data are subject to subsequent **revision**. Table 3.3 shows estimates for GNP for 1991 shown in successive Blue Books. The revisions here are small, being of the order of £2 billion (about one half of one per cent of GNP) but even this small revision is quite large relative to the average growth of GNP which is around 2.2 per cent.

Secondly, one suspects that the size of the **black economy** or **cash economy** is substantial. The black economy comprises all those services paid for in cash or kind which are never recorded and hence escape the attention of both the Inland Revenue and the national income statistician. However, the omission of these cash transactions from the national accounts constitutes a serious error only if they are growing or shrinking in importance over time.

Summary

This chapter has presented a Keynesian analysis of the workings of the macroeconomy. This analysis is partly axiomatic and partly paradigmatic. The axiomatic part is reflected in the way that the national accounts are drawn up. The relationships between the variables which the accounts display are true by definition. Thus we can write:

$$Y = C + I + G + X - M \qquad \text{[3.8 repeated]}$$

and this equation is a definition accepted by all rather than an interpretation associated with a particular school of thought.

However, part of the analysis of this chapter should be viewed as paradigm rather than axiom. It represents a particular view of the way the macroeconomy works, a view which is challenged by other schools of thought. In particular, the *importance* which Keynesians place on injections and withdrawals as determinants of aggregate demand would be challenged by the monetarists who place much greater emphasis on the role of the money supply. There is moreover another paradigm which concentrates less on demand and more on supply side factors. These will be examined in subsequent chapters.

Key terms

Review questions

3.1 What impact will the following have on aggregate demand, *ceteris paribus* (up/down/no change)?
(a) An increase in public spending on new roads.
(b) The issue of a new high-yield security which encourages people to save more.
(c) The publication of a CBI survey which reports favourable business prospects for the next six months.

3.2 Here are six statements about the probable effect on the economy of an increase in demand. Consider whether each of them could be correct and under what circumstances they could be correct.
(a) The increase in demand will cause a subsequent increase in spending on imported goods. Therefore domestic firms won't benefit at all.
(b) The increase in demand will result in increased incomes which in turn will mean that people will save more. So domestic firms still don't benefit.
(c) The increase in demand will mean that firms can sell more. They will therefore increase their production and take on more workers.

(d) The increase in demand will mean that firms can sell more. They are therefore likely to run down their stocks of finished goods. Production will not increase.

(e) If the increase in demand results in higher incomes people will have to pay more income tax. So they won't be able to spend any more than they did previously.

(f) If demand goes up, firms will take advantage of the situation to put up prices.

3.3 *Ceteris paribus*, what impact will the following have on aggregate demand?
   (a) The government reduces its expenditure on Trident missiles by £50m.
   (b) Student grants are increased by a total of £50m.
   (c) The Government spends £50m more on pensions financing it by increasing taxes on the higher paid by the same amount.
      Which of the three above will have the biggest impact on aggregate demand?

3.4 'If savings go up the increased flow of loanable funds will result in a fall in interest rates. This will encourage extra investment. So savings always equals investment.' What is wrong with this statement?

3.5 Which of the following explains why investment may not increase if the rate of interest falls. Because:
   (a) Most firms have their own funds anyway so they have no need to borrow.
   (b) Investment is interest inelastic.
   (c) The cost of funds is less important to firms than future sales prospects.
   (d) People save less when the rate of interest falls and therefore funds may not be available.

3.6 State which of the following constitutes investment from a macroeconomic point of view.
   (a) A company builds a new factory.
   (b) A private individual buys Krugerands.
   (c) A jeweller buys gold.
   (d) A company buys a new car for one of its sales staff.
   (e) An individual buys a new car to get to work.

3.7 In recessions net investment often becomes negative.
   (a) What does this mean?
   (b) Why does it occur?

3.8 You are given the following figures on national output (GNP) and Gross Domestic Fixed Capital Formation (investment). Assume that replacement investment is equal to 10 in each time period and that the behaviour of new investment can be approximated by an accelerator model of the form:

$$I_t = \alpha \Delta Y$$

where $\Delta Y = Y_t - Y_{t-1}$, i.e. income (or output) in this period minus income last period, and α is the accelerator coefficient.

Period	1	2	3	4	5	6	7
GNP	100	100	110	120	130	127	127
Investment	10	10	40	40	40	?	?

(a) What is the value of the accelerator coefficient?

(b) What will investment be in periods 6 and 7?

3.9 Suppose that an economy is initially in equilibrium at a level of national income of £600m per year. Suppose then that an additional export order of £10m is received.

(a) What is the initial impact of the economy?

(b) Assuming that on average people spend only 80 per cent of their last pound's worth of income, to what level will income have risen after three rounds?

(c) If, on average, people spent 90 per cent of their extra income (rather than 80 per cent) would the increase in national income brought about by the exports be more than previously or less?

3.10 Which of the following will have the largest expansionary effect on Aggregate Demand and which will have the smallest?

(a) A reduction in employee's National Insurance Contribution amounting to a total reduction in the government's tax take of £10m.

(b) An increase in retirement pensions involving the government in additional expenditure of £10m.

(c) A reduction in taxation for the higher paid amounting to a total reduction in the tax take of £10m.

3.11 GNP is the value of all the goods and services produced in the economy in a given year. How does this differ from NNP (Net National Product)?

3.12 Would an increase in any of the following result in an increase in measured GNP?

(a) Wives' housekeeping allowances.

(b) Children's pocket money.

(c) Student grants.

(d) Retirement pensions.

(e) Lecturers' salaries.

3.13 Given the following information prepare a set of National Accounts showing:

(a) Total domestic expenditure.

(b) GDP at market prices.

(c) GNP at market prices.

(d) GNP at factor cost.

(e) National Income (i.e. net national product).

The figures have been jumbled up to make it more difficult for you. All figures are in £ bn.

Exports: 56

Net property income from abroad: 1

Taxes on expenditure: 30

Government spending on goods and services: 38

Value of physical increase in stocks and work in progress: 3

Consumers' expenditure: 116

Subsidies: 4

Imports: 54

Capital consumption: 22

Gross domestic fixed capital formation: 34

3.14 (You need a calculator for this.)

The GDP deflator is akin to a price index which shows how prices in the economy are increasing. The value of the deflator for the period 1986 to 1996 is shown below:

1986	1987	1988	1989	1990	1991	1992	1993	1994	1995	1996
79	83	88	94	100	106	111	115	117	120	123

(a) What would be the price in 1996 of a bundle of goods which cost £10 in 1990?
(b) What was the rate of inflation in 1991?
(c) What was the rate of inflation in 1992?
(d) What was the rate of inflation in 1993?

GDP (in current prices) since 1986 looks like this (all figures to the nearest £ billion):

1986	1987	1988	1989	1990	1991	1992	1993	1994	1995	1996
349	424	471	516	551	576	599	631	669	704	742

Using the GDP deflator given above, prepare a series for GDP at constant 1990 prices.

(e) By how much in real terms did GDP in 1991 exceed GNP in 1990?
(f) By how much in real terms did GNP in 1993 exceed GNP in 1989?
(*Source*: *UK National Accounts*, 1997 edition, Tables 1.7 and 1.2)

3.15 In each of the following cases state whether you should use:

- current price estimates;
- constant price estimates;
- either can be used.

(a) Assessing what proportion of total expenditure goes on government spending.
(b) Working out the rate of growth of output.
(c) Determining what the trade balance is.
(d) Working out the rate of growth of government spending.

4 Money

This chapter looks at the nature of money, how the stock of money is defined and how in theory it is controlled by the authorities. The link between the financing of public spending and the money supply is explored. Theories about the influence which money has on the economy are examined in detail. The monetarist view about the importance of the money supply in economic activity is contrasted with that of the Keynesians.

4.1 Definition of the money supply: the case base and credit money

Money, it is said, makes the world go round, though this is disputed. Those of a more romantic nature attribute this role to love. Both money and love share the common characteristic that neither is easy to define, but there the similarity ends.

In attempting to define what money is, economists normally start off by saying that money possesses three **functions**. It is:

- a medium of exchange
- a store of value
- a unit of account.

The last of these may require some explanation. What it means is that money is a unit by which the value of an object can be measured. The weight of an object can be measured in grammes, its length in centimetres, its temperature in degrees Celsius ... and its value in £s.

In the past all sorts of different things have been used as money, including precious metals, salt (the word *salary* comes from a Latin word meaning salt) and cattle (the word *pecuniary* comes from the Latin word for cattle). To be accepted as money these various things would have to perform all of the functions listed above and in addition they should ideally possess certain desirable characteristics of a good money substance – namely that they should be easily portable, divisible, durable – but above all acceptable and scarce.

The definition of the money supply is to some extent somewhat arbitrary. There are a variety of different definitions to choose from and there are no strong prior reasons for choosing any one of them. Two main measures are now in use in the UK which are known as M0 and M4. The narrowest definition of money is M0. This corresponds, more or less, to the amount of cash – that is, notes and coins – in the system. The widest definition, M4, comprises, in addition to cash all accounts at banks and building societies regardless of whether they bear interest and how much notice is required to withdraw funds. The official definitions of the aggregates, together with an approximate indication of their size, are shown in Table 4.1.

It is worth emphasising that the definitions of 'the money supply' are to some extent arbitrary. The definitions have been frequently revised particularly in the 1980s when the process of **financial deregulation** led to innovations in banking practices which rendered the old definitions obsolete. Of particular note was the monetary aggregate known as M3 which comprised cash and accounts at UK banks. It did not, however, include accounts at building societies. In mid-1989 the Abbey National Building Society, a major financial institution, changed its legal status from that of a building society to that of a bank. This resulted in a major discontinuity in the statistical series for M3 since all of the 'money' in the accounts of the Abbey National, previously excluded from M3, were henceforth included. This was the major event which led to the abandonment of the use of M3 which had up until then been the then Government's most important financial indicator. All of this suggests that the dividing line between money and other assets which are not money is not at all clear-cut and the definition of the money supply owes more to convention than to any real difference between the various money-like substances.

We can, however, make a very clear distinction between the **cash-base** of the system, which is money issued by the central bank, and **credit money**, which is

Table 4.1 The main monetary measures

M0

The 'wide monetary base' consists of notes and coins in circulation outside the Bank of England *plus* banks' operational deposits with the Banking Department of the Bank of England.

Notes and coins comprise over 99% of the total which in June 1997 stood at about £25.5 billion.

M4

The UK non-bank, non-building society private sector is known as the 'M4 private sector'. The monetary aggregate known as M4 comprises the M4 private sector's holdings of sterling notes and coin and all sterling deposits at UK banks and building societies. The total amount outstanding at June 1997 was £728.6 billion made up as follows:

notes and coin	21.5
non-interest bearing bank deposits	38.9
other bank retail deposits	295.7
building society retail shares and deposits	126.9
bank wholesale deposits	235.3
building society wholesale deposits	10.3
M4 total	**728.6**

Source: derived from *Bank of England Quarterly Bulletin*, February 1996, Statistical Appendix and *Financial Statistics*, August 1997, Tables 3.1C and D.

money created by the commercial banking system through the process of **multiple credit creation**, explained below.

4.2 The process of multiple credit creation

Currency is the so-called cash base of the system. It is sometimes called **high powered money**. It is money created by the central bank, in our case the Bank of England, and the amount in existence can therefore be directly controlled. Credit money, on the other hand, is money created by the commercial banking system through the process of credit creation. If a bank grants one of its customers an overdraft it has thereby increased the stock of credit money. The stock of credit money is not directly controlled by the Bank of England, and this may have important implications for the ability of the central bank to control the overall money stock.

We can illustrate the principle whereby the banks create credit money with the following example, sketched out in Fig. 4.1, although the practice is somewhat different, depending as it does on the particular institutional arrangements.

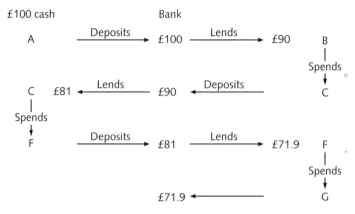

Figure 4.1 Multiple credit creation

Suppose that individual A deposits £100 cash with her bank, and that the bank knows that A, who is a creature of habit, never withdraws more than 10 per cent of her total deposit at any time. The bank can therefore safely lend out the other 90 per cent (or £90 in this example), which it will do quite willingly since it is a profit-seeking institution whose main source of revenue is the interest charged to borrowers. Thus, it will want to lend out as much as possible, subject to the requirement that it must retain enough cash to satisfy any withdrawal that A is likely to make. The bank therefore lends £90 to B, who uses the money to buy goods valued at £90 from C, who promptly banks the receipts. Provided C, like A, is not expected to withdraw more than 10 per cent of their holdings at any one time, the bank will then re-lend the other 90 per cent (90 per cent of £90 = £81) to another customer, D, who uses it to buy goods from E who banks the receipts, and so on.

By the time this process gets to the letter G in Fig. 4.1 the total amount of money in existence is £100 + £90 + £81 + £71.9 = £342.9, of which £100 was the cash originally in existence, and the other £242.9 is credit money created by the banking system.

If the process continued, until we had run out of letters and way beyond, we would find that altogether £900 of credit money could be created from the original £100 cash. You can check the arithmetic involved here – but only if you can remember the formula for the sum of a geometric progression.

Our analysis has been conducted in terms of creatures of habit who never withdraw more than 10 per cent of their holdings at any time – clearly an unrealistic assumption to make for any one individual. However, what is untrue for one individual may well be true for all the bank's customers taken as a group – on average no more than 10 per cent of total money holdings are ever withdrawn at one time. Thus, the bank would be quite safe in making advances up to the limit of its 10 per cent **cash ratio**. This is known as **fractional reserve banking**.

4.3 The control of the money supply via control of the cash base

In the past, commercial banks have been obliged by the Bank of England to adhere to a cash ratio of the sort described above. However, as we have seen, banks get their income from lending money at interest, and they will therefore try to lend as much as possible, so as to make their profits as large as possible, and to this end commercial banks seek ways to circumvent the reserve ratio imposed upon them by the central bank. The response of the central bank is to change the regulations – to modify the reserve requirements – so as to maintain more effective control on the supply of money. Thus the reserve requirements have been changed by the Bank of England on numerous occasions.

A milestone in this process was the publication in 1971 of the *Competition and Credit Control* arrangements, brought in because the cash ratios which had been in existence had proved to be an ineffective method of controlling banks' multiple credit-creating activities. The CCC arrangements were defined not on the ratio of cash to total liabilities, but on the ratio of a narrowly defined range of liquid assets to total liabilities. However, commercial banks also found ways around these regulations – mostly by juggling around the assets in their portfolio of 'liquid assets' – and these arrangements were superseded in 1980 by a form of **monetary base control**. Under this system, the Bank of England controls the monetary base – that is, principally cash (notes and coins) plus some balances which the commercial banks are obliged to hold at the Bank of England. This control of base money directly affects each bank's liquidity position, that is, the extent to which it is able to fulfil its immediate obligations to creditors. 'Normal banking prudence' will then ensure, in theory, that the banks will not overstretch themselves by lending too much, but the liquidity position of each bank is also supposed to be monitored by the Bank of England. Thus the system of monetary base control which evolved after 1980 was akin to a cash ratio system except that there was no externally imposed cash ratio to which the banks had to adhere. Rather there was a self-imposed **prudential ratio** set by each individual bank which would reflect that bank's overall liquidity position both immediately and in the near future. The Bank of England monitors this overall liquidity status rather than concentrating on any particular cash or liquid asset ratio.

An alternative method of attempting to control monetary growth is to operate not on the *supply* of money but on the *demand* for it. By increasing the rate of interest at which it is willing to lend, the Bank of England can bring about an increase in the overall level of interest rates, which will, in theory, reduce people's willingness to borrow money. That is, the increase in interest rates reduces the demand for money. If this happens, then banks will not be able to create as much credit money as they would like, simply because people are not prepared to borrow at the higher interest rates.

There is a two-fold difficulty with such a policy. First, the higher the rate of interest, the greater the incentive for banks to lend money to customers since the greater the profits they can thereby earn. Secondly, the high interest rates have an effect – often an adverse one on many other ares of the economy. For example, higher interest rates will, *ceteris paribus*:

- cause an appreciation of the exchange rate (if it is floating) or upwards pressure on a fixed rate;
- lead to a reduction in investment spending (that is, domestic fixed capital formation) which may adversely affect the long-term rate of growth;
- make borrowing more expensive – and since the government is itself normally a borrower this will have implications for the financing of public spending. This is discussed in the next section.

4.4 Financing public spending

Public expenditure can be financed in one of three ways. First, the government can levy taxes, either direct taxes on income, or indirect taxes on expenditure. Secondly, the government can borrow money from the public using a variety of **debt instruments** – Treasury Bills, which are short-term loans redeemable after three months, Treasury Bonds, which are longer-term loans, National Savings schemes, Premium Bonds and so on. If neither of these methods of finance is acceptable, for reasons discussed below, then the government may resort to a third alternative which is to finance spending through a process which involves an increase in the money supply. This third alternative is what is sometimes called 'printing money' though it is a misleading expression since, as we shall see, the monetary expansion involved does not necessarily take the form of an increase in notes in circulation.

In any particular year, the amount by which the government's tax revenue falls short of its spending requirements is known as its borrowing requirement – the so-called **Public Sector Borrowing Requirement** (**PSBR**). If the borrowing requirement is positive in any particular year this will result in an increase in the size of the **National Debt**, which is the total amount of government debt outstanding at any particular time, and includes both current borrowing and debt accumulated from previous years. Normally the government succeeds in meeting most of its borrowing requirement by borrowing from the public by the issue of Treasury Bills and so on. In some circumstances, however, it may be unable to persuade people to buy government securities without offering very high rates of interest, which it may be unwilling to do, and in this case it may resort to the third alternative, which involves an increase in the money supply. This is discussed in the next section.

4.5 The connection between government spending and the money supply

To recap, we have just seen that government spending can be financed either by:

- taxation;
- borrowing from the public;
- a process which involves monetary expansion – 'printing money'.

To see how these various forms of financing will affect the money supply, consider first the effect of an extra £10 m of public spending which is financed by taxation. The extra government spending adds £10 m to the supply of money – pensioners receive more in their weekly pension, teachers get a salary increase and so on – but this is exactly cancelled out by a £10 m decrease in the supply of money brought about as a result of the increased taxes that people have to pay to government. Thus, we say that the *monetary effect is neutral.*

Similarly, if the government finances spending by borrowing, the increase in the money supply brought about by the extra spending is offset by an equal decrease in the money supply which results when the public lend the government money by purchasing National Savings Certificates, Treasury Bills and so on. The monetary effect is again neutral.

Even though these methods of financing do not result directly in any increase in the money supply, they may have certain undesirable effects. Raising taxes in order to pay for increased public expenditure is understandably unpopular since, other things being equal, it reduces people's real disposable income. If income tax is increased then take-home pay falls, and if VAT is increased the increase in the price level which this brings about reduces the real value of a given money income. Thus, in both cases, people's ability to purchase goods and services with their income is reduced, and consumption in real terms will fall. This will lead to a fall in society's welfare, which may or may not be offset by the increase in social welfare brought about by the increased public spending. The reduced consumer spending may also have deleterious long-term effects on investment in those consumer goods industries which are most affected by the fall in demand.

Lastly, it has been claimed that direct taxes have a disincentive effect on work effort. It should be noted that there are no prior reasons for supposing that this will necessarily be the case. If the individual's objective is to obtain a certain amount of post-tax income, then an increase in income tax will mean that he or she has to work harder to meet their objective. What is more likely, however, is that the individual will seek ways of avoiding the payment of income tax, either by tax avoidance (which is legal) or tax evasion (which is illegal). They may, for example, prefer to take part of their income in the form of benefits-in-kind, or 'perks', which are either not taxed as highly as money income or not taxed at all. Company cars and expense account lunches are examples of tax avoidance. Alternatively, slightly lower down the social scale, the individual may resort to 'moonlighting' or taking on jobs for which they are paid in cash and which they do not declare to the Inland Revenue.

There are also undesirable side-effects which result from the use of borrowing from the public to finance government spending. The money which the government borrows may be funds which would otherwise have been spent on consumption, or they may be funds which would otherwise have been lent to some other sector, such as private industry. If this is the case, the government spending is said to have displaced or **crowded out** the investment in private industry which would otherwise have taken place. The assumption implicit here is that there is a fixed amount of investable funds and, if the government pre-empts a large part of those funds, there will be fewer funds left for other sectors. We consider this crowding-out hypothesis in more detail later.

The way in which the government attracts investment funds is to offer interest rates which are higher than those the investor can get elsewhere. This, of course, leads to an increase in the overall level of interest rates, which is undesirable for a number of reasons. First, as we have already noted, it may lead to a fall in the investment undertaken by private sector firms, and this, in the long run, may have adverse effects on productivity growth and on the growth of output. Secondly, the increased interest rates lead to an increase in the price index (and may thus contribute to inflation), since they increase the cost of borrowing generally and, in particular, they increase the cost of borrowing for house purchase, which is the largest single item in many people's expenditure. The high interest rates will also increase industry's costs and these increased costs may be passed on in the form of increased prices, thus exacerbating the inflationary effects. Moreover, high interest rates increase the burden of debt of the government, which means that the government will have to raise more money just to pay the increased interest charges. And lastly high interest rates may affect the exchange rate.

To summarise, we can say that financing government spending through taxation or by borrowing from the public, although it does not increase the money supply, may have undesirable side-effects.

Because of the damaging effect of high interest rates, the government may resort to raising funds in a way which results in monetary expansion (that is, by 'printing money'). If the government cannot persuade the *public* to buy Treasury Bills at the going rate, it can sell them to the *banking sector*. The banks may treat these Bills as part of their reserve assets so that they do not have to reduce their lending to customers. They have merely replaced one type of liquid asset (cash) with another (Treasury Bills) so their liquidity position remains unchanged.

Now, if the government uses the money it has raised by this means to finance spending, there will be a net increase in the money stock, since the increase in government spending is not this time offset by a corresponding decrease in people's bank balances as a result of increased tax payments or increased lending to the government. This increase in the money supply will have some influence on the economy – most probably it will contribute to inflation. This we discuss in the following sections.

4.6 The money supply as a determinant of aggregate demand

The **monetarist** school, which was particularly influential in the 1980s, would claim that, as a matter of empirical fact, variations in the level of aggregate demand can be explained better by variations in the money supply, rather than by the Keynesian explanation which emphasises injections and withdrawals. Inflation, monetarists would argue, is the inevitable result of a situation in which the money supply is expanded too fast, allowing aggregate demand to exceed the capacity of the economy to produce goods. They point out that every single inflation in history has been associated with an expansion of the money supply. Since an over-expansion of the money supply is the one factor which is common to *all* inflationary situations, then the cause of inflation must be attributed to excessive monetary growth.

The monetarists thus elevate the money supply to a position of prime importance in macroeconomics, a position which it formerly occupied before the Keynesians relegated it to a more inferior role.

4.7 The quantity theory of money

The pre-Keynesian (or 'classical') thinking about the role which money plays in determining economic activity is often illustrated by reference to the so-called **Quantity Theory of Money**. The famous **Equation of Exchange**

$$MV = PT \tag{4.1}$$

states that the money supply (M) multiplied by its velocity of circulation (V) must always be equal to the number of transactions (T) multiplied by the average price of each transaction (P). Since one pound coin creates one pound's worth of spending every time it changes hands, MV must therefore represent total spending in the economy, or aggregate demand. What this equation is therefore saying is that the total amount of money spent on buying goods and services in the economy in the year must be equal to the total value of all the goods and services sold in the economy in the year. As such, it is tautology. It is similar to, though not the same as, the statement we make in microeconomics that, when trade takes place in the market for a particular good, the amount demanded (the amount bought) must equal the amount supplied (the amount sold).

The quantity theory of money, in its crudest form, used the Equation of Exchange to show that if V (the velocity of circulation) and T (the physical volume of goods produced) were fixed, then there would be a directly proportional relationship between variations in the money supply and variations in the price level. A 10 per cent increase in the money supply would result in a 10 per cent rise in the price level.

Clearly, once one has accepted the crucial assumption that the velocity of circulation of money is fixed, then aggregate demand is determined solely by the money supply. The way in which the classical economists justified this assumption of a fixed velocity was to argue that, since it depended upon institutional factors which would change only slowly over time, then in the short run the velocity could be treated as fixed. These institutional factors – the length of payment periods (that is, whether people are paid daily, weekly or monthly), the nature of the banking system (for example, the speed at which cheques can be cleared through the banking system, bank opening hours, the extent to which credit cards are accepted as a means of payment) – will certainly remain relatively fixed in the short run, but Keynes argued that the velocity did not depend solely on these institutional factors. He went further in fact, to argue that the velocity of circulation was a quite unstable magnitude, so that a given money stock could finance widely differing levels of aggregate demand, depending on the velocity of circulation.

4.8 Keynesian and monetarist views of the role of the money supply

We have seen how the monetarist school claimed that, throughout history, inflation is always associated with an increase in the supply of money. It may seem paradoxical that Keynesians would not dispute this as a statement of fact. What they would dispute is the fact that, simply because there is an *association* between increases in the money stock and inflation, increases in the money stock are necessarily the *cause* of inflation.

Both schools would agree that there is a correlation between increases in the money stock and increases in aggregate demand and that, in a situation in which the economy is utilising all the available resources of labour and capital, real output cannot be increased. In such a situation an increase in aggregate demand will result in inflation or a rise in spending on imported goods, or both. The fact that a correlation exists between changes in the money stock and changes in aggregate demand is not particularly surprising. It is difficult to see how spending can increase unless there is an expansion of the money supply, but correlation is not proof of causality. The causality could run from the rise in the money stock to the rise in aggregate demand or, equally logically, it could run in the opposite direction, from the rise in aggregate demand to the rise in the money stock. The monetarists, while accepting this point, argue that, if it can be shown that increases in the money supply *precede* increases in aggregate demand, then this, on the face of it, is evidence that the causality runs from the money supply to aggregate demand, and not the other way round. A number of prominent monetarists have attempted to show, in the contexts of the American and British economies, that changes in the money supply do in fact precede changes in aggregate demand. The Keynesian riposte has been first of all to dispute the validity of the statistical evidence, and secondly to point out that precedence in time is not proof of causality. To illustrate this, they point to the increase in the money supply which occurs in November and December each year, which is followed by a sharp rise in consumer spending. The cause of this is the spending frenzy engendered by the Christmas season (supported, if not invented, by the advertising industry), rather than the increase in the money supply *per se*. This is a clear example of the monetary authorities anticipating an increase in spending and therefore expanding the money supply so that consumers and traders will not run short of cash.

The general Keynesian view, therefore, is that the money supply is a passive variable. It responds to increases in aggregate demand (and may even anticipate them) but it does not play an active role in determining economic activity.

4.9 The transmission mechanism

The dispute between the Keynesians and the monetarists about the role played by the money stock in determining the level of economic activity has taken various forms. First, as we have seen, the statistical evidence has been disputed. Secondly, the mechanism whereby changes in the money supply induce changes in aggregate demand – the so-called **transmission mechanism** – has been argued about at length.

Historically, Keynesians have explained the transmission mechanism as follows. The interest rate is the price of borrowing money. This price is therefore determined by the demand and supply of money, as in Fig. 4.2.

The demand for money is shown to be inversely related to interest rates. This is because holding money involves an **opportunity cost**, which is the interest that

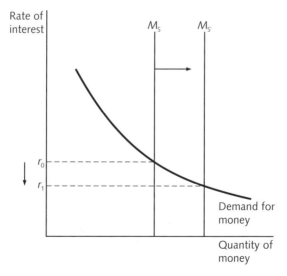

Figure 4.2 An increase in the money supply causes interest rates to fall

could have been earned by putting the money in an interest-earning account at a bank or building society. As interest rates rise, so the cost of holding money rises and people will wish to hold less – that is, the demand for money will be less. The supply of money is represented by a vertical line. This implies that it is not dependent upon interest rates. Rather it is **exogenously fixed** by the monetary authorities at some particular level, and does not vary as interest rates vary.

An increase in the supply of money, shown by a rightward shift of the money supply curve, will lead to a drop in equilibrium interest rates. This fall in interest rates will encourage investment spending (fixed capital formation), since, as we have seen, this type of spending is influenced by interest rates. Investment is itself a component of aggregate demand. Hence we conclude that an increase in the money supply leads to an increase in aggregate demand through the interest rate effect on investment.

In this view, the link between the money supply and aggregate demand is somewhat tenuous – hence the view that money is not very important in determining aggregate demand. If the transmission mechanism is of this form, then it is likely to involve considerable time lags and a large amount of uncertainty.

Interest rates, for example, are affected by other factors, and they may not fall. Even if interest rates do fall, investment may not be very responsive to such falls. Thus, if the money supply can only affect aggregate demand via this somewhat roundabout process then it does indeed appear to be a rather unimportant variable.

4.10 The monetarist view of the transmission mechanism: portfolio balance

The Keynesian account of the transmission mechanism given above would be disputed by the monetarists. Their version relies upon the concept of **portfolio balance**. The individual is assumed to have a variety of different ways in which to hold his or her wealth. One way of categorising the various forms of wealth holding is in terms of the liquidity spectrum such as that shown in Fig. 4.3. Figure 4.3 illustrates some of the more important forms of wealth holding, though many more are possible. For example, reading from the left in Fig. 4.3 we see that the most liquid form of wealth holding is cash. The main costs involved in so doing are first the interest that is forgone and, secondly, the loss of purchasing power that results from the falling value of money in inflationary times. The main benefit to be derived from holding wealth in the form of cash is convenience – you do not have to bother to go to the bank if you wish to make a purchase, since cash is universally accepted as a means of payment. Holding cash may, however, involve some risk of theft. Putting your money in a bank account reduces the risk of theft, but may also involve some loss of convenience.

The important point, however, is that the costs and benefits associated with each of the various forms of wealth holding will differ from one individual to another – or, at least, their *assessment* of the costs and benefits will differ. But each individual

Liquid ← → Illiquid

Form of wealth holding	Cash	Current account at bank (non-interest bearing)	Interest-bearing account at bank or Building Society	Bonds, e.g. local authority bonds	Shares	Physical assets, e.g. cars, TVs, boats	'Real property' houses
Costs	Interest forgone / – Value eroded by inflation / – Risk of theft	Interest forgone / – Value eroded by inflation / – May not be accepted as means of payment	Loss of liquidity – cannot withdraw money immediately	Less liquid than bank – money tied up	Risky – could go down in value – may be difficult to sell without incurring capital loss	Very illiquid	Very illiquid
Benefits	Convenience	Less risk of theft than cash	Rate of interest	Usually higher rates of interest than bank	May go up in value	Yields stream of services / – Value not eroded by inflation	Yields stream of services / – May appreciate in value

← Money → ← Financial assets → ← Physical assets →

Figure 4.3 A wealth portfolio

will weigh up the costs and benefits of each form of wealth holding and will then proceed to arrange their wealth portfolio in a way that yields them maximum **utility** (that is, yields them maximum personal satisfaction). This condition will be satisfied when it is impossible to increase utility by rearranging their portfolio, for example, by holding more bonds and fewer shares. Their portfolio will then be in a state of equilibrium or balance.

Now consider the effect of an increase in the money supply. Some individuals will now find themselves holding more cash than previously, and this will disturb the equilibrium in their portfolios, which are now too liquid. They will embark on a process of **asset substitution**. In an attempt to re-establish equilibrium in their portfolios, these individuals will use part of their money to buy assets – and this spending spills over not merely to financial assets but also into the realm of physical assets and even on to goods and services which are not normally considered as assets at all. As this spending takes place, so it may change the costs and benefits (either real or perceived) of the various forms of wealth holding, causing further adjustments to be made to get back to a state of portfolio balance.

The basic idea, then, is that an increase in the supply of money causes an increase in spending, as individuals attempt to re-establish equilibrium in their wealth portfolio. The resultant increased spending on any particular asset or class of assets cannot be predicted with accuracy, since the process of portfolio adjustment involves subjective assessments of the costs or benefits associated with very many different types of wealth holding. However, in the aggregate, the monetarists would argue, the increased spending resulting from monetary expansion is clearly discernable in empirical studies.

4.11 Portfolio balance: the Keynesian view

In explaining the transmission mechanism, most contemporary Keynesians would probably now accept the portfolio balance view – with one important difference. For the Keynesians, the increase in the money supply directly affects other financial assets, but the effect does not spread directly to the realm of physical assets, as the monetarists would claim it does. Rather, any impact which monetary expansion or contraction ultimately has on demand in other sectors of the economy occurs as a result of the changes brought about in the market for financial assets. For example, an increase in the supply of money will result in some portfolios becoming excessively liquid and, in an attempt to correct this imbalance, part of the cash will be used to purchase financial assets. The increased demand for financial assets will cause their price to rise and this, in turn, will cause their **yield** to drop (for reasons explained below). Following the fall in interest rates in the bond market other interest rates will fall and, in response to this, both consumption and investment spending will increase. Thus, even though the contemporary Keynesians acknowledge the validity of the portfolio balance approach, they still maintain that the effect that monetary factors have on spending is indirect, operating via interest rate changes in financial markets.

Before proceeding, we pause briefly to explain how in theory these interest rate changes are brought about by increased spending in financial markets. Consider a **bond** (that is, a fixed interest security) whose **nominal price** is £100. Suppose it pays interest of £10 per year, thus giving it a **nominal rate of interest** of 10 per cent. If the bond's *actual market value*, as distinct from the nominal price, is £100 then it will yield an actual return of 10 per cent. But suppose now that its market value increases to £200 because of a strong demand for such securities. Since it gives a return of only £10 per year, its actual yield will now fall to 5 per cent per year (that is, $\frac{10}{200} \times \frac{100}{1}$). This demonstrates that the market price of fixed interest securities is inversely related to their yield. Thus if bond prices go up, the interest rate on bonds will go down.

So this Keynesian variant of the transmission mechanism can be summarised as follows. Increases in the money supply result in increased spending in the bond market. This causes an increase in the price of bonds, which in turn results in a drop in interest rates. As a result, investment spending – and possibly consumer spending – will rise. Note how in this view interest rates are **endogenously** determined – that is, they are determined in the money market by the demand and supply of money, rather than being fixed **exogenously** by the monetary authorities.

4.12 Keynesians and monetarists – waxing and waning

In the immediate post-war period Keynesianism was the conventional wisdom of academics and governments alike. Spawned in the depression years of the 1920s and 1930s, the message of Keynesianism was one of hope; governments could spend their way out of a recession and thereby eliminate the scourge of unemployment. There is absolutely no doubt that the Keynesian medicine worked. And it was easy for Keynesianism to win the hearts and minds of the people, for the medicine was pleasant to take. Just inject more spending into the economy and prosperity will follow with no nasty side-effects – or so it seemed at the time.

However, in the late 1960s and 1970s, the disease which seemed to be attacking the economies of the Western world was of a different kind. Inflation was becoming the major concern. The Keynesian prescription for this was a much more bitter pill to swallow. Deflation, with its attendant slow-down in the growth of prosperity and consequent rise in unemployment, meant that, to get well again, the patient had to undergo a rather painful treatment. Moreover, the treatment seemed to be becoming increasingly ineffective. It was almost as if the patient had developed an immunity to the drugs that the Keynesian doctors prescribed, so that larger and larger doses of deflation and reflation were required to bring about the desired effect. Could a new treatment be found?

It was in these circumstances that the monetarists started to gain intellectual and ideological support. True, the medicine that they prescribed would be no more pleasant to endure but it might, some thought, be more effective. The monetarist diagnosis of the problem attributed the cause of the disease, in part at least, to the medicine that had been prescribed in the past. The behaviour of governments in increasing public spending had, they claimed, had a four-fold impact. First, in as much as it had been financed by borrowing, it had made it increasingly costly and difficult for governments to service the ever growing burden of the National Debt. Secondly, increasing public borrowing had tended to pre-empt the lion's share of the available loanable funds, crowding out private sector investment and thus hindering the growth of the private sector. Thirdly, in as much as increasing public spending had necessitated monetary expansion, this had resulted directly in inflation, which had engendered inflationary expectations among employers and employees alike, which had made the eventual curtailment of monetary expansion more difficult to achieve. And, fourthly, the increasingly active role of the State in providing supportive services for individuals and firms had led to a decline in the traditional values of self-reliance and self-advancement by one's own efforts. This moral degeneration had manifested itself at the personal level in a belief that the individual had the right to be maintained by the State, and at the company level by the belief that the State should cushion the firm from the unpleasant effects of market forces.

In the battle that raged between the Keynesians and the monetarists during the 1970s and early 1980s the Keynesians may have won the intellectual skirmishes but the monetarists won control of the political high ground. In Britain in particular, the Conservative Government was wedded to the idea that the level of demand in the economy was determined by the money supply. The mid-1980s was probably the heyday of monetarism but by the beginning of the 1990s it became obvious that the promises which it held out for controlling aggregate demand by the simple control of a particular monetary aggregate were simply not borne out in practice, and support for this form of monetarism fell away.

Summary

The money supply consists of high powered money (cash) issued by the central bank and credit money created by the commercial banks through the process of multiple credit creation. The central bank controls the overall stock of money through its control over the cash base.

The money supply may be related to the way in which public spending is financed – if the government is forced to borrow from the banks rather than from the public this may lead to monetary expansion.

Classical economists used the Quantity Theory of Money to explain the role that money plays in the economy. Nowadays there are more sophisticated versions of the transmission mechanism between the stock of money and the flow of spending which emphasise the notion of asset substitution and portfolio balance.

Key terms

Review questions

4.1 What are the three functions of money?

4.2 Explain in what circumstances the following were (or could have been) used as money, and consider the drawbacks of so doing:
 (a) cigarettes;
 (b) salt;
 (c) cowrie shells;
 (d) cows;
 (e) coffee;
 (f) gold coins.

4.3 What are the two most commonly used official definitions of the money supply in the UK? Explain what they mean.

4.4 Explain what the following terms mean:
 (a) PSBR.
 (b) The National Debt.
 What is the link between the two?

4.5 Which of the following are ways of financing a budget deficit?
 (a) Selling Treasury Bills.
 (b) Persuading the public to buy more National Savings Certificates.
 (c) Printing more £5 notes.
 (d) Selling off assets.
 (e) Selling local authority bonds.
 (f) IMF loan.
 (h) Persuading the public to buy more 'Ernie' Bonds.

4.6 In the Quantity Theory of Money

$$MV = PT$$

What do the four symbols, M, V, P and T, stand for?
What factors might determine the magnitude of V and why therefore might V change (according to Keynes)?
What is likely to happen to V in a hyperinflation?

4.7   The following causal chain represents the interest rate effect on investment of an expansion in the money supply:

increase in money supply
↓
effect on interest rates
↓
effect on investment
↓
effect on Aggregate Demand

Indicate in each case the direction of the supposed effect and what other factors may be present to reduce (or eliminate) the expansionary effect of an increase in the money supply.

4.8   Which of the following statements most nearly describes the view of the transmission mechanism between money and spending held by (a) a contemporary monetarist and (b) a contemporary Keynesian:
(a) An increase in the money supply will cause a reduction in interest rates and this in turn will stimulate investment.
(b) An increase in the money supply means people have more income and they base their consumption spending on their income.
(c) An increase in the money supply will result in some people's wealth portfolios becoming too liquid. Hence they swap money for goods in an attempt to re-establish equilibrium in their portfolios.
(d) An increase in the money supply will result in some people's wealth portfolios becoming too liquid. Hence they buy fewer liquid financial assets, e.g. bonds. This causes an increase in the price of bonds and hence a fall in interest rates.

4.9   Consider an individual whose portfolio of assets is currently in equilibrium. What effect on his holdings of various types of asset will result from the following:
(a) an increase in the rate of inflation which is expected to continue;
(b) increasing optimism on the stock market;
(c) an increase in bank charges for overdrawn balances.

4.10 What will happen to the market price of a bond whose nominal value is £100, which pays 10 per cent of its nominal value annually, if market interest rates rise to 15 per cent?

4.11 Explain the distinction between Bonds and Bills, e.g. Treasury Bonds and Treasury Bills.

4.12 The extreme Keynesian view is that the money supply is unmeasurable, uncontrollable and irrelevant. Explain why they take this view.

5 The labour market: employment and unemployment

5.1   Some terms defined
5.2   Voluntary and involuntary unemployment
5.3   Interim summary
5.4   The determinants of the level of employment and unemployment
5.5   Monetarist views of the determinants of unemployment
5.6   Keynesian views of the determinants of unemployment
5.7   Marginal Productivity Theory
5.8   Structural and frictional unemployment
5.9   Unemployment as an indicator of the level of economic activity

This chapter explores the way in which economists have tried to explain the determinants of the level of unemployment in an economy. It defines the meaning of various terms which are found in the official statistics relating to the labour market and attempts to link those measured magnitudes with the theoretical constructs used by economists within the major paradigms.

5.1 Some terms defined

What determines the level of unemployment in the economy? In trying to answer this question a difficulty we face initially is how to define what is meant by the term 'unemployment'. The published unemployment statistics record those people who register themselves as being available for work but currently without work. These unemployed people indicate their availability for work by 'signing on' each week at their local employment office, which they have to do in order to claim unemployment benefit. In the UK in mid-1997 the figure for the number of unemployed and claiming benefit was around 1.7 million. The total population of the UK (that is, England, Wales, Scotland and Northern Ireland) was about 59 million and the working population slightly less than half that – about 28 million.

65

Unemployment expressed as a percentage of the workforce is thus estimated to have been about 6 per cent.

However, as the figures above show, more than half the population of Britain is not working, or more exactly is not in the employed labour force. Such people are said to be **economically inactive** – that is, they do not form part of the **working population**. What then determines the size of the working population? This is *not* equal to the **population of working age** – that is men aged 18–65 and women aged 18–60. To this figure must be added those people who go on working past the normal retirement age – some MPs, judges, university professors and self-employed people – but one must also subtract those in full-time further and higher education, in prison, those who because of some physical or mental disability are unable to work, and those who *choose* not to be in the workforce. This last group will include married women who do not go out to work, preferring instead to remain at home to look after children or other family members. It will also include some men and women who prefer not to work because their income from social security benefits is almost as great as – or in some cases greater than – the income that they could earn from full-time employment. The unemployment which these last two groups are experiencing could be defined as **voluntary unemployment** – they prefer not to work given the circumstances in which they find themselves. But these last two groups may be treated quite differently in the official statistics. The full-time housewives and carers will not be treated as part of the working population even though the task of child-rearing or caring for an elderly relative may be particularly onerous, and they will not be counted in the unemployment statistics, since they do not register themselves as unemployed and available for work. They therefore do not form part of what is called the **economically active population**. Those people in the second group, however, would normally register themselves as unemployed in order to qualify for social security benefits. Thus, even though they choose to be unemployed in the same way that the housewives do, they may be counted as part of the 'economically active population' and they will be counted in the unemployment statistics as involuntarily unemployed.

By way of summary, a glossary of the more important terms used in official classification is shown in Table 5.1.

The term 'voluntary unemployment' should not be taken to imply that those so classified are necessarily satisfied with the circumstances in which they find themselves. The housewife, for example, may be anxious to go out to work but unable to do so because of the inadequate nursery school provision in her area. Similarly, the father of a large family who finds that he can derive a higher income from social security than he can earn in full-time employment may regret that his employment earnings potential is so low and resent the lack of status that society affords him as an unemployed person.

The fact that we have suggested that some people who could work prefer not to do so implies no moral condemnation of them, whether they be fathers of large families, unmarried mothers, people who stay home to look after aged relatives, or people with substantial inherited wealth. The choice of whether or not to engage in paid employment is a decision which each individual makes, having regard to his

Table 5.1 Glossary of terms

The economically active – people in employment plus the unemployed as measured by household surveys and censuses.

The economically inactive – people who are not economically active, e.g. full-time students who neither have, nor are seeking, paid work and those who are keeping house, have retired or are permanently unable to work.

The population of working age – males aged 16 to 64 years and females aged 16 to 59 years. (In Britain men qualify for state retirement pension at the age of 65, women at the age of 60.)

The activity rate – the proportion of the population of working age who are economically active.

The total labour force – the economically active (this could also be called the *workforce*).

The workforce in employment – employees in employment, self-employed, HM forces and participants on work-related government training programmes. (Critics of the former Conservative Government claimed that the inclusion of this last group served to reduce the unemployment total artificially.) Note also that some of those in employment will not be part of the population of working age.

Unemployment – the definition varies according to the source of the statistics. In the UK the Labour Force Survey uses the ILO (International Labour Office) definition which treats as unemployed those of working age, available for work and who have been seeking a job in the last four weeks. An alternative definition used by administrative sources treats as unemployed those people claiming and receiving the *Jobseeker's Allowance* (formerly known as Unemployment Benefit – the name was changed in 1997 at which time new regulations were brought in which meant that fewer people would qualify for the Allowance than had qualified for the old Unemployment Benefit).

Unemployment rate – the percentage of the 'workforce' who are 'unemployed'. Because of differences in definitions this rate can vary according to the source of the statistics. For example, in March 1996 unemployment in the UK was 7.9% according to national definitions but 8.4% according to standardised OECD definitions.

Source: derived from *Social Trends* and *Employment Gazette*.

or her own circumstances. They will take into account not only the potential income to be earned but also the degree of job satisfaction likely to be experienced. The individual will also take into account the *opportunity cost* of working – what has to be given up in order to earn income from employment. In some cases, this opportunity cost (which may be non-pecuniary) may be so high in comparison with potential net earnings from employment that the rational individual chooses not to enter the labour market.

Figure 5.1 shows **activity rates** for males and females for 1971 and 1996. The activity rate shows the percentage of the population that is in the labour force. As can be seen in the figure, over the last 25 years there has been a slight decline in male activity rates and a marked increase in female activity rates. Notice also that in 1996 both male and female activity rates decline sharply after the age of 55, reflecting the increasing incidence of 'early retirement' – which may itself be a

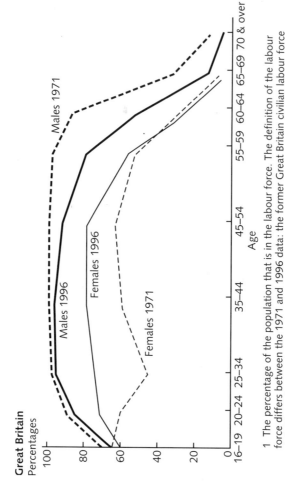

Great Britain
Percentages

Males 1971

Males 1996

Females 1996

Females 1971

100

80

60

40

20

0

16–19 20–24 25–34 35–44 45–54 55–59 60–64 65–69 70 & over

Age

1 The percentage of the population that is in the labour force. The definition of the labour force differs between the 1971 and 1996 data: the former Great Britain civilian labour force definition of unemployment has been used to produce the 1971 data while for the 1996 data the ILO definition has been used and members of the armed forces have been included.

Figure 5.1 Economic activity rates by gender and age, 1971 and 1996

euphemistic expression. As the figure shows, the phenomenon of early retirement is more evident now than it was 25 years ago.

Most importantly, note that activity rates reflect a *choice* that individuals make – albeit a choice constrained by circumstances. The reasons for choosing economic inactivity in preference to economic activity are multifarious. The results of surveys of the labour force which attempt to establish exactly what these reasons are should be treated with a degree of scepticism since respondents may not reveal their underlying motivations to the interviewer, even if they themselves are aware of them. However, the results of one such survey are shown in Table 5.2.

5.2 Voluntary and involuntary unemployment

As we saw in Chapter 3, where we looked at the pre-Keynesian views on the determination of the level of savings and investment, the classical view of the workings of the macroeconomy relied heavily on demand and supply analysis – the so-called Theory of Value. It was natural for the classical economists to apply the same sort of reasoning to the study of the labour market, which is what we do here.

In analysing the labour market we assume, for simplicity, that labour is a **homogeneous** commodity – an hour of one employee's time is equivalent to an hour of any other employee's time. This simplifying assumption will be relaxed later when we consider the problem of structural unemployment.

In Fig. 5.2 we measure, on the horizontal axis, the quantity of labour demanded and supplied and, on the vertical axis, the price of labour (the wage rate). It is important to note that this is measured in *real terms*, that is, it is the money wage divided by the price index.

Table 5.2 Reasons for economic inactivity: percentages by gender, autumn 1996

	Males 16–64	Females 16–59	All of working age
Looking after family or home			
One or more children under school age	1	28	19
One or more other children	2	15	10
Dependent adult relative	3	5	4
Other reasons	0	8	5
All looking after family or home	*7*	*55*	*39*
Student	30	15	20
Temporarily sick or injured	4	2	3
Long-term sick or injured	49	19	29
Discouraged worker	4	4	4
Other reasons	6	5	5
All reasons	**100**	**100**	**100**

Source: Labour Force Survey, Office for National Statistics, quoted in *Social Trends*, 27, 1997.

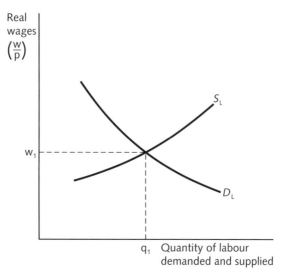

Figure 5.2 The labour market

The number of people offering themselves for employment (the supply of labour) is assumed to be positively related to real wage rates. The higher the reward for work, other things being equal, the greater the number of people who will want to work. This will not necessarily be true in all circumstances, but it is a convenient working hypothesis.

The demand for labour is shown as being inversely related to the price of labour, implying that the demand for labour will fall as the price of labour increases.

The equilibrium level of employment q_1 is thus determined by the intersection of the demand and supply curves, and this occurs at the equilibrium wage rate w_1. At this wage rate, q_1 people will offer themselves for employment, and this will be equal to the number of people that employers are willing to hire at that wage rate. Thus there is no unemployment, or rather there is no **involuntary unemployment**.

Now consider what would happen if the demand for labour shifted to the left, implying a fall in the demand for labour, as in Fig. 5.3. If real wages are flexible downwards, then a new equilibrium level of employment will be established at q_2 at a real wage of w_2. Actual employment has, of course, fallen by $(q_1 - q_2)$ but this movement along the supply curve represents a fall in the number of people *willing* to work, that is, a rise in *voluntary* unemployment, and these individuals, you will recall, like the housewives who stay at home to look after families, are not recorded in the official unemployment statistics.

Although this analysis appears to be sound enough, you may be left with a nagging suspicion that all is not quite as it should be. If employment falls from q_1 to q_2, is not this fall in employment equivalent to an increase in unemployment, whether one calls it voluntary or involuntary? This objection is only valid if the size of the workforce is in some sense fixed. 'Full employment' could then be defined as

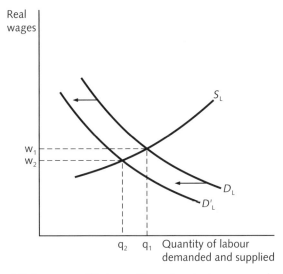

Figure 5.3 A new equilibrium with no involuntary unemployment

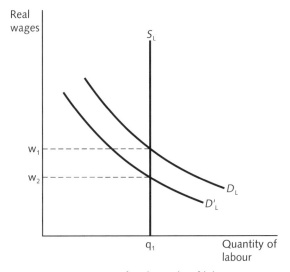

Figure 5.4 A fixed supply of labour

a situation in which all of the workforce was employed and any level of −1employment less than this would be defined as an unemployment situation. If this were the case, the supply curve of labour would be perfectly inelastic, as in Fig. 5.4. q_1 would represent the total workforce, all of whom would have to be employed for the situation to qualify as being 'full employment'.

In those countries where the State took it upon itself to direct people's lives, it may have been possible to define the size of the workforce in some unambiguous

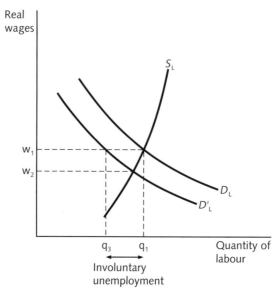

Figure 5.5 Involuntary unemployment emerges if wages are sticky

way. However, in capitalist economies such as our own, individuals are free to choose whether or not they will enter the labour market. However, for those readers who still find the concept of voluntary unemployment difficult to accept, a compromise can be reached. Henceforth, the supply curve for labour will be drawn as a relatively steep curve, indicating that the number of people offering themselves for employment is relatively insensitive to changes in wage rates. In terms of our model, the supply of labour can then be treated as something which has a relatively fixed magnitude.

To continue with our analysis, consider what would happen if wages did not fall, as a result of a shift in the demand for labour, but remained at w_1 as in Fig. 5.5. Actual employment would then fall to q_3 and unemployment equal to $(q_1 - q_3)$ would emerge. All of this unemployment could be regarded as involuntary since the number of people who would like a job at this wage rate is smaller than the number of jobs on offer. It is important to note that this is a disequilibrium situation. The existence of involuntary unemployment occurs as a result of the **downward inflexibility of wages**, which prevents them falling to the equilibrium level w_2.

This was the explanation that the pre-Keynesian economists gave for the existence of unemployment. They regarded it as a disequilibrium phenomenon caused by monopolistic elements in the labour market which prevented the real wage from falling as it ought to do. They argued, however, that the market would eventually adjust to the new equilibrium position and 'full employment' would be restored. It was not necessary for the government to intervene to bring unemployment down as, in the long run, the market would adjust of its own accord.

This argument, though seemingly logical, is now widely regarded as fallacious, for a number of reasons.

First, the demand for labour is what is known as a **derived demand**. It is derived from the demand for the final product which the labour helps to create. The sum of the demands for all the goods and services in the economy – aggregate demand – thus determines the total demand for labour. By far the largest component of aggregate demand is the consumption spending of the workers themselves. Thus, it is argued, if wages fall then aggregate demand will fall, further reducing the demand for labour and creating more unemployment. This objection is not necessarily correct, however. Aggregate demand may not fall because the rise in incomes of the newly employed workers may more than compensate for the fall in incomes of the existing workers.

Secondly, it is argued that wages *never* fall, so that an analysis that says they ought to is flying in the face of reality. This point is easily answered, however, since we are here talking about *real* wages and not money wages. Real wages fall when the rate of price inflation exceeds the rate at which money wages are increasing.

Thirdly, this way of interpreting the behaviour of the labour market is criticised for being unrealistic and out of touch with the way that wage rates are determined in contemporary society. In the real world, it is argued, most wage rates are determined as the result of a process of collective bargaining between the parties involved. The employees' side may be highly organised and able to wield monopoly power, or it may be fragmented and weak. The employer's side similarly may be unified and strong, or fragmented and relatively powerless to resist union demands. The bargaining strengths of the two parties will determine the nature of the wage settlement. In addition, a third party (the government) may influence the outcome of the bargaining process.

This last point is important. In the late 1990s even after 18 years of Conservative rule during which the 'frontiers of the state have been rolled back', a sizeable fraction of the workforce in Britain is still employed in what could loosely be termed the 'public sector'. In that sector wage rates and employment levels are determined not so much by market forces – the pressures of demand and supply – as by institutional factors and administrative decisions. Thus, the number of teachers that a school employs, or the number of nurses employed by a hospital, will depend upon the funds made available from central government, and on directives and policies about required class sizes, waiting lists in hospitals and so on. Teachers' salaries, and those of doctors, nurses, the police and so on, will be agreed nationally by a process where arguments about relativities and differentials play a more important role than arguments about labour shortages or oversupply.

Finally, to what extent do the official unemployment figures capture the theoretical distinction we have made between voluntary and involuntary unemployment? In theory, the official statistics record only involuntary unemployment but they may also erroneously include some voluntary unemployment. Moreover – and this is a much more serious shortcoming – some people who are available for work and are actively seeking it may not register themselves as unemployed, because for one reason or another they are not eligible for the Jobseeker's Allowance and do not wish to subject themselves to the indignity of claiming state welfare benefits. Thus, the unemployment statistics may over- or under-estimate the true level of involuntary unemployment.

5.3 Interim summary

We set out to try to explain the determinants of the level of unemployment. We saw that in our theoretical models we could distinguish between voluntary and involuntary unemployment but that the official statistics may over-record or – more likely – under-record the existence of involuntary unemployment.

A more fruitful line of enquiry may be to ask what determines the level of *employment*. This, we saw, could be explained in terms of the demand and supply of labour. If we can treat the supply of labour as being fixed (invariant with respect to wage rates) then the level of unemployment will be determined as a *residual* – it will be the difference between the level of employment and the size of the workforce (the fixed supply of labour).

What determines the demand for labour? As we saw above, the demand for labour is determined by the level of aggregate demand. In Chapters 3 and 4 we discussed the views of two major competing schools of thought – Keynesian and monetarist – about what determines the level of aggregate demand. We noted there that the level of aggregate demand was crucial in determining the rate of inflation. We can now see that the level of aggregate demand is equally important in determining the demand for labour, which will in turn influence the level of employment, which in its turn influences the level of unemployment.

Even in the public sector where the demand for labour is not directly the result of the spending on those goods and services that labour helps to produce, the demand for labour is nevertheless influenced by the level of aggregate demand. In the Health Service, for example, the demand for labour will be determined by the amount of funds which the government allocates for health care. In a recession, when the level of aggregate demand is low, government tax revenues will be correspondingly low and, because funds are short, expenditure cuts can be expected in all government departments, including those concerned with health care. Thus, the state of demand in the economy indirectly affects the demand for labour in the public sector.

5.4 The determinants of the level of employment and unemployment

We argued above that, in an advanced capitalist society, the price of labour cannot be explained solely in terms of market forces. Wage rates, we argued, are the result of a complex bargaining process between parties with varying degrees of monopoly power where attitudes and expectations play an important part in shaping the final outcome. Suppose therefore that for the purpose of this analysis we treat wage rates as being *exogenous*, that is, determined outside the demand and supply model.

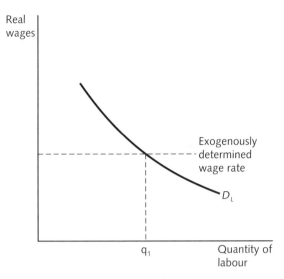

Figure 5.6 An exogenously determined wage rate

It would then follow that the level of employment will be determined solely by the demand for labour, as in Fig. 5.6.

To summarise, we have argued that aggregate demand is the principal determinant of the demand for labour, and that – with a fixed supply – the demand for labour determines employment levels.

Having identified what determines the level of *employment*, we can now proceed to state that – with a fixed supply of labour – the level of unemployment must be determined as a residual. It is equal to the number of people who wish to work (at the going wage rate) minus the number of jobs which the economy sustains. The level of unemployment is thus affected by the level of demand in the economy. *Ceteris paribus*, the higher the level of aggregate demand, the higher will be the demand for labour and the higher the level of employment. The lower, therefore, will be the level of unemployment.

It is a mistake, however, to regard the level of unemployment as being *exclusively* determined by aggregate demand since the supply of labour is equally important. The supply of labour is itself determined by a complex set of socio-economic factors in addition to the obvious fact that it will be affected by changes in the size of the population and its age-structure. These socio-economic factors are partly responsible for the varying *activity rates* which we encountered earlier (Figure 5.1). Remember that the activity rate is defined as:

$$\frac{\text{total employed} + \text{registered unemployed}}{\text{total population of working age}}$$

and it thus measures the fraction of the total population of working age who are economically active.

5.5 Monetarist views of the determinants of unemployment

Up to now, the analysis we have presented has been eclectic, owing no particular allegiance to either Keynesian or monetarist camps. We now want to highlight the crucial differences between these two schools in their analysis of the determinants of unemployment. This section discusses monetarist views, and the following section the Keynesian view.

Monetarists would accept wholeheartedly the foregoing analysis of the labour market. They believe that real wage and employment levels are determined in the labour market and that the market *clears*, that is, it is in equilibrium. They distinguish, however, between short-run and long-run equilibrium. Short-run equilibrium is a situation in which **expectations** are incorrect and hence are unfulfilled, whereas in long-run equilibrium the expectations of all the parties involved are correct anticipations of future events.

The suppliers of labour will be interested in the real wage. Similarly, firms will hire labour only as long as the wage they have to pay is less than the value of what that labour can produce. In other words, they too will be interested in the real wage – the money wage relative to the money value of the extra output that the labour can produce. Monetarists believe that this real wage is flexible in the long run (for example, if money wages fall less than prices, then real wages fall). This flexibility ensures that in the long run a **market-clearing** real wage will rule in the labour market, ensuring full employment or, more exactly, no involuntary unemployment. Any registered unemployment that remains will be 'natural', since the economy will be at the 'natural level' of unemployment.

Assume now, however, that the government undertakes expansionary policies designed to reduce the level of unemployment. The effect will be first of all to increase demand in the market for goods and services, pushing up prices. The demand for labour, therefore, increases because each employee becomes more productive in the sense that the *value* of goods which they produce per hour will rise. The disequilibrium situation in the labour market caused by the increased demand for labour causes money wages to rise and this results in an expansion of supply as more individuals opt voluntarily for labour rather than leisure. Thus, employment levels increase, along with money wages and prices.

Note, however, that this short-run effect will occur only if workers can be fooled into supplying more labour by an increase in money wages alone, in a situation in which *real wages* remain unchanged, prices and wages having increased at the same rate. Workers, in this case, are said to suffer from **money illusion**. In the longer run, however, they realise that increased prices have completely offset the increase in money wages and they therefore revert to their former behaviour. Those who had recently entered employment drop out again, preferring leisure to labour at this real wage. This fall in the supply of labour results in labour shortages and consequently a further rise in money wages. This increase in money wages, which may also be a temporary increase in real wages, leads to a fall in the demand for labour, the net result being that the economy falls back to the **natural level of unemployment**.

The dynamics of the situation, that is, how the economy arrives at the long-run equilibrium position, may be involved and uncertain. The essential point, however, is that deviations from the natural level of unemployment are purely temporary phenomena. In the long run, real wages determine both the amount of labour demanded and supplied and hence the 'natural rate of employment', as in Fig. 5.7.

In the long run, neither of the curves in Fig. 5.7 is altered by the sort of reflationary policies we have been considering, since each curve is based on the rational maximising behaviour of individual firms and individual workers. The supply of labour is based on the labour-leisure choice facing each individual worker. This choice can be influenced by government policies, which make the reward for working higher relative to the reward for not working. A cut in income tax, for example, or a decrease in unemployment pay and social security benefit would have this effect. The demand for labour is based on the profit-maximising actions of firms in hiring labour up to the point where the cost of hiring additional labour exceeds the value of what that labour can produce. This analysis is known as **Marginal Productivity Theory** since the demand for labour depends upon the extra output – the marginal product – which each additional worker can produce. Marginal productivity theory lies at the heart of the neo-classical and monetarist analyses of the labour market and, as we shall see, it is the point at which critics have focused their attack. Note that, according to this analysis, the demand for labour depends upon the real wage and therefore it cannot be permanently raised by expansionary macroeconomic policies, since such policies result in wages rising

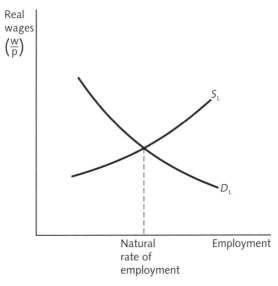

Figure 5.7 The natural level of employment

in line with prices, leaving real wages unchanged. The demand for labour would increase permanently as a result of increased investment in new machinery, for example, which makes labour more productive, but the increased demand for labour brought about by reflationary policies will be purely temporary, and hence such policies cannot reduce unemployment permanently. Rather, monetarists have argued, they result in accelerating inflation of both wages and prices.

To summarise, the common feature which distinguishes the monetarist approach centres around the use of the word 'market'. For monetarists, a market is a device for allocating resources which, in the absence of government regulation, functions smoothly and efficiently. It is a self-equilibrating mechanism, through which the transmission of appropriate signals to both buyers and sellers ensures that supply and demand are brought into equality by movements in prices. This concept of a market is an intellectual construction of sparkling clarity and elegant simplicity. However, although it is an amazingly powerful analytical tool, it may also serve to block thought and hinder scientific progress because, for some people, it has transcended *theory* and become belief. Consider the following:

> I believe that God created the heaven and the earth.
> I believe in the market mechanism.

There is no difference in the meaning of the word 'believe' in each of these two sentences. In neither case does it mean: 'I have a theory that...' Rather it means: 'I support intellectually and emotionally, and accept the view that...' History is littered with examples where belief has stood in the way of understanding and scientific knowledge. In the seventeenth century, Galileo was imprisoned for supporting the Copernican theory, that the planets revolved around the sun, because the theory was incompatible with the Church's belief that the earth was the centre of the universe. Galileo knew that all the evidence was incompatible with the Church's belief but it is extremely difficult to argue with belief, whether it relates to the nature of the universe or the nature of the labour market.

5.6 Keynesian views of the determinants of unemployment

When we say that monetarists believe in the market mechanism, this statement has enormous philosophical and methodological implications. Keynesians, in contrast, accept that *some* markets work as self-equilibrating, smoothly functioning devices but they question whether the market for labour behaves in this way. Although they concede that a market for labour exists, in the sense that there is a demand for labour and a supply, they point to the imperfections inherent in the market, which may prevent it clearing. On both the supply side and the demand side of the market, there are monopolistic elements which can influence wages and employment levels. Money wages, they point out, are notoriously **sticky** in a downwards direction, and even real wages may exhibit such a tendency since institutional factors allow workers to resist cuts in their real wages.

More importantly, they argue that there is not one market for labour, but a number of distinct markets. Each market is separated from the rest by geographical, occupational and institutional factors. Thus, bus drivers in Birmingham and shop assistants in London constitute two **non-competing groups**.

Moreover, if we take any particular occupational group – say local authority manual workers – there may also be two distinct markets – an **internal labour market** comprising existing employees, and an **external labour market** comprising potential employees, all those who are actively or not-so-actively considering employment in this occupation. The internal market is governed by a different set of administrative procedures from that existing in the external market and, although the two markets are interconnected, the internal market is to a lesser or greater extent shielded from the competitive forces to which the external market is exposed.

In addition, some Keynesians would question the validity of Marginal Productivity Theory which underlies the analysis of the demand side of the labour market. The debate here is sufficiently important to warrant further investigation, which we do in the next section.

5.7 Marginal Productivity Theory

Consider the following example, where a shop manager whose objective is to maximise the profit he achieves from his shop can hire as many sales assistants as he wishes at the going rate. Generally speaking, the more staff he has, the greater the sales revenue from the shop, but the more staff hired, the smaller will be the *extra* contribution of each additional assistant. There will come a point when additional staff will actually reduce sales, not because the extra staff are less efficient or more surly, but simply because the size of the shop is fixed and the number of potential customers to be served is limited. In other words, the staff get in each other's way and put off the customers. Clearly, there are too many staff in this situation, but what is the optimal number to hire?

Suppose that the shop manager knows the relationship between the number of staff hired and the shop's output (or sales revenue) as in Table 5.3, columns 1 and 2. The manager can therefore calculate the *extra* output (or extra revenue) attributable to each additional assistant. This extra revenue is shown in column 3 where it is referred to as the **value of the marginal product**.

The optimal number of staff which the manager wishes to hire will depend upon the wage rate. Suppose the going rate is £60 per week. The first assistant will be worth hiring because he or she adds £100 to revenue but only £60 to costs, thus increasing profits by £40. Similarly, the second and third assistants add more to revenue than they do to cost, so that they too will be hired. But the fourth assistant adds only £55 to revenue and a further £60 to costs, so that by employing him or her the manager will be reducing the shop's profits. Hence, the fourth assistant will

Table 5.3 Relationship between number of sales assistants and sales

Number of assistants	Output (Sales revenue) (£ per week)	Extra output (Value of marginal product) (£ per week)
1	100	100
2	180	80
3	245	65
4	300	55
5	320	20
6	320	0
7	310	−10

not be employed. When the wage is £60, the manager will hire three assistants. That is, the demand for labour is three.

However, if wages rise to, say, £70 per week but the productivity of the assistants remains unchanged then the third assistant will no longer be employed because the wage paid exceeds the value of the extra output – the marginal product – created. At the higher wage of £70, the demand for labour drops to two.

In fact, the value of the marginal product curve is the manager's **demand curve for labour**, since it shows how many assistants will be hired at each wage, as in Fig. 5.8. If the four points in Fig. 5.8 were joined up, they would constitute a demand curve for labour. In our particular example, this is a step function rather than a smooth curve, but one can readily appreciate that what Fig. 5.8 illustrates is an inverse relationship between the demand for labour and the wage rate.

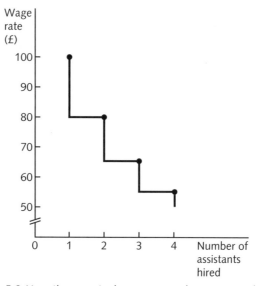

Figure 5.8 How the marginal revenue product curve is derived

This then is the microeconomic foundation of the neo-classical (or monetarist) analysis of the demand side of the labour market. Some Keynesians, while accepting that the analysis is logically consistent in the very restricted context of our example, deny that it can be validly applied in the real world, particularly in the macroeconomic context. There are a number of reasons for this.

First, Keynesians argue that the assumption of profit maximisation may be unrealistic, particularly for labour employed in the public sector. Secondly, even if one accepts that profit maximisation is the goal that firms pursue, to do so successfully requires that firms possess much more information about costs and revenues at the margin than they could ever hope to have in practice. The informational requirement is too great. In other words, it is impossible for firms to calculate the extra revenue attributable to the marginal employee. Thirdly, the analysis presumes that all other factors of production are held constant – for example, the size of the shop cannot be increased, the number of checkouts is fixed and so on. In reality, a shop manager wishing to expand would be more likely to purchase increased amounts of *all* the factors of production rather than holding all the factors fixed, save one. In the real world many technologies are characterised by **fixed factor proportions** and **indivisibilities**. For example, it takes one person to drive a bulldozer – three-quarters of a person is not enough and two people is too much. In short, critics of marginal productivity theory argue that, though the analysis may be internally consistent, it is a poor model of the determination of the demand for labour in contemporary societies, because it can only be applied to a very limited range of circumstances.

5.8 Structural and frictional unemployment

In our analysis so far we have made the simplifying assumption that labour is a homogeneous commodity. This assumption was necessary to enable us to discuss the demand for labour and the supply of labour in aggregate terms, but in reality, of course, labour is not all of the same kind. Different people possess different skills and abilities which suit them for some forms of employment and not for others. This can give rise to a situation in which there is a mis-match between the demand for labour and the supply, not in terms of the numbers of people wanting work and the number of jobs offered, but in terms of the skills possessed by the people wanting jobs and the skills required by the employers. In one particular geographical area there could be, for example, a high and rising demand for bus drivers coexistent with severe unemployment among spot-welders. In such a situation, an overall expansion of demand in the economy will do little to alleviate the problem of unemployed spot-welders. The unemployment that exists in this case is due to structural factors rather than any overall deficiency in aggregate demand.

Structural unemployment, so called, arises either because there is a mis-match of skills available and skills required, or because there is a mis-match between the location where the jobs are available and where the unemployed labour is to be found. This second type of structural unemployment could be described as **regional unemployment**, to emphasise the fact that unemployment, as it exists in the UK, is very much a regional phenomenon – Northern Ireland, the North of England and Wales typically have unemployment rates higher than the rest of the UK and substantially higher than in the South East of England or East Anglia. Unemployment in these less-favoured areas could be reduced by an overall expansion of demand – so, in this sense, it is still valid to think of it as being caused by a deficiency of aggregate demand, but, if such a policy were pursued, the result would be to cause the labour markets of the prosperous South East to become overheated, leading to wage-push inflation long before the unemployment in the less-favoured areas had been mopped up. Governments, therefore, sometimes prefer to use policies which discriminate in favour of the less prosperous areas in order to try to reduce the disparities in unemployment rates between areas. Such **regional policies** have taken a variety of forms, including policies designed to encourage the creation of new jobs in the less-favoured regions through the provision of grants or other forms of financial incentives to employers.

Disparities in unemployment rates persist through all the stages of the business cycle, as Fig. 5.9 illustrates. Whether the national level of unemployment is high or low, certain regions always have unemployment rates above the national average, and the unemployment that persists in these regions when the rest of the economy is buoyant should therefore be ascribed to regional factors rather than to deficiencies of aggregate demand.

It should be noted that the two types of structural unemployment – the skills mis-match and the geographical mis-match – often occur together, the effect of one

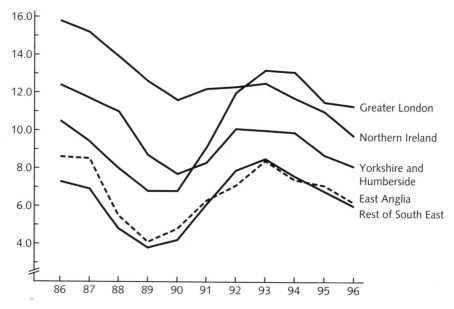

Figure 5.9 Unemployment rates in selected regions, 1986–96

reinforcing the other. In many cases, a whole area may be heavily dependent on one industry that is experiencing decline or rapid technological change which reduces the need for labour. This has occurred in Britain in the West Midlands, an area heavily dependent on the motor industry. As the motor industry has declined in importance as an employer of labour, so unemployment rates in the West Midlands – once one of the most prosperous areas of the country – have risen relative to other areas.

Technological change, which reduces the demand for labour, produces what is sometimes referred to as 'technological unemployment'. This has become particularly associated with the so-called microelectronic revolution, though, in fact, its causes are much more widespread.

'Technological' unemployment has, in fact, been proceeding more or less rapidly since the dawn of time, though arguably – the process has now speeded up – it did, after all, take over one hundred years before the invention of the musket made the archer redundant. It is important to note, however, that in any dynamic economy – that is, one in which the pattern of consumer demand changes over time and in which technology also changes – a certain amount of temporary unemployment is, more or less, inevitable. Such **frictional unemployment** arises because employees do not have perfect information about job vacancies and employers do not have perfect information about available unemployed labour. It therefore takes time to find a job and the unemployment statistics will always record some people who are in the process of changing jobs. Such frictional unemployment can be minimised by improving the flow of information – for example, by improving the services offered by Job Centres – but can never be totally eliminated. Indeed, without a certain amount of frictional unemployment, changes in employment patterns could not occur.

5.9 Unemployment as an indicator of the level of economic activity

The level of unemployment is often taken as a crude indication of the state of aggregate demand in the economy. High levels of unemployment tend to be associated with situations in which the level of aggregate demand is relatively low and the economy is experiencing a recession; conversely, low levels of unemployment tend to be associated with a buoyant economy where the level of economic activity is high. Although this is a general tendency, it does not, however, follow as a matter of course. The level of economic activity determines, other things being equal, the demand for labour. This, together with the supply of labour, in turn determines the extent of unemployment.

The level of unemployment is more correctly thought of as the state of excess supply of labour and this may be more accurately measured by taking account of registered vacancies as well as registered unemployment. In Britain the Department of Employment publishes estimates of vacancies but it is acknowledged

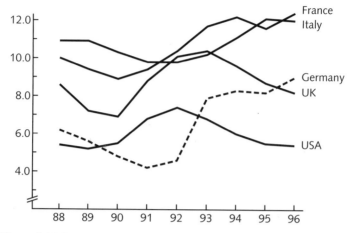

Figure 5.10 Percentage unemployment in various countries, 1988–96

that the statistics may be inaccurate because of under-reporting. That is, firms may not notify the Job Centres when they have vacancies, preferring instead to recruit labour by other means. The extent of under-reporting may vary systematically with the unemployment rate.

It is accepted, however, that movements in unemployment rates do measure, albeit in a rather crude way, the state of demand in the economy. We should not be surprised to learn therefore that unemployment rates in different countries tend to move together, just as unemployment rates in different regions of the same country tend to move together. That is, in all of those countries linked by trade, unemployment rates tend to move in the same direction at the same time, as if moved by a common force. This force is, of course, the level of world economic activity. However, some economies appear to be better able to hold unemployment in check than others. Figure 5.10 illustrates this.

We have now identified three different types of unemployment – demand deficient, structural and frictional unemployment. It is, of course, not possible to say whether any one particular unemployed person is experiencing structural, frictional or demand deficient unemployment, since the 'types' of unemployment are explanations of the phenomenon rather than mutually exclusive categories. Rather, the purpose of distinguishing the different types of unemployment is to identify their cause as an essential step in devising appropriate policies for alleviating the problem.

Summary

If one applies demand and supply analysis to the labour market, a distinction can be made between involuntary and voluntary unemployment. The existence of involuntary unemployment can be viewed as a disequilibrium phenomenon caused by real wages being sticky downwards.

The unemployment rate measures claimant unemployed as a percentage of the total labour force, which is equivalent to the working population but not equivalent to the population of working age. The activity rate measures the proportion of the population of working age who choose to be economically active. The remainder – the economically inactive – can be thought of as being voluntarily unemployed.

The use of demand and supply analysis as a complete explanation of how the labour market works tends to be acceptable to monetarists but Keynesians regard it as overly simplistic. They point to such things as internal markets where the terms on which labour is bought and sold are different from those on external markets.

Marginal Productivity Theory is an essential element of the analysis. The demand for labour is the marginal revenue product curve.

In addition to the unemployment caused by deficiencies in aggregate demand, unemployment also arises as a result of structural and frictional factors.

Key terms

economically inactive	66	Marginal Productivity Theory	77
working population	66	sticky (money wages, downwards)	78
population of working age	66	non-competing groups	79
voluntary unemployment	66	internal labour market	79
economically active population	66	external labour market	79
activity rates	67	value of the marginal product	
homogeneous commodity	69	(of labour)	79
involuntary unemployment	70	demand curve for labour	80
downward inflexibility of wages	72	fixed factor proportions	81
derived demand	73	indivisibilities	81
expectations	76	structural unemployment	81
market-clearing	76	regional unemployment	82
money illusion	76	regional policies	82
natural level of unemployment	77	frictional unemployment	83

Review questions

5.1 'An increase in employment levels of 1 million implies an equal reduction in the numbers of the unemployed.' What is wrong with this statement?

5.2 How do you measure the fraction of the total population of working age who are economically active? What do you think has happened to this statistic in recent years? Why?

5.3 Registered unemployment is supposed to measure the extent of 'involuntary unemployment' in the economy. State why it might either overestimate or underestimate the true extent of such 'involuntary unemployment'.

5.4 Given the official population census classifications, where would you place the following persons in terms of their employment status?
   (a) Persons detained in HM prisons.
   (b) Non-working housewives.
   (c) Full-time students.
   (d) Part-time students.

(e) A 61-year-old man recently made redundant.

(f) A 61-year-old woman recently made redundant.

(g) A chronically sick person incapable of working.

(h) A relative who stays at home to look after the above.

5.5 *Ceteris paribus*, what effect will each of the following have on the level of employment in the private sector (adopt a conventional Keynesian view of the determinants of employment).

(a) a cut in income taxes;

(b) an increased propensity to spend on imported goods;

(c) an increase in the number of traffic wardens employed.

5.6 'If people would agree to work for lower wages the unemployment problem would be solved.' Which of the following responses to this quote is most nearly correct?

(a) People never agree to work for lower wages because trade unions keep wages up.

(b) If people already in employment took a wage cut, their incomes would fall and hence spending would fall. This would further depress the demand for labour.

(c) The statement is correct because people have been pricing themselves out of jobs recently by asking for wage increases that exceed productivity increases.

5.7 Which of the following statements are correct:

(a) At the natural rate of unemployment there is no demand deficient unemployment.

(b) The natural rate of unemployment could be reduced if unemployment benefit and social security benefit were abolished.

(c) For the father of twelve dependent children the opportunity cost of working is very high.

5.8 What evidence suggests that the natural rate of unemployment rose in the 1980s?

5.9 The difference between the number of people that want jobs at the prevailing wage rate and the number of jobs available is known as:

(a) The natural rate of unemployment.

(b) Voluntary unemployment.

(c) Involuntary unemployment.

(d) Registered unemployment.

5.10 A tomato farmer can hire tomato pickers at £20 per day and the relationship between pickers and yield is given below:

Number of pickers	Tomato output (£)
1	60
2	110
3	135
4	154
5	164
6	169
7	170
8	170

If the farmer wants to maximise his profits he should hire only:

(a) one tomato picker because he or she picks the most;

(b) three tomato pickers because the fourth costs more than he or she produces;

(c) seven tomato pickers because that maximises output.

The tomato pickers' union, in an attempt to make its members better off, manages to enforce a legal minimum wage of £26 per day. If our profit-maximising farmer complies, which of the following will be correct:

(a) Each of the tomato pickers our farmer had previously hired will become better off.

(b) The quantity of tomato output will fall.

(c) Unemployment among tomato pickers will increase.

If we had information on the number of pickers who would be hired at each wage rate we could trace out a schedule which would be the demand for tomato pickers' labour. This would depend on the value of their marginal product (VMP).

Say whether the following statements are true or false. If false, correct them:

(a) The maximum wage that tomato pickers can earn is limited by the value of their marginal product.

(b) An increase in the market price of tomatoes will lead to a fall in the demand for tomato pickers' labour.

(c) If the supply of pickers is completely inelastic (i.e. fixed), the wage that they earn will not reflect their productivity.

(d) If employers were able to discriminate (i.e. pay each worker a different wage), the wages of each worker would be equal to the value of their marginal product.

(e) This analysis assumes that other factors of production are variable.

(f) In the long run pickers will be paid in accordance with what they produce.

5.11 Give examples of:

(a) regional unemployment;

(b) structural unemployment;

(c) demand deficient unemployment.

Are these categories mutually exclusive?

5.12 Table 5.5 shows percentage unemployment in various regions of the UK.

Table 5.5 Unemployment in selected regions

	East Anglia	Greater London	Rest of South East	Yorkshire & Humberside	Northern Ireland
1986	8.6	10.5	7.3	12.4	15.8
1987	8.5	9.4	6.9	11.7	15.2
1988	5.5	8.0	4.8	11.0	13.9
1989	4.1	6.8	3.8	8.7	12.6
1990	4.8	6.8	4.2	7.7	11.6
1991	6.3	9.1	6.1	8.3	12.2
1992	7.1	12.0	7.9	10.1	12.3
1993	8.4	13.2	8.5	10.0	12.5
1994	7.4	13.1	7.6	9.9	11.7
1995	7.1	11.5	6.8	8.7	11.0
1996	6.2	11.3	6.0	8.1	9.7

Source: derived from *Regional Trends* 1996 and 1997. Figures are ILO unemployment rates.

(a) Which area has the highest unemployment rate?
(b) Do you think the unemployment that existed in that area in 1989 was due to cyclical factors (i.e. was it 'demand deficient' unemployment?). If not, what was it?
(c) How would you classify the unemployment that existed in East Anglia in 1993?
(d) If income taxes were reduced, *ceteris paribus*, would this reduce the rate of unemployment in Greater London?

6 The labour market and inflation

Preview

Increases in wage costs are often a key element in the inflationary process. As part of their counter-inflation strategy some governments have supplemented demand-management policies with policies aimed at directly restraining the growth of wages by so-called incomes policies. This chapter examines the difficulties associated with attempting to control wage-push inflation by direct controls. It also examines a key piece of economic theory known as the Phillips curve.

6.1 Wage inflation

In Chapter 2 we saw how the causes of inflation could be explained in terms of demand pressures or in terms of autonomous increases in costs such as wage costs. It was argued that autonomous increases in costs would result in a sustained increase in prices only if the level of demand was allowed to expand to enable the same volume of goods to be bought at the higher prices. If aggregate demand were fixed, increases in wage costs would lead to falling output and employment. In practice, however, we recognised that there is often considerable political pressure on governments to allow the level of demand to expand, and thus prevent the unemployment that would otherwise occur.

Since the Keynesian revolution some 50 years ago it has been widely accepted that governments have the responsibility for maintaining a level of effective demand which is sufficient to ensure the full or reasonably full employment of resources, particularly labour resources. Thus, for the first half of the post-war period, at least, the maintenance of 'full employment' was arguably the government's top priority, not just in the UK but in almost all advanced market economies. Since high levels of unemployment were embarrassing for governments, there was an expectation among the electorate that the government would take steps to alleviate the problem. This means that there was an expectation that the government *would* allow the level of demand to rise to prevent unemployment.

In such a situation autonomous increases in costs, particularly wage costs, may be an important determinant of the rate of inflation. Thus the use of the term **wage inflation** which implies that the cause of the increases in the price level can be traced to increases in wage costs. This explanation of the causes of inflation, however, implicitly assumes that the government will act in an **accommodating fashion**, allowing demand to expand. Economic agents – firms, individual workers, trade unions – will generally take this view about the government's likely action. Thus the trade union *expects* that an increase in wage rates will not lead to a fall in the demand for its labour because the increased wage costs will be passed on in the form of higher prices. The employer *expects* that, as a result of the increased costs which have been passed on to customers in the form of higher prices, the demand for the firm's product will not fall because there will be an increase in purchasing power and because the firm's competitors are also announcing similar price increases. Thus, everyone expects inflation to continue, and wage increases are therefore negotiated which ensure that inflation does indeed continue. Deflationary demand management policies could in theory prevent inflation from proceeding and thus change people's expectations. But this process of changing people's expectations by holding down the level of aggregate demand would involve a painful period of adjustment, with high unemployment and falling living standards for a time at least. Hence, for most governments whose time horizon is necessarily short, the price (in terms of political popularity) of getting inflation down is too high, and they cannot afford to pay it.

6.2 Pay restraint policies

Hence governments sometimes resort to other means which appear to offer a way out of the dilemma. One such alternative is a **pay restraint** imposed by the government on the earnings of individual groups of workers. These **wages policies** or **incomes policies** were an important part of government counter-inflation policy in Britain during the post-war period up until 1979. The rationale for these policies was that, if wage costs could be held down in the short run, this would bring down the rate of price inflation. This would, in turn, reduce the expected rate of inflation, and hence the wage increases negotiated in the following time period would be more modest. Thus, a progressive reduction in the rate of inflation would be achieved.

There are, however, certain difficulties inherent in the operation of incomes policies, and the remainder of this section is devoted to a discussion of the problems involved in using these forms of pay restraint as an instrument of macroeconomic management. The effectiveness of such policies in reducing wage inflation is also discussed.

Statutory or 'voluntary'

In what is fundamentally a free enterprise economy it is not really feasible to enforce laws governing the price to be paid for a particular good or service unless the overwhelming majority of the populace believe those laws to be just, and thus voluntarily comply with them. The difficulty is not in putting the laws on the statute book – any government with a parliamentary majority can do that. The difficulty is in enforcing the laws. By analogy, it is easy to pass a law making the use of seat belts in cars compulsory, but extremely difficult to enforce it. It would require an enormous amount of resources (a policeman on every street corner) to ensure that no one broke the law. In such a case people either act within the law voluntarily or they break the law with impunity apart from the tiny minority who are unlucky enough to get caught. Moreover, if people believe in the wisdom of wearing seat belts they will do so whether or not the law tells them to, and in this case the law is superfluous.

At this point, however, the analogy between the wearing of seat belts and the actions of employees in seeking to increase their income breaks down. In the seatbelt case you are asking people to behave in a way which is, in fact, in their own interest. The major beneficiary is the individual who wears the belt though society as a whole may experience some benefit in terms of a smaller burden on the National Health Service. In the latter case, however, by asking individuals to refrain from seeking wage increases, you are asking them to behave in a way which runs counter to their own best interests, though society as a whole may benefit from it. If it were universally agreed that this act of self-sacrifice would, in fact, benefit society, it might be possible for sufficient moral suasion to be exercised to persuade the individual to act against his or her own interests, but since there is no such universal agreement that wage restraint will bring down the rate of inflation and preserve real living standards, such moral suasion is weak and ineffective.

Because of the inherent difficulties with policies which attempt to restrain pay in a formal, statutory way, governments have often opted for what have been euphemistically called 'voluntary' incomes policies. They are 'voluntary' in the sense that no legislation has been placed on the statute book, though governments have attempted to ensure compliance with their directives by a variety of means. In Britain in the 1970s this took the form of tri-partite agreements reached between the government, the employers' organisation – the CBI (the Confederation of British Industry), and the employees' organisation – the TUC (the Trades Union Congress), which at that time was much more powerful and influential than it is today. However, since neither the CBI nor the TUC had any power to compel its members to abide by the agreements, the effectiveness of the agreements depended to a large extent on the degree to which a consensus existed about the desirability of wage and price restraint. In the event there was insufficient consensus for the agreements to have much effect.

Sanctions

Whether the incomes policy is statutory or voluntary, it will be difficult to enforce. First, as we have already noted, the administrative cost of monitoring the millions of pricing decisions that are made in the economy every year is very high. Second is the problem of what sanctions can be applied to those who do not abide by the government's directives.

In the past, society has punished those who transgress the law in a variety of ways – fines, imprisonment, deportation, hanging and so on – and the motive for so doing has been threefold. First, to set an example so that others will be more easily persuaded not to break the law *(pour encourager les autres)*. Second, to ensure that some restitution takes place and, third, so that society can extort retribution from the lawbreaker. Although the retributive motive figures prominently in some people's attitudes towards trade union legislation, it is the other two motives which concern us here. Clearly, whatever sanctions are taken, to be effective they should encourage others not to break the law in the same way and they should take from the lawbreakers the fruits of their illegal act.

In the context of a wage settlement in excess of some agreed guideline one can attempt to impose a fine, the magnitude of which is related to the degree to which the wage settlement was deemed to be excessive. A very real problem arises, however, as to who should pay the fine – the employee or the employer – since both were party to the illegal act. A second and more serious problem arises if one or both parties refuse to pay the fine. The only sanction that then remains is imprisonment and, although the imprisonment of trade union officials is not an uncommon occurrence in some countries, the undesirability of such a solution is obvious.

An alternative solution is to use the income tax system to tax away wage increases in excess of the government's directive. Such a tax-based incomes policy would, of course, require a substantial increase in the resources of the Inland Revenue. The feasibility of such a scheme is open to question and has never been attempted in the UK.

Formulating the policy

The limit on wage increases can be in the form of either a lump sum or a fixed percentage increase (or some combination of the two). There could possibly be some relaxation of the controls for the low paid.

Wage increases which could be wholly financed through increased **productivity** could be encouraged. If these were genuine productivity increases then **wage costs per unit of output** would not rise despite the rise in wages. Keeping down wage costs, as distinct from wages, is the objective of the incomes policy. The danger of relaxing controls in this way, however, is that in many occupations, labour productivity –

defined as the value of output per unit of labour input – is difficult to measure, or difficult to improve, or both. In teaching, for example, the value of output cannot be measured. It would be possible for teachers to teach bigger classes but this does not necessarily increase the teacher's productivity, since the quality of the education that is given to each child might deteriorate. An incomes policy which encourages 'productivity deals' would discriminate against groups such as teachers. If, however, the salaries of groups such as teachers were allowed to increase under some sort of 'comparability principle' then there would be a tendency for the general level of wage increases to be lifted to the level of those industries where productivity increases are easiest to secure. In other occupations where, as we have seen, it may be difficult to measure productivity, the possibility of measuring it in some spurious fashion is opened up, and this provides employers and employees with the opportunity of circumventing the controls by negotiating spurious productivity deals.

For these reasons a **wage freeze** may be a simpler and more effective policy. Whatever form of incomes policy is imposed, however, the distribution of earnings between different occupations will be affected, or one could say *distorted*, by the policy. In the absence of any sort of government policy on incomes, occupational differentials will ultimately be determined by market forces. The forces of demand and supply, or **relative scarcity**, must in the long run determine the wage that any particular type of labour can command. Over time, relative scarcities will change and thus occupational differentials will change also. For example, 50 years ago the average wage of blue-collar workers was less than that of the lowest grade of white-collar worker. Nowadays, the situation is reversed. This change has not been brought about by the increased recognition of the nobility of manual labour; it merely reflects changes in the relative scarcities of the two types of labour.

In essence, it is impossible for any form of incomes policy to be sufficiently flexible to allow the pattern of differentials to change in response to changing relative scarcities. Thus, the application of an incomes policy leads to a pattern of differentials which is different from that which would be produced in the absence of any such policy. This may be an explicit objective of the policy. For example, it could be argued that the differentials between highly paid workers and low paid workers are too great and should be narrowed by allowing larger increases for low-paid workers. Implicit in this view is the belief that the set of differentials produced by the market mechanism is undesirable, and that the incomes policy should try to amend it. The success of an incomes policy can thus be judged by the extent to which it modifies the set of differentials that would have existed in the absence of the policy – that is, the set of earnings differentials that would be produced by the unfettered workings of the market mechanism.

Is a consensus possible?

Wage control is frequently associated with industrial unrest, which often has far-reaching consequences. The 'May events' in France in 1968 and the fall of the Conservative Government in Britain in 1974 and the Labour Government in 1979 were all caused, in part at least, by industrial troubles brought about by incomes policies. As a result, many people have asked whether there might not be a less painful way of agreeing on differentials. Is it not possible, they ask, for a society to arrive at a consensus view on the pattern of differentials. In essence they are asking the question whether, given the size of the national cake, it is possible for everyone to agree how that cake should be divided up. Is there any criterion which would be universally accepted, by which an impartial arbiter could work out how much a nurse should earn relative to a doctor, an accountant or a shop worker?

The answer to this question is yes, but it will prove to be a disappointing answer, as we shall presently show. In order to appreciate the answer fully, however, we need to consider the question of how wage differentials are in fact determined in our society, and whether or not there is an economically founded pattern of wage differentials.

First, however, it may be useful to look at the data on earnings differentials in Table 6.1 since these are the earnings relativities that we shall try to account for.

Table 6.1 Average earnings – full-time males on adult rates

	Average gross weekly pay (April 1996)
Police officer (inspector and above)	700.2
Police officer (sergeant and below)	486.3
Mechanical engineers	532.0
Software engineers	519.7
Medical practitioners	852.7
University and polytechnic teaching professionals	577.0
Legal professionals	727.3
Legal associate professionals	488.0
Chartered and certified accountants	536.4
Marketing and sales managers	644.7
Laboratory technicians	337.9
Social workers, probation officers	372.9
Draughtspersons	359.5
Computer analysts, programmers	470.7
Nurses	370.0
Security guards	264.1
Bar staff	186.6
Telephone salespersons	261.7
Painters and decorators	264.4
Plumbers, heating engineers	370.1
Tyre and exhaust fitters	226.4
Bus and coach drivers	249.9
Farm workers	235.7
Hotel porters	177.7
Cleaners, domestics	201.5
All manual occupations	301.3
All non-manual	464.5
All occupations	391.6

Source: New Earnings Survey 1996, Part A, Table 8.

6.3 How does the market mechanism determine wages?

The price that any particular factor of production can command must ultimately depend on its scarcity. In other words, the laws of demand and supply are inexorable. Like the law of gravity, which states that there will be a mutual attraction between two bodies proportional to their masses, the laws of supply and demand (which were discovered rather than invented by economists) state that, when goods or services are traded on markets, there exists an *equilibrium* price which is determined by the forces of demand and supply. Transactions can take place at prices which differ from the equilibrium price, but there will normally be a tendency for prices to move towards the equilibrium. Thus, in the labour market, though short-term aberrations are possible, in the long run the reward that any particular type of labour receives will depend upon the forces of demand and supply. Thus, there exists an economically founded pattern of wage differentials.

This much would be agreed by most economists, though not all. It represents the view of the mainstream of economic theory (what is normally called neo-classical economics) to which most practitioners of the art and teachers of the discipline subscribe. There are, of course, alternative views – such as the Marxist interpretation – but here we content ourselves with a more detailed examination of the neo-classical analysis of wage differentials.

Consider three groups of workers – airline pilots, doctors and nurses. How can neo-classical economics explain the earnings of these three groups of workers? Consider first the labour market for airline pilots, illustrated in Fig. 6.1.

We can argue that there will be an equilibrium wage, W_e, for pilots' services, and that the actual wage will tend towards this equilibrium level. Thus, if the actual wage is less than W_e, say W_L, there will be an excess demand for pilots. Airlines will

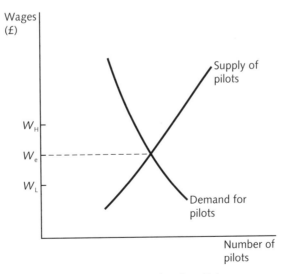

Figure 6.1 The market for pilots

find they cannot service all their schedules with their existing staff and they will try to hire more staff, attracting them away from other employers by offering higher wages. Thus, the actual wage will tend to move up towards the equilibrium. Similarly, if the actual wage is above the equilibrium level, say at W_H, there will be an excess supply of pilots. In their wage negotiations pilots will now be in a weak bargaining position, since there are now more people seeking jobs as pilots than there are jobs available. Thus, pilots' wages will tend to decline, perhaps not in absolute terms (though this is possible if their wages do not keep pace with inflation), but more likely in *relative* terms, that is, relative to other groups of workers.

However, if the equilibrium wage is in fact determined by demand and supply, we then have to ask what determines the demand for and supply of pilots.

Clearly, the demand for pilots is derived from the demand for air travel. If no-one wished to travel by air, there would be no demand for commercial airline pilots. Similarly, the greater the demand for air travel the greater the demand for pilots. They are an essential **factor of production** which, together with other factors of production – air stewardesses, mechanics, air-traffic controllers and so on – combine to produce a service which the consumer is willing to purchase. Thus, when the customer buys a ticket, they are buying the services of all these people.

The **elasticity of demand** for airline pilots will depend, among other things, on the degree to which they constitute an *essential* factor of production. This goes part of the way to explaining why pilots earn more than other crew members, since it is impossible to provide air travel without pilots, but feasible to do so without stewards.

The supply of pilots depends upon a different set of factors from those which determine demand. To become an airline pilot one has to possess certain attributes – good health, good eyesight, a higher than average IQ, a head for heights and so on – and this immediately disqualifies the majority of the population from becoming pilots. The more stringent the entry qualifications, the fewer the number of people that will be able to meet them. Thus, even though they might be attracted by the high salaries that pilots earn, and by the attractive uniform, people who do not possess the necessary attributes cannot become pilots. The supply of pilots is thus fairly *inelastic* – it is not very responsive to changes in wages or, to put the same thing in another way, a large increase in wages is required to call forth a small increase in supply.

The supply of pilots is further restricted by the establishment of a professional organisation – a pilots' trade union – which can limit entry into the profession, or establish operating standards and procedures which are more stringent than is strictly necessary for safety reasons. If the union is well organised and successful, the effect of this will be, in terms of our analysis, to push the supply curve to the left, thus raising the equilibrium wage for pilots as in Fig. 6.2.

Taking all these factors together, we could argue that, because there is a high demand for pilots, because the demand is inelastic and because the supply of pilots is inelastic, this will tend to keep the equilibrium wage high and rising.

Doctors are another group who earn high wages. Unlike airline pilots, however, the service that they help to produce is not sold to consumers, since in Britain

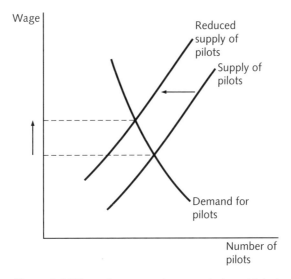

Figure 6.2 Wages increase when supply is restricted

under the National Health Service medical care is provided free, or almost free, to consumers and financed out of general taxation. Thus, the demand for doctors does not depend upon market forces; rather, it is the result of a complex set of decisions taken by hospital administrators, civil servants, government ministers and so on. Nevertheless, we can still describe the demand for doctors as a derived demand since they are, in effect, a factor of production which combines with other factors to produce health care, a service for which consumers would be willing to pay. Indeed, the very existence of private medicine in Britain illustrates that consumers are willing to pay for health care. However, because health care is provided publicly by the NHS, the government in effect decides when it allocates spending how much health care will be produced and consumed. In so doing, the government also determines the demand for doctors, though if the services of the doctors became very expensive we might expect hospital administrators to substitute other factors of production – technicians, nurses, clerical staff and so on – in order to minimise the cost of producing a given amount of health care. The degree to which doctors can be substituted by other factors of production will determine the elasticity of demand for doctors. As with airline pilots, where we argued that, because of the essential role they played, the elasticity of demand for their labour would be low, so with doctors we could argue that the demand for their services will be inelastic because of the essential role they play in providing health care.

On the supply side, we can argue that the supply of doctors will be highly inelastic for the same reasons that the supply of pilots is inelastic, namely that to become a doctor requires high academic qualifications, a lengthy training period and so on, and that this disqualifies most of the population from taking up jobs as doctors, however much they might be attracted by the high salaries. As with pilots, the establishment of a professional organisation, or doctors' trade union, can restrict the supply of doctors still further – imposing minimum entry requirements into the profession over and above what would be required to safeguard the interests of the patient.

Thus, an analysis of the labour market for doctors would look similar to that for pilots in Fig. 6.1, the combination of an inelastic demand and an inelastic supply ensuring a high equilibrium wage.

The wages that nurses earn in the NHS on the other hand are quite low. If the wage that they earn is, in fact, the equilibrium wage (and we discuss this below) then the fact that the equilibrium wage is low must be because the demand for nurses is low in relation to the supply of nurses.

As with doctors, the demand for nurses within the NHS is determined not by market forces but by a set of administrative decisions. The demand for nurses is still a derived demand, since they too combine with other factors (including doctors) to produce health care. The elasticity of demand for nurses will depend upon how easily the services of a trained nurse can be substituted by other factors of production – ancillary staff, ward orderlies and so on – and on *a priori* grounds we could argue that they will be less essential and hence face a more elastic demand for their services than doctors or airline pilots.

A more marked difference is apparent on the supply side of the market, however. The entry requirements into the training schools are much lower than for doctors or pilots, there is a highly elastic supply of foreign-trained nurses and, with no effective trade union organisation to restrict the supply of nurses by imposing strict entry requirements or restrictive codes of conduct, the supply of nurses in Britain is highly elastic. Hence a small increase in wages calls forth a greatly increased supply, thus ensuring that the equilibrium wage remains low.

By this stage some readers will have been moved to indignation. Surely nurses should be paid more than they are at present? How can one seek to justify the low pay of nurses in terms of the workings of the so-called laws of demand and supply?

In response to this understandable indignation, the neo-classical economist would reply that what the above analysis has attempted to do is explain *why* some occupations earn more than others. The analysis does not attempt to say what differentials *ought* to exist, nor does it say that the existing differentials are 'just' or 'fair'. This is the way the market mechanism works. To say that the laws of demand and supply are 'unfair' is rather like saying that the law of gravity is unfair because bodies with a larger mass exert a larger gravitational pull.

If nurses formed a strong trade union and succeeded in restricting the supply of nurses, this would, *ceteris paribus*, raise the equilibrium wage and the actual wage would in the long run rise towards the equilibrium level. The particular economic analysis we have been using does not suggest that the higher wage is more justifiable or less justifiable than the lower one. It merely explains how in the long run relative scarcity, or the laws of demand and supply, determine the wage that a particular occupational group can command.

6.4 A consensus solution

We asked earlier whether it was possible for a consensus to emerge as to how the national cake should be divided up between the various occupational groups. Was it possible, we wondered, for an impartial arbiter to establish a set of criteria that could be used to work out how much each group of workers ought to earn relative to other groups?

Suppose that our impartial arbiter does establish some formula which everyone is persuaded to accept through some process of mass hypnosis. The formula could take into account variables such as the number of years' education or formal training required to do the job, the degree of physical or mental skill or physical strength required, the degree of unpleasantness associated with the job, the health risks and so on. Each of these variables could have a weighting associated with it, so that for each occupation the formula could be used to arrive at a single number which would thus represent the consensus view as to what this particular occupational group ought to be paid.

Suppose that all wage differentials established by the formula are accepted by all, but there arises a shortage of, say, bus drivers. What is to be done? It appears that greater financial incentives have to be paid to persuade people to become bus drivers. But how can this be done? Can the formula be changed in some way so that bus-driving scores a higher number? Clearly, either the weightings in the formula have to be changed or else additional variables have to be included in the formula, together with their associated weightings. Over time the formula could be adjusted and, given enough time, a formula could be arrived at which ensured that in each occupation there was neither an excess demand nor an excess supply of labour. Certainly, this formula would be very complicated, containing many hundreds of different variables, including things such as the degree of skill involved in any particular job, society's evaluation of the worth of the good or service that this labour helped to create, and how important a contribution any particular type of labour made in producing that good or service. Ironically, the set of wage differentials that would be produced by the super-formula would be identical to the set of differentials produced by the market mechanism. This is not surprising, since the many hundreds of variables which our formula would take into account would be precisely those variables which determine the supply of and demand for any particular type of labour. We would have established a surrogate price system.

6.5 Can intervention permanently modify earnings differentials?

LASC LIBRARY LRS

The foregoing analysis should not be interpreted as suggesting that the set of earnings differentials produced by the market mechanism is the only possible set. Government intervention, through an incomes policy or minimum wage

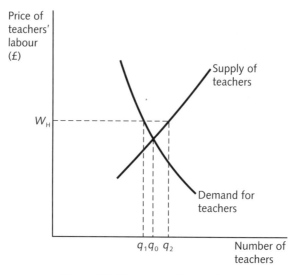

Figure 6.3 The market for teachers

legislation, can affect differentials but there will be a tendency for equilibrium differentials to be restored when the policy is relaxed. In certain circumstances, however, it is possible to argue that government policy could permanently affect wage differentials. Consider the labour market for school teachers. The demand for school teachers will be inelastic, being the result of government policy, but since local authorities have some leeway as to what pupil-teacher ratio to apply, whether to provide nursery schools and so on, the demand for teachers will be affected by their salary levels. These salary levels will be determined more or less exogenously by a process of wage bargaining. What would be the effects on the labour market for teachers of a campaign which succeeded in securing a wage as high as W_H in Fig. 6.3? This is a disequilibrium situation and in the foregoing analysis we have argued that in the long run *price* will adjust to bring the market back into equilibrium.

It is possible, however, that the variable which adjusts to bring the market back into equilibrium is *quantity* not price. At a wage of W_H only q_1 teachers will be employed. This means that, if the market was formerly in equilibrium (when q_0 would have been employed), there will be a reduction in the numbers of teachers employed of $(q_0 - q_1)$. This reduction may be brought about by early retirement, or by natural wastage, or some redundancies may be involved. At the same time, the increase in wages will produce a movement along the supply curve so that the number of people wishing to be employed as teachers increases to q_2. There is thus substantial unemployment of $(q_2 - q_1)$.

The effect of this will be two-fold. First, the government may instruct teacher training institutions to reduce their output of newly trained teachers since there is little point in training new teachers when there is already a 'teacher surplus'. Secondly, teaching will become less attractive as a career since teachers will no

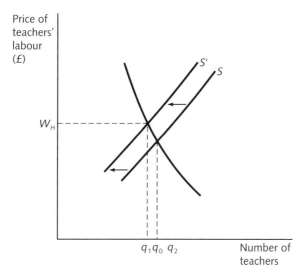

Figure 6.4 Equilibrium restored by a reduction in supply

longer enjoy the security of employment which they formerly had. Thus the number of people wishing to be trained as teachers may fall.

In the long run both of these effects will tend to reduce the supply of teachers, that is, to push the supply curve of teachers to the left as in Fig. 6.4 so that the teacher surplus is eliminated and the market is brought back to equilibrium at the new higher equilibrium wage for teachers. Thus, government policy has succeeded in effecting a permanent increase in the salaries that teachers receive, relative to other groups.

Whether the labour market for teachers is brought back to equilibrium by price adjustments or by quantity adjustments is impossible to tell *a priori*, depending as it does on the circumstances of the particular case. The purpose of this analysis has been to show that intervention – either in the form of incomes policy or minimum wage legislation – can permanently affect the earnings for some groups and modify differentials since, although the forces of demand and supply are very strong, they can be channelled in one direction or another by conscious government policy.

6.6 The macroeconomic effects of pay restraint

We have spent some time discussing what could be called the microeconomic effects of pay restraint policies. That is, whether or not in the long run they can lead to a set of earnings differentials different from that which would have occurred in the absence of such a policy. In the purely macroeconomic context, however, the effect of an incomes policy is judged solely in terms of whether or not the policy reduces the rate of price inflation, and questions of distributive justice or allocative efficiency are not relevant. How can we judge the effectiveness of incomes policy in moderating the rate of inflation? It is not sufficient merely to compare the rate of inflation in those years when the policy was in operation with those years when it was not, since incomes policies have only been introduced when the rate of inflation has been high. What one needs is a **counterfactual analysis** to estimate what the rate of inflation would have been in the absence of a pay restraint policy and compare this with the rate of inflation that actually occurred with the policy in operation. The difference between the two could thus be ascribed to the effects of incomes policy. What is needed therefore is a model that can be used to predict the rate of inflation from the values of certain other variables in the economy. As an illustration of the technique that could be used, it will be helpful at this point to introduce the **Phillips curve**.

6.7 The Phillips curve

First of all it will be convenient to introduce a bowdlerised version of the Phillips curve to illustrate the main features before we look at some of the more esoteric issues connected with it.

The article by Professor Phillips[1] published in 1958, which was to provoke an enormous amount of subsequent research and criticism, was the result of an empirical investigation of the relationship between the rate of change of money wages and the level of unemployment. Phillips collected statistics for the British economy for the period 1861-1957 on these two variables, and plotted them on a graph such as that shown in Fig. 6.5. Using regression analysis, he fitted to this set of points the curve which now bears his name. Most of the observations appeared

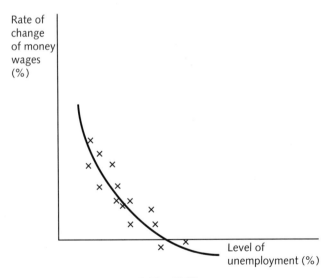

Figure 6.5 The Phillips curve

to lie quite close to the fitted line, apart from exceptional periods – such as periods of rapidly rising import prices. There appeared therefore to be a fairly stable relationship between the level of unemployment and the rate of wage inflation in Britain. Similar investigations were conducted for other countries, which revealed similar relationships remaining stable over long time periods.

If the Phillips curve had been as simple and as unambiguously correct as was at first supposed, it would have been an enormously important discovery. Like the physical sciences the social sciences seek to establish **stable functional relationships** between variables. In physics, for example, Boyle's law tells us that there is a stable relationship between the volume, the temperature and the pressure of a gas. We can then use our knowledge of this stable relationship to 'explain' real world phenomena – such as the fact that gases become cold when they are allowed to expand – though it is a rather restricted type of 'explanation' since it relies on the acceptance of the general law to explain the particular event. So, in economics, if it were possible to demonstrate the existence of a stable relationship between one measurable variable and another, one could 'explain' changes in one variable in terms of changes in the other.

We could also use this relationship to predict, say, the rate of wage inflation that corresponds to any particular level of unemployment. For example, in Fig 6.6 if the level of unemployment is, say, 1 per cent, the Phillips curve model predicts that the rate of wage inflation will be 7 per cent.

We can use this as a way of measuring the effectiveness of incomes policies in moderating the rate of inflation. If, for example, in a particular year in which an incomes policy was in operation, the average level of unemployment was 2 per cent, we could predict from the Phillips curve that the rate of wage inflation would be 3 per cent. If the actual rate of wage inflation was, say, only 2.5 per cent, then

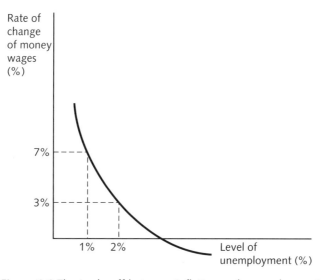

Figure 6.6 The trade-off between inflation and unemployment

the difference between the two could be ascribed to the moderating influences of the policy. In other words, the policy would have succeeded in reducing the rate of wage inflation by 0.5 per cent.

6.8 Evidence about the effectiveness of intervention

Tests based on this principle have been used to try to assess the impact of various forms of pay restraint on reducing inflation. In practice, the models used have been more complicated than simple Phillips curve relationships. That is, they have used additional variables, not just unemployment levels, to predict the rate of inflation. In essence, the technique remains the same, however. First, construct a model which will predict the rate of wage inflation, given the values of certain other variables. Secondly, in those years when a formal policy of pay restraint is in operation, compare the 'predicted' rate of inflation with the actual rate. The difference between the two can then be ascribed to the effects of the policy.

Obviously, there are difficulties which the researcher encounters in trying to apply this method, not the least of which is how to decide whether incomes policy is 'on' or 'off'. (For example, do 'calls for restraint' constitute policy 'on', or is incomes policy only 'on' when it has the backing of the law?) The results of published research tend to suggest some modest success for incomes policies, as Table 6.2 shows. The effects are rather erratic, however, since, if the results are to be believed, in some periods incomes policy actually leads to a higher rate of inflation than would otherwise have occurred. Overall, in most periods the rate of inflation does not seem to be significantly lower than it would have been in the absence of the policy.

Although some form of incomes policy was in operation in Britain for a substantial part of the post-war period up until 1978, formal policies have not been part of the political agenda since that time. Such policies were anathema to Margaret Thatcher, for whom any interference with the workings of the free market was to be avoided. Her successor John Major shared the same beliefs about the undesirability of intervention and in 1997 the incoming Labour party was keen to show that it would not repeat the interventionist policies which had been such a key feature of previous Labour administrations.

6.9 Criticisms of the Phillips curve

We conclude this chapter with a more detailed look at the Phillips curve. Earlier we introduced the Phillips curve to illustrate the sort of techniques that could be used to estimate the effects of incomes policies. Its place in economics is much more important than this, however, and the debate as to whether or not a stable relationship exists between unemployment and wage inflation has received considerable attention since Phillips first published his findings. The reason for this is two-fold.

First, in some years, combinations of high unemployment and high inflation have been observed which do not lie on the Phillips curve, but somewhere to the

Table 6.2 Estimated effects of incomes policy on the rate of wage inflation – results of two studies conducted by Lipsey-Parkin and Hines

+ =	number of quarters in which inflation was higher than predicted
− =	number of quarters in which inflation was lower than predicted
$\hat{E}$ =	estimated effect of incomes policy (% p.a.) mean
$\sigma_{\hat{E}}$ =	a measure of the degree of variability of the rate of inflation around its mean value. To be reasonably confident that incomes policy produces a significant reduction in inflation, the measured reduction should be at least twice as big as $\sigma_{\hat{E}}$. In the Lipsey-Parkin study, for example, reductions in the rate of inflation of less than 2×1.058 could be the result of chance factors rather than the result of the incomes policy. Thus only in the early years 1948 (3rd quarter) to 1950 (3rd quarter) was there a significant reduction in inflation.

		Lipsey-Parkin			Hines		
	Incomes Policy Years	+	−	$\hat{E}$	+	−	$\hat{E}$
1	1948Q3-1950Q3 1949Q1 (Hines)	0	9	−2.369	0	7	−1.440
2	1956Q1-1956Q4	2	2	−1.050	2	2	−0.073
3	1961Q3-1967Q2 −1968Q2 (Hines)	11	13	−0.127	14	14	−0.050
4	1968Q3-1969Q4 Hines only	–	.	–	2	4	−0.056
	All periods	13	24	−0.772	18	27	−0.267
		$\sigma_{\hat{E}} = 1.058$			$\sigma_{\hat{E}} = 0.851$		

Source: R. G. Lipsey and M. Parkin, 'Incomes policy: a re-appraisal', in M. Parkin and M. T. Sumner (eds), *Incomes Policy and Inflation* (1972) p.101, Manchester University Press.

right of it. Thus, it was said, the Phillips relationship had 'broken down'. This criticism, however, is the result of an incorrect reading of Phillips' original work. He anticipated that the relationship between unemployment and changes in money wages would not hold good during periods when import prices were rising very rapidly. Because the late 1960s and 1970s were periods of rapidly rising import prices, it is not surprising that the model breaks down for those years. In the 1980s and 1990s the relationship has tended to re-appear.

The major criticism of Phillips' work, however, relates to an alleged failure to distinguish between *real* and *money* wage increases. This is discussed in the next section.

6.10 The vertical Phillips curve

Writers such as Phelps[2] and Friedman[3] argued that Phillips was fundamentally incorrect in trying to discover a relationship between unemployment and the rate of change of money wages. The variable which is determined by the level of unemployment, they argued, is not the rate of change of money wages, but the rate of change of *real* wages, that is, money wages deflated by the change in the price index. Phillips' original hypothesis had been that, for any commodity or service, when the demand is high relative to the supply of it, we expect the price to rise, the rate of rise being greater the greater the excess demand. In the labour market, he argued, excess demand can be measured by the level of registered unemployment (the two will be negatively correlated) and this will therefore determine the rate of change of the price of labour, which he took to be money wages. Friedman, however, argues that the price of labour is, in fact, real wages – that is, money wages relative to what those wages can purchase.

If this is the case, it is argued, there will be not one Phillips curve but a whole family of such curves, each corresponding to a particular rate of price inflation as in Fig. 6.7. Consider what would happen if the economy were initially operating at a level of unemployment of U_N with no price inflation, and the government, in an attempt to reduce unemployment, expands demand. The effect will be felt initially in the goods market but will rapidly be transmitted to the labour market where the expansion of demand for labour reduces unemployment to U_0 but also pushes up wages by, say, 2 per cent. That is, we move north-west along the zero price inflation Phillips curve. However, because of excess demand in the goods market, prices begin to rise by, say, 2 per cent, and the economy therefore shifts to the 2 per cent price inflation curve.

We can see from Fig. 6.7 that, with 2 per cent price inflation, a money wage increase of only 2 per cent will cause the level of unemployment to rise again towards U_N. The reason for this is that, to preserve a level of unemployment of U_0, increases in *real wages* of 2 per cent would be necessary, but since prices are now rising by 2 per cent, the *money wage* increase of 2 per cent is equivalent to a zero per

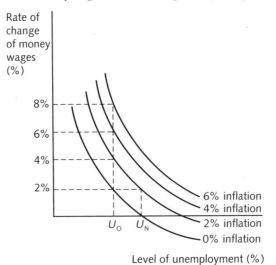

Figure 6.7 A 'family' of Phillips curves

cent increase in real wages – the real wage increase compatible with a level of unemployment of U_N.

If the government expands demand again, attempting to reduce unemployment to U_0, the economy will now move along the 2 per cent price inflation curve. Money wages increase by 4 per cent, as do prices, and the level of unemployment drifts back towards U_N as we shift to the 4 per cent price inflation curve, and so the process continues.

This analysis suggests, then, that trying to keep the level of unemployment down to U_0 results in a continually increasing rate of inflation. Only by allowing the level of unemployment to rise to U_N (where the zero price inflation Phillips curve cuts the axis) can the rise in the rate of inflation be halted. Friedman calls this the **natural level of unemployment**. It is that level of unemployment which is consistent with a steady – that is, non-increasing – rate of inflation. Some writers have called this the **non-accelerating inflation rate of unemployment** or **NAIRU** for short. The rate of inflation could be zero per cent or 4 or 10 per cent, but the crucial point is that labour market conditions are such that there is no tendency for the rate of inflation to increase. To achieve a reduction in the rate of inflation from an initially higher level requires that the level of unemployment be held above U_N so that the level of demand in the labour market is reduced to a sufficient extent to bring about a fall in real wages.

There are two further implications which follow from this analysis. First, the **trade-off** between inflation and unemployment, which the Phillips curve appeared to illustrate, now disappears. There is no longer a downward sloping relationship between inflation and unemployment. Since the level of unemployment continually drifts back towards the natural level, the Phillips curve, if it exists at all, should be thought of as a vertical line at U_N, as in Fig. 6.8, illustrating that in the long run

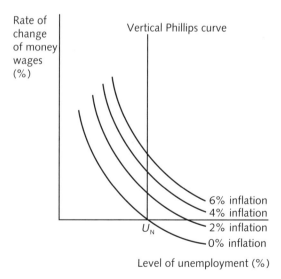

Figure 6.8 The vertical Phillips curve

society can choose either a high rate of inflation coupled with the natural rate of unemployment or a low rate of inflation coupled with the natural rate of unemployment. In other words, as far as the level of unemployment goes, there is no choice at all in the long run.

Secondly, and more importantly, this analysis highlights the importance of **expectations** in the inflationary process. If people expect a certain rate of price inflation, they incorporate this into their money wage claims. The higher the expected rate of inflation, the higher the increase in money wages which they will seek. Thus, expectations play a reinforcing role in sustaining the inflationary process once it has got under way.

The role of expectations is something which is stressed by Friedman and other monetarists. They point out that, once the government has allowed an inflationary situation to develop, it will be extremely difficult to reduce the rate of inflation because people acquire expectations of inflation which lead them to behave in such a way that inflation does, in fact, result. The rate of inflation can only be reduced if expectations are changed and this can only be brought about, Friedman argues, by reducing the level of demand so that unemployment rises above the natural level.

Bringing down the rate of inflation by keeping the level of unemployment somewhere above its natural level may be a protracted process, since expectations change only slowly in response to events. However, the process by which expectations are adjusted can be speeded up, Friedman argues, by the widespread use of **indexation** of wage settlements. Indexation means that current money wage increases will be tied to the current increase in the cost of living. Thus, the money wage increases which occur will depend upon the current rate of inflation, rather than on some expectation of future rates which is itself determined by some average of past rates. In other words, workers bargain for increases in real wages, and the increases in money wages which they actually receive will depend upon whatever real wage increase they have negotiated, plus whatever the rise in the cost of living turns out to be.

Note, however, that indexation in itself does not reduce the rate of inflation – it merely speeds up the process of moving from a higher rate of inflation to a lower one. The basic causal mechanism is the restraint of demand via control of the money supply. Therefore indexation is a two-edged sword, since, if the growth of the money supply is not controlled sufficiently, then widespread indexation will cause the rate of inflation to accelerate even faster than it would otherwise have done.

One serious criticism that can be levelled at Friedman's theory of the **vertical Phillips curve** is that the analysis does not tell us how high a level of unemployment is required to prevent accelerating inflation – that is, it does not tell us what level of unemployment corresponds to the 'natural level'. We can define the natural level of unemployment as that level which is compatible with non-accelerating inflation, but this will probably depend on institutional factors within the economy. A generous system of social security and unemployment benefits, Friedman argues, will increase the natural level of unemployment.

Summary

Direct controls on prices and (more often) on wages are sometimes used as a supplement to demand management policies to control inflation. In the post-war period various forms of pay restraint were employed, some of them 'statutory' and some 'voluntary'. Such controls are difficult to administer and may distort earnings differentials. Evidence suggests that the rate of inflation was not lowered significantly as a result of such policies.

The Phillips curve illustrates what was thought to be a stable functional relationship between the rate of change of wages and the level of unemployment. Friedman and other monetarists dispute that there is any trade-off between inflation and unemployment. For them the Phillips curve is vertical and the economy will always return to the natural level of unemployment.

Notes

1 Phillips, A. W. (1958) 'The relation between unemployment and the rate of change of wage rates in the United Kingdom 1862–1957', *Economica* 25 (November): 283–99.
2 Phelps, E.S. (1970) *Microeconomic Foundations of Employment and Inflation Theory*: Norton.
3 Friedman, M. (1968) 'The role of monetary policy', *American Economic Review* 58 (March): 1–17.

Key terms

Review questions

6.1 Some economists argue that inflation can be caused by autonomous increases in wage costs. Explain what is meant by the term *autonomous* in this context.

6.2 The following are all types of wage/price restraint policies which have been attempted in Britain or in other European countries. What are the drawbacks (and the advantages) of each particular form?
(a) wage freeze;
(b) freeze on earnings and prices;
(c) lump sum increase in wages;
(d) fixed percentage increase;
(e) wage restraint with special allowances for the low paid and/or special duties, e.g. unsocial hours;
(f) policies which allow wage increases which can be covered by productivity increases.

6.3 In what ways can firms circumvent controls on
(a) wages;
(b) prices?

6.4 The following factors may affect (to a greater or lesser extent) wages for different occupational groups.
(a) market forces, i.e. relative scarcity;
(b) notions of social status;
(c) notions of comparability;
(d) power of determining your own wages;
(e) equity;
(f) trade union bargaining power.
Consider which of these factors are important in determining wages for the following occupational groups:
(a) computer programmers;
(b) printing workers;
(c) teachers;
(d) footballers in Division 2;
(e) cabinet ministers;
(f) ministers in the Shadow Cabinet;
(g) accountants;
(h) water workers;
(i) judges;
(j) actors.
If relative scarcity is thought important, assess the elasticity of demand for the labour in question and the elasticity of supply.

6.5 Is the Phillips curve compatible with a demand-pull or a cost-push interpretation of inflation?

6.6 Suggest reasons why the Phillips curve may have 'broken down' in the 1970s and reappeared in the 1990s.

6.7 Why didn't they have inflation in the USSR until perestroika?

The balance of payments and the determination of the exchange rate

Preview

This chapter explains how exchange rates are determined. It distinguishes between fixed and floating exchange rates and discusses the merits of the various policies which can be used to correct a balance of payments deficit. It also explains how the Balance of Payments accounts are drawn up.

7.1   The equilibrium exchange rate

In Chapter 1 we assumed that our desert island was completely isolated from outside influences, whereas the British economy, which is the real subject of our study, is in reality subject to many such external influences. We are a relatively small country operating in a big world. Thus, the world economic climate affects the British economy, but the state of the British economy has little impact on the rest of the world. It is important to understand the world economic environment within which the British economy operates, and moreover to understand the nature of the links that we have with the rest of the world. These links, of course, are primarily in the form of trade between Britain and the rest of the world, but, in addition to flows of goods and services across international frontiers, there are also flows of capital (that is, money) for which there is no corresponding good or service rendered. The international payments system forms the backdrop against which the action takes place. The purpose of this chapter is to describe that backdrop.

The essential feature which distinguishes **international trade** from **domestic trade** is that, with the former, different currencies are involved. The following section examines how the value of one currency in terms of another is determined.

Suppose we look at the market for pounds sterling. Every working day transactions take place on foreign exchange markets at prices which ensure that the market is **cleared**. Since for every transaction there must be a buyer and a seller, the function of the foreign exchange dealers is to adjust prices in such a way that the number of pounds which people wish to buy at the prevailing price is exactly equal to the number which (different) people wish to sell at that price. Normally, as with any other commodity, the lower the price the more pounds can people be persuaded to buy. Thus, to find a buyer for his sterling the broker has only to drop his price – though hopefully not below his buying price, otherwise he will make a loss.

In Fig. 7.1 the vertical axis measures the sterling **exchange rate**, or the price of pounds in terms of other currencies. We have chosen the Deutschemark as our yardstick, though we could have chosen the dollar, the franc, the yen or any other currency. The horizontal axis has an implicit time dimension. It measures the number of pounds demanded and supplied *per unit time* – per day, if you like. Figure 7.1 shows conventional **demand and supply curves**,[1] indicating that the higher the sterling exchange rate the more sterling will people wish to sell and, conversely, the cheaper sterling becomes the more will people wish to buy. This behaviour is essential to ensure a stable market, though there are occasions on which contrary behaviour is observed. For example, in speculative situations, a fall in the value of the pound may induce people to sell more sterling, not less, since they fear a further decline in the exchange rate and hence a capital loss to the holders of sterling. For the moment we shall regard such behaviour as merely short-run aberrations to the more logical pattern, though, as we shall see later, such aberrant behaviour may be rather common in the real world.

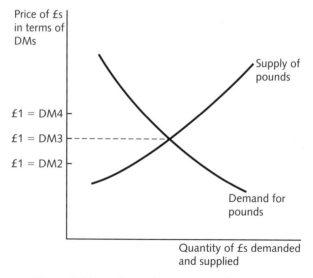

Figure 7.1 How the exchange rate is determined

Why do people wish to buy and sell sterling? British exporters want to be paid for their goods in sterling, since they cannot pay their workforce, pay the rent for their factory or pay their own suppliers in foreign currency. Even if British exporters agree to accept payment for their exports in, say, marks, they will have to convert these marks to pounds when they receive them. Thus, we say that they will enter the foreign exchange market and buy pounds (that is, demand pounds) and sell marks (that is, supply marks). In practice, of course, they will not do so in person but will instruct their bankers to act as agents for them.

Thus the demand for pounds comes principally from the demand for British exports. The more we in Britain export, the greater will be the demand for pounds on foreign exchange markets to pay for them.

In the same way, when British residents buy imported goods from Germany, those imports will ultimately have to be paid for in deutschemarks. Therefore, the importer will have to buy marks and pay for those marks in pounds (that is, demand marks and supply pounds). The supply of pounds thus emanates principally from the demand for goods being imported into the UK.

Apart from **visible trade** there is also so-called **invisible trade**, which consists of services such as insurance, banking, tourism and shipping. This invisible trade has exactly the same effect on the demand and supply of pounds as visible trade and is, in fact, very important for the British economy since historically we have had a surplus on invisibles (that is, we exported more than we imported).

There is a third set of items which affect the demand and supply of pounds – the so-called **capital account** transactions. If, for example, a German resident wishes to purchase shares in ICI (a British company), he will have to buy those shares in pounds, thus augmenting the demand for pounds on the foreign exchange market. This transaction thus has the same effect on the market for pounds as a British export. However, when the German resident receives dividends on the shares purchased, which will be paid in pounds, he will convert these pounds into marks (that is, he will supply pounds to the foreign exchange markets) and the receipt of these dividends therefore has the same effect as a foreign import into Britain.

In summary

The **balance of payments accounts** record all the transactions involving the purchase or sale of sterling during a certain period (say, the previous month, quarter or year). It can be subdivided as follows:

Visible trade + invisible trade = **Balance of Trade**

This is similar to the balance on **Current Account** (the distinction is explained in section 7.6 below)

Balance of payments = Balance on Current Account
+ Balance on Capital Account

7.2 Fixed and flexible exchange rates

With the demand and supply schedules depicted in Fig. 7.1, the equilibrium exchange rate (that is, the rate at which the demand and supply of pounds is equal) would be £1 = DM3. Consider what would happen if the demand for pounds increased as shown by a **shift** in the demand curve to *D'* as in Fig. 7.2. (The reasons why such a shift might occur will be discussed later.) The equilibrium exchange rate will increase to DM4 = £1 and, provided the exchange rate is perfectly free to vary, the market exchange rate will in fact appreciate to this level. In practice, however, the exchange rate may not be free to vary in this way because governments, for a variety of reasons, have an interest in manipulating the exchange rate. It is convenient to describe two different exchange rate regimes – **fixed exchange rates** and **flexible** (or **floating**) exchange rates. These are, in effect, polar cases and the sort of policy pursued in practice may be somewhere in between these two extremes.

As the names imply, a flexible exchange rate policy is one in which the exchange rate is determined from day to day by the forces of demand and supply. No attempt is made by the monetary authorities to intervene in foreign exchange markets and the prevailing exchange rate is always the equilibrium one (that is, the one which equates the market demand for pounds with the market supply of pounds). At the other extreme is a fixed exchange rate policy which is one where the monetary authorities are committed to maintaining a particular **par value** or **parity**. On any particular day, of course, it would be most unlikely if this official par value were the same as the equilibrium exchange rate. At the official exchange rate there will either be too many pounds being offered for sale relative to the number that people wish to buy, or too few – that is, there will be either an **excess supply** of

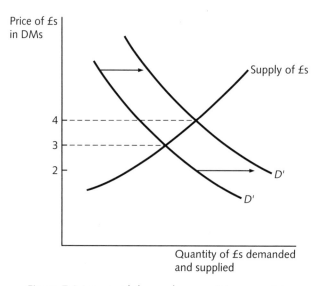

Figure 7.2 Increased demand causes £ to appreciate

pounds or an **excess demand**. In the former case the Bank of England has to buy up the excess supply of pounds that nobody else is willing to purchase at the prevailing price. It will have to pay for them in foreign currencies. In the latter case, when there is an excess demand, the Bank of England will supply the extra pounds needed. Normally it will do this quite readily since it receives payment in foreign currencies and this will enable it to replenish or increase its **reserves** of foreign currencies, which is often regarded as a healthy situation. This is discussed more fully in section 7.3 below.

We illustrate the former case (excess supply of pounds) in Fig. 7.3. At the official exchange rate of £1 = DM3, the amount of pounds demanded is q_D and the amount supplied q_S. There is thus an excess supply. Under a flexible exchange rate system the pound would depreciate, that is, fall in value, to a new exchange rate of DM2.5 = £1, at which level the demand for pounds is equal to the supply at q_e. Under a fixed exchange rate system, however, the monetary authorities will buy up the excess supply of pounds, thus increasing the demand for pounds by $(q_S - q_D)$. This can be shown by a rightward shift of the demand curve by this amount (that is to D').

By convention, the terms **appreciation** and **depreciation** are used to describe an increase or decrease in the value of a floating currency. **Devaluation** and **revaluation** are the terms used to describe a step change in the value of a currency that is nominally fixed in value (that is, a change in par values). Thus with flexible rates, as we move up the vertical axis in Fig. 7.3, the pound is appreciating in value (you get more marks for your pounds), and the mark is depreciating in value.

From 1944 to 1972 the British economy operated under a fixed exchange rate regime, though there were periodic devaluations. From 1972 to 1990 the exchange

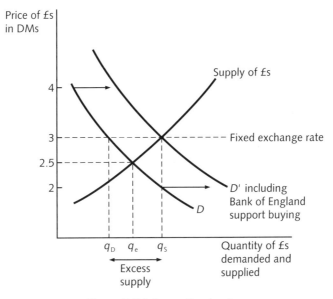

Figure 7.3 Intervention buying

rate was allowed to float. What this meant in practice was not that the Bank of England totally abstained from intervention on foreign exchange markets, but that it officially abandoned its commitment to any particular exchange rate. In fact, during this period there was still continuous intervention in foreign exchange markets by the Bank of England, but the purpose of this intervention was not to preserve any particular parity. Rather it was to modify the speed at which the exchange rate moved up or down, or to buy currencies when they were being offered at cheap rates.

In 1990 the pound entered the **exchange rate mechanism** of the **European Monetary System** which is a fixed exchange rate system. The parity chosen was DM2.95 = £1 and the Bank of England was then committed to intervening to prevent the actual exchange rate deviating from this parity by more than 6 per cent. On 16 September 1992 – a date which has come to be known as **Black Wednesday** – the weight of selling pressure against sterling forced its exit from the e.r.m. The fixed exchange rate policy was abandoned and the exchange rate floated down, reaching a low of little more than DM2.2 in the mid-1990s. In 1997 a combination of factors resulted in sterling floating up again to around DM3.0.

7.3 The accumulation of reserves

To operate a fixed exchange rate policy it is necessary to hold stocks of foreign currencies which can be used to buy up one's own currency when the situation demands it. A balance of payments deficit is financed in this way. That is, when the demand for pounds on the capital and current accounts taken together falls short of the supply of pounds, the shortfall is made good by the Bank of England. In this sense the balance of payments *always* balances (that is, the number of pounds bought equals the number sold, but this is ensured through Bank of England **intervention**).

Balance of payments surpluses therefore involve the accumulation of foreign exchange reserves, which is not in itself praiseworthy since these reserves do not earn interest for the country holding them. It is normal to wish to avoid persistent deficits, however, since this involves a run-down in reserves and a stage will eventually be reached when, with reserves exhausted, the country is forced to borrow additional reserves from other central banks – in Britain's case from other European central banks – or from the **International Monetary Fund (IMF)**, which acts like a banker to the central banks, lending money to central banks to help them maintain their fixed exchange rates.

It is important to note, however, that the accumulation of reserves does not increase society's welfare directly. The ultimate aim of all economic activity is consumption. The accumulation of claims on other countries – for this is what foreign exchange reserves are – does not directly increase consumption, though it does provide the opportunity of cashing in these claims at some time in the future, thereby enabling the economy to enjoy a once-and-for-all increase in consumption. In the **mercantilist** era in the seventeenth century the wealth of an economy was judged by the amount of gold it had accumulated, and thus the accumulation of such wealth was the ultimate objective towards which the nation strove. Although the vestiges of the mercantilist tradition still survive, this view is now regarded as incorrect. The amount of gold possessed by the *individual* may indeed measure his or her wealth, but what is true for the individual is not true for society. The wealth of a society is measured in terms of its productive capacity, its ability to produce a stream of consumption goods and services for the benefit of its citizens. Many countries, particularly developing countries, have chosen policies designed to promote a rapid expansion of productive capacity and this has usually involved heavy borrowing from abroad. In other words, they have allowed other countries to build up huge claims on their economies. This is not necessarily a case of 'living beyond one's means' however – rather, it may represent an effective stratagem for development.

7.4 Exchange rates and purchasing power parities

The market exchange rate, as we have seen, is determined by the demand for and supply of a currency on foreign exchange markets, manipulated to a greater or lesser extent by central banks. Ultimately, however, we would argue that the exchange rate between two currencies must reflect the **internal purchasing power** of those currencies relative to one another or what is known as the **purchasing power parity**. Suppose the exchange rate between pounds sterling and French francs is, for example, £1 = 8Fr. There must be some relationship between what can be bought in the shops in France for 8Fr and what can be bought in the shops in Britain for £1. Take a particular commodity, such as a jar of coffee, which costs, say, £1 to buy in Britain. The cost of this same item in France will not be exactly 8Fr, but it can be argued that it cannot diverge too much from that price. If the price of coffee in France was substantially less than 8Fr (say 5Fr) and it were possible for jars of coffee to be traded without restrictions between France and Britain, then it would be profitable to buy up coffee in France and export it for sale in Britain. The effect of this would be to increase French exports and increase British imports, thus increasing the demand for francs and the supply of pounds on foreign exchange markets. *Ceteris paribus,* this would lead to an appreciation in the value of the franc and a depreciation in the value of the pound, assuming that exchange rates were perfectly free to vary. If coffee were the only thing that was traded between Britain and France the franc would appreciate against the pound to £1 = 5Fr. In the real world where thousands of commodities are traded, or could be traded, between Britain and France, the exchange rate must, in the long run, reflect the difference in the price of a typical **basket of goods** in France and a similar basket of goods in Britain. Thus there will be a tendency for exchange rates to reflect purchasing power parities.

In reality, however, market exchange rates will not be equal to purchasing power parities. There are five main reasons for this. First, not all goods and services are capable of being exported and imported. Physical goods such as cars, television sets, food and so on can be traded internationally, but things such as houses, the services of the local garage or the window cleaner cannot. Thus market exchange rates only reflect internal purchasing power to the extent that an individual's income is spent on goods which are, or could be, traded internationally.

Secondly, few countries allow completely free trade in all those goods and services which are, or could be, traded. For a variety of reasons governments may impose trading restrictions – quotas or levies – on imports. To the extent that this reduces international trade, it also reduces the extent to which market exchange rates will reflect the internal purchasing power of a currency.

Thirdly, the market prices of goods and services are affected by sales taxes. If, for example, France imposes a higher rate of sales tax on coffee than Britain does, then the price of coffee in the shops in France will remain higher than in Britain.

Fourthly, even though exchange rates may be nominally floating, they are seldom completely free to vary. If we take the other extreme, where exchange rates are rigidly fixed, then the export of coffee from France to Britain, which we described in our previous example, will not tend to make the franc appreciate. Instead it will cause a run down of foreign exchange reserves at the Bank of England to pay for the imports from France.

Fifthly, companies may be willing to accept large differences in profit margins between the different markets on which they sell. For example, on markets in which they face a lot of competition from rival suppliers companies may be willing to accept lower margins than on other markets where competition is not so fierce. A well-documented example of this is in the market for new cars where at various times there have been substantial differences in profit margins (as reflected in prices) between various countries of the EU which is supposedly a free-trade area.

As Table 7.1 shows, in the early 1980s a car purchased in Britain was rather more expensive than an identical model purchased in most other European countries. In fact, it was almost twice as expensive in Britain as it would have been if purchased in Denmark. The price differential was not explained by differences in national sales taxes (since the prices shown are net of tax). Rather, it was related to differences in the degree of competition in the various national markets.

Classical economists argued that the price of identical goods sold in different markets would in the long run be equalised by the forces of competition. They

Table 7.1 Comparative car prices in the EEC (prices are pre-tax)

	UK	WG	F	I	NL	B	L	IRL	DK
1975	100	97.8	101.3	103.4	93.4	90.2	91.3	93.1	86.4
1980	100	80.7	80.3	87.0	74.1	76.7	73.7	82.0	64.7
1981	100	72.0	71.7	–	65.6	65.2	64.5	83.3	53.3
1982	100	75.1	72.4	77.2	71.9	61.4	62.8	93.3	55.0
1983	100	83.0	81.0	87.0	–	72.0	–	–	–
1984	100	85.0	88.0	93.0	–	77.0	–	–	–

Source: Garel Rhys 'Economics of the Motor Industry' in *Economics*, Winter 1988.

called this the **Law of One Price**. Table 7.1 provides startling evidence that, in the short run at least, the law does not hold. It also provides some evidence about how firms set prices. Clearly, it is more profitable for firms to sell on some markets than on others, and what this implies is that companies do not base their prices on production costs – rather the price they charge is based on 'what the market will bear' – that is, they charge relatively high prices where demand is inelastic and lower prices where demand is more elastic.

Of course, while these price differences exist there is an incentive for enterprising individuals or companies to buy up goods on markets where they are cheap for resale on markets where they are expensive. Inasmuch as this does occur, there will be a tendency for the Law of One Price to reassert itself, either through movements in exchange rates, or through movements in profit margins and prices. This in turn will have an impact on domestic rates of inflation in the countries concerned, a point to which we return later.

7.5 Policies to correct payments imbalances

The balance of payments, as we have seen, always balances, but this is only achieved through the intervention of the central bank, either buying or selling currency as it sees fit. Without these official transactions, however, if there is a continual tendency for the supply of pounds to outstrip the demand for them, then we can talk of a **payments imbalance** – in this case a balance of payments deficit. Such payments imbalances, if they are chronic, give cause for concern and some action must be taken to redress the imbalance. We shall confine ourselves to a discussion of the problems caused by balance of payments deficits, though it is worth noting that those countries who experience chronic surpluses appear to find it equally difficult to remove them.

A balance of payments deficit – that is, an excess supply of pounds on foreign exchange markets – can be tackled in a variety of ways. The main types of policy are set out below. It should be noted that all of the policies mentioned will probably be effective in eliminating a balance of payments deficit provided they are applied sufficiently strictly, but that all of them involve undesirable side-effects. It is because of the seriousness of these side-effects that some policies are either not rigorously applied, or are not applied at all. The policy maker may feel that attaining a balance of payments equilibrium is a less important objective than, say, reducing inflation, reducing unemployment or promoting economic growth. In macroeconomics there is often a **conflict between objectives**, and we shall discuss this more fully later.

Raising interest rates

By bringing about an increase in interest rates, the Bank of England can attract foreign capital into the country. The world capital market is often said to be competitive, which means that international investors will place their money wherever it can find the highest return. Thus, if British interest rates rise relative to those in other countries, this will increase the demand for the bonds and bills offered for sale by public and private institutions in Britain. In order to purchase these bonds, foreigners will first have to acquire sterling. Thus the sale of a bond to an overseas purchaser is just like an export since it adds to the demand for pounds.

Restrictions on capital movements; incomplete convertibility

If a currency can be bought or sold for whatever purposes and in whatever amount, that currency is said to be freely **convertible**. In practice, many countries place restrictions, either temporary or permanent, on convertibility since this is one way of relieving balance of payments difficulties. Typically, there may be restrictions on the freedom to export capital, or on citizens' rights to sell (their own) currency when they go abroad. In 1967, for example, the British Government introduced restrictions on the amount of sterling (then £50) which British tourists could take abroad with them on holiday. Some form of exchange control was practised in Britain until 1979, when it was abandoned by the then Conservative government, who believed that the workings of the market in foreign exchange should be unfettered.

Reducing domestic demand

By increasing income taxes the government can reduce the post-tax incomes of those in employment. Similarly, the incomes of other members of society can be held down by reducing spending – or reducing the growth of spending – on pensions, social security benefits and so on. In so far as a proportion of people's incomes will be spent on imported goods, a fall in incomes will necessarily bring about a fall in spending on imports. Reducing domestic demand – what is known as **domestic deflation** – is one of the most important instruments used by governments to reduce balance of payments deficits.

There is a major drawback with this policy, however, in that, although it may be effective in reducing spending on imports, it also reduces spending on *domestically produced* goods and this may have deleterious effects on some of the other objectives of macroeconomic policy, particularly the level of unemployment.

Quotas, import tariffs and export subsidies

An import **quota** is a restriction placed on the amount (measured either in value terms or in physical units) of a particular commodity which importers are allowed to bring into the country. Clearly, the smaller the quota, the less will be imported, and the greater will be the beneficial effect on the balance of payments. An import **tariff** is a tax on imported goods, which may be levied on all imported goods or on just a few specific items. This has the effect of making imports more expensive relative to domestically produced goods, and domestic consumers will therefore tend to switch their spending away from imports and towards domestically produced goods. An **export subsidy**, which again can either be specific or general, is any measure such as a tax concession or a preferential loan granted to exporters which is designed to make exporting more profitable and hence encourage the growth of exports.

It should be noted that, if all countries adopted these policies, then the policies would be self-defeating and international trade would be reduced. Because of this, it is often claimed that such defensive policies are 'anti-social' in some global sense, and invite **retaliatory action** from other countries which could lead to a **trade war**. Moreover, they run counter to agreements freely entered into, for example those of the World Trade Organisation (WTO), the successor to GATT (the General Agreement on Tariffs and Trade) which was set up to negotiate mutual tariff reduction.

Changing the exchange rate

The effect which a devaluation has on the balance of trade is somewhat more difficult to predict, being the subject of some debate both on the theoretical level and on the empirical level. Here we present two models of how a devaluation could, in theory, improve the balance of trade.

Model One: devaluation makes exports cheaper

It could be argued that a fall in the exchange rate would immediately result in a rise in the price of imported goods (causing domestic consumers to buy fewer imports) and a fall in the price of British exports (causing a growth of British exports), the two effects combining to produce an improvement in the balance of trade. Things are not quite so simple, however. The price of what we buy from abroad relative to the price of what we sell abroad is known as the **terms of trade** and the devaluation clearly worsens the terms of trade. Thus to pay for the same volume of imports we now have to export more than previously since relative prices have moved against us.

The extent to which a devaluation will improve the balance of trade depends, among other things, on the degree to which the demand for imports and the demand for exports are sensitive to price – in other words, on the **price elasticity of demand for imports** and the **price elasticity of demand for exports** (see appendix A if you are not confident about what this means). Consider the import side. The price elasticity of demand for imports is defined as:

% change in quantity of imports bought
――――――――――――――――――――――
% change in price of imports

If this elasticity is just unity (strictly speaking minus one) then it implies that a 10 per cent devaluation, which results in a 10 per cent rise in the price of imported goods will lead to a 10 per cent fall in demand for imports. Thus expenditure, in pounds, on imported goods, remains unchanged – and therefore the supply of pounds to the foreign exchange market resulting from this is unaltered. By a similar line of argument, in order for a devaluation to reduce the supply of pounds to the foreign exchange market, the demand for imports would have to be *elastic* (that is, elasticity greater in absolute value than one).

Clearly, therefore, we cannot argue that a devaluation will inevitably reduce a balance of trade deficit. The degree of responsiveness of both the demand for imports and exports to price changes is the crucial determining factor. It has been argued that these elasticities are low in the short run so that the immediate effect of a devaluation is to worsen rather than improve the trade balance. Only when consumers, both at home and abroad, adjust themselves to the changed set of relative prices – and this will occur only slowly – does the balance of trade start to improve. This produces a phenomenon known as the **J-curve** effect, illustrated in Fig. 7.4. It is generally reckoned that it may take one or two years before the beneficial effects of a devaluation are felt, though these things are difficult to measure with any degree of certainty.

Model Two: devaluation makes exporting more profitable

As we saw in section 7.4, the sorts of goods which constitute the most important part of foreign trade, namely manufactured goods, are often sold on markets where the price is administered or manipulated by the seller rather than being determined by the interaction of demand and supply as it would be on a competitive market. Following a devaluation, an exporter therefore has a choice of cutting the price, in foreign currency terms, of his exports, or keeping the same price, in which case exporting becomes more profitable to him. An example will help to illustrate the point.

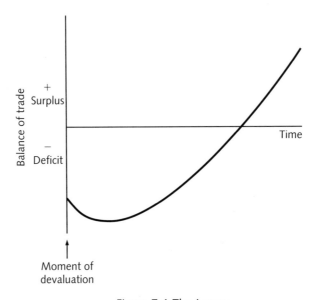

Figure 7.4 The J-curve

Let us imagine that a Rover Metro sells at £9000 in Britain and that in Germany the same car sells at DM27 000. Rover choose this price, taking into account the price at which comparable cars from rival manufacturers sell on the German market. They probably want to ensure that it is priced 'competitively'; that is, that its price is comparable with the price of cars with which it competes for sales. Now, with an exchange rate of £1 = DM3, the export revenue accruing to Rover is exactly $\dfrac{27\,000}{3}$ = £9000 per car and thus Rover would be indifferent as to whether they sold the car on the UK market or on the overseas market. In practice, they might prefer to sell on the home market since the cost of home sales would probably be lower.

Now suppose the pound is devalued to £1 = DM2.7 (again choosing easy numbers to illustrate the principle involved). Rover may choose to keep the DM price of the car at DM27 000 as before, since this is their favoured selling price taking into account all those factors which their marketing managers tell them are important. At the new exchange rate, export revenues are now $\dfrac{27\,000}{2.7}$ = £10 000 per car, making overseas sales much more profitable than domestic sales, even taking into account the slightly higher cost of selling overseas. Thus the profit-seeking company will direct its energies to increasing exports, which it hopes to do not by cutting prices but by increasing expenditure on advertising and so on.

On the import side, the effect of the sterling devaluation will be to make exporting to Britain less profitable. To continue with our example, the price of Volkswagen cars sold in Britain will have been chosen taking into account the price of competing products. If the price of Volkswagen cars on the British market goes too high, then sales will dwindle; therefore a devaluation of the pound will probably not result in any change in the price of Volkswagen cars sold on the British market, or at least the price may not rise by the full amount of the devaluation. The number of marks received by the German exporter for each car sold in Britain will, however, fall. Thus exporting to Britain becomes less profitable and, other things being equal, this will reduce the flow of imports into Britain.

In practice, the effect of a devaluation on the balance of trade will occur both through the process of model one and model two – model two being more applicable to those goods sold on oligopolistic markets (where the seller has some discretion in price setting) and model one being more applicable to those goods sold on competitive markets (where the seller has little discretion as regards his selling price). It should be noted, however, that in both cases the beneficial effects of the devaluation on the balance of trade may take quite some time to manifest themselves.

Moreover, the beneficial effects depend on the devaluation actually bringing about a change in relative prices – that is, the price of British goods relative to foreign goods. This may not occur because, in addition to being affected by the exchange rate, relative prices will also depend upon relative inflation rates – that is, the rate of domestic price inflation in Britain relative to the rate of price inflation overseas.

Let us say, for example, that it takes eighteen months for the beneficial effects of a devaluation on the balance of trade to occur. If, during this period, the rate of domestic inflation is higher than the rate of inflation overseas, this will reduce the extent to which the devaluation actually succeeds in changing relative prices. If the two effects are of equal weight, the devaluation of the exchange rate being exactly cancelled out by the higher rate of domestic inflation relative to that overseas, then at the end of the eighteen-month period nothing will have happened in **real terms**. The exchange rate will have fallen, but domestic prices and money incomes will have increased more rapidly than overseas, so that the amount of foreign currency that can be purchased with the average persons's income will be unchanged. We could say that the **real value of the currency** was unchanged.

7.6 The Balance of Payments accounts

The term 'Balance of Payments' is often used rather loosely, to refer to one of a number of different balances relating to overseas payments. Before we explain in detail what each of them is we should note that the *balance* on any account is the difference between **debits** and **credits**. If Rover exports one of its cars to France, this adds to the demand for pounds on foreign exchange markets, since at some stage the French francs used to purchase the car in France will have to be converted to pounds. Thus this purchase leads to an increase in the supply of francs and an increase in the demand for pounds. By accounting convention, this is known as a credit on the UK Balance of Payments accounts. If you remember that *exports* add to the *demand* for pounds and are shown as a *credit*, then you can work out that imports add to the supply of pounds and are shown as a debit.

The balance which is easiest to understand is the **visible trade balance**. Visible trade consists of things like cars, coal and coconuts (and also goods beginning with other letters of the alphabet). In 1996 visible exports were about £166 billion and visible imports about £179 billion, giving a visible deficit of approximately £13 billion. It will help to give some idea of the order of magnitude to know that gross national product in 1996 was about £752 billion so that the visible deficit in that year was quite small – less than 2 per cent of GNP.

From these figures one can, however, immediately appreciate the very 'open' nature of the UK economy. We could say, roughly speaking, that about one pound in every four spent in the shops in Britain is spent on imported goods.

The next balance to consider is the **invisible trade balance**. Invisible trade consists not of goods but of services – principally financial services such as insurance and tourism, civil aviation and sea transportation. In 1996 total credits – that is, total earnings from invisible exports totalled around £51 billion and total debits (invisible imports) were about £44 bn, giving a surplus on invisible trade of about £7 billion. Note that the surplus on invisible trade goes some way towards offsetting the deficit on visible trade – but unfortunately not far enough because visible trade is more than three times as large in value terms as invisible trade.

A confusion over nomenclature often arises with the use of the term 'trade balance'. Some authors use it to refer just to visible trade: others include invisible receipts and payments as well. The 'trade figures' published monthly and widely reported in the media always refer to visible trade only – they are often shown on the television news against a backdrop which includes a picture of dockside cranes, which is clearly intended to explain this fact. It would be more correct, however, to apply the word 'trade' to goods *and services* sold abroad (and purchased from abroad) – that is, to use the term to refer to both visible and invisible transactions.

To add to this confusion, the **current balance** is not the same thing as the **trade balance**, even if the trade balance is defined to include invisibles. The reason for this is that there are some transactions which take place on foreign exchange markets which are clearly not of a capital nature – that is, they do not involve a change in the ownership of assets – but which equally clearly are not related to trade, which basically means selling goods or services to somebody. The most significant of such items is **interest, profits and dividends** or **IPD** for short.

Consider the following chain of events. A German resident purchases shares in British Gas. Her bank will have to convert Deutschemarks into sterling. This will add to the demand for pounds and therefore will be shown as a credit. It will be shown on the *capital account* of the balance of payments because it involves a change in the ownership of an asset and this will therefore have some implications for the future. This is basically how we distinguish between a current account item and a capital account item. A current account item occurs in the year in question and no further flows across exchanges result from it in subsequent years. A capital account item in contrast involves a change in the ownership of an asset. In future years the new owner of this asset will receive a stream of earnings as a result of the ownership of such property and these earnings may themselves result in foreign exchange market transactions. In our example the German resident who now owns the shares will receive dividends, probably twice yearly, for as long as she holds the shares. These dividends are of course declared and paid in pounds. But pounds are of no use to a German resident – she needs Deutschemarks to spend in the shops in Germany. Thus she will instruct her bank to convert these pounds into marks. At this point a transaction takes place on the foreign exchange market. Effectively, the German resident will be selling pounds and buying marks. Like a Volkswagen motor car produced in Germany and sold in the UK this adds to the supply of pounds on foreign exchange markets and will thus be recorded as a debit.

In 1996 the total credits on IPD were about £96 billion, almost all of which was private sector (that is, non-governmental) receipts. Note that £96 billion is a large amount – almost twice as large as total receipts from services (financial services, tourism etc.). Total debits of IPD in 1996 were about £86 billion, giving the UK a positive balance on IPD of about £10 billion.

The only other significant item on the current account was **'transfers'**. Credits were about £7 billion in 1996, debits about £12 billion. Transfers represent transactions for which there is no *quid pro quo* and closer inspection of the accounts reveals that this balance of minus £5 billion was made up largely of the UK's net contribution to the European Union. We thus arrive at the current account balance. Total credits, total debits and the balance are summarised in Table 7.2.

Table 7.2 UK Current Account 1996 (£bn) (estimates are rounded to the nearest £ billion)

	Credits	Debits	Balance
Visible trade	166	179	−13
Services (total)	51	44	+7
of which			
business services	27	12	+15
travel	13	17	−4
sea transport	6	5	−1
civil aviation	6	7	−1
general government	0.4	3	−2
Interest, profits & dividends	96	86	+10
Transfers	7	12	−5
Totals (current account)	**320.1**	**320.6**	**−0.4**

Source: UK Balance of Payments Pink Book 1997, Table 1.4.

Table 7.3 UK Capital Account 1996 (£bn) (estimates are rounded to the nearest £ billion)

	Debits	Credits	Balance
Portfolio investment	−61	28	−33
Direct investment	−28	21	−7
Lending/borrowing overseas by UK banks	−63	75	12
Lending/borrowing overseas by UK residents other than banks	−66	95	28
Change in official reserves	..	0.5	..
Totals	−219	217	−2

Source: UK Balance of Payments Pink Book 1996, Table 7.1.
Note: the column totals do not sum correctly because of rounding errors and the omission of certain minor items.

Note that by chance in 1996 the current account was almost exactly in balance. More often the current account has a deficit, which is sometimes quite large.

Note also that approximately half of total credits come from visible trade. The remaining half comes from all the other items, which are sometimes lumped together and called 'invisibles'.

We now turn to Capital Account transactions. These, as we have already seen, are transactions involving a change in the ownership of assets. In 1996 the total value of transactions undertaken was around £218 billion (compare this with transactions totalling about £320 billion on the current account). Table 7.3 simplifies the relevant tables in the Balance of Payments Pink Book.

The interpretation of debits and credits, minus signs and plus signs on the Capital Account can be rather confusing. However, we can consider the first item by way of illustration – portfolio investment. This relates to the acquisition of financial assets such as shares in a company. As can be seen, portfolio investment overseas by UK residents was £61 billion. This is shown as a debit (minus sign) since UK residents had to purchase foreign currency – that is, sell sterling – in order to spend this money overseas acquiring foreign assets. The flow in the opposite direction – portfolio investment in the UK by overseas residents – was £28 billion. These overseas residents had to acquire sterling in order to purchase UK assets and hence the transaction is shown as a credit (plus sign). Lending overseas by UK banks is shown as a debit (−£63 billion) and borrowing from abroad by UK banks is shown as a credit (+£75 billion). Note that in 1996 the capital account was also approximately in balance – there was a small deficit of £2 billion.

Note also from Table 7.3 that two types of 'investment' are distinguished – **portfolio investment** and **direct investment**. As stated earlier, portfolio investment relates to the acquisition of financial assets such as bonds or shares. In contrast the term 'direct investment' refers to expenditure on *fixed capital formation* – for example, spending on purchasing new machines or building a new factory.

We are now in a position to add together the balances on the current and the capital account. This gives us the 'overall' balance of payments. In theory the balance on the current account and the balance on the capital account added together should equal the change in reserves. This is so because the balance of payments must always balance. That is, the balance must be zero. This follows, because there are two sides to every transaction – a buyer and a seller. The total number of pounds bought must be equal to the total number of pounds sold. Unfortunately, things in reality are not so clear cut, and we need a 'balancing item' to make the debits equal the credits. As Table 7.4 shows, in 1996 this balancing item was quite small – about £2 billion. The Pink Book explains the need for this item as follows:

> Since the two entries made in respect of each transaction are generally derived from separate sources and the methods of estimation are neither complete nor precisely accurate, the two entries may not match each other precisely or may fall within different recording periods. Furthermore with timing variations it is possible that entries which correspond in foreign currency terms are converted to sterling at different rates of exchange. In order to bring the total of all entries to zero an additional entry, the **balancing item**, is therefore included to reflect the sum of all these errors and omissions.
>
> *UK Balance of Payments 1990*, page 7.

Table 7.4 Summary Balance of Payments 1996 (£bn)

Current account balance	−0.4
Capital account balance*	−2.2
Balancing item	+2.6
*includes £0.5 change in reserves	

Source: UK Balance of Payments Pink Book, 1996, Table 1.1.

It is worth noting before we conclude that the way in which these accounts are presented has changed quite a lot over the last few years. The accounts no longer distinguish a 'Balance for Official Financing' as they used to do. It is also worth noting that the accuracy of the statistical estimates may be worse not better than in 1979 when Mrs Thatcher came to power. One of her first acts was to disband the Exchange Equalisation Account of the Bank of England whose task it was to engage in this 'official financing' and of course to record and monitor flows across the exchanges.

Summary

The equilibrium exchange rate is determined by demand and supply on foreign exchange markets. The value of a floating exchange rate will be market determined in this way. However, the value of a fixed exchange rate is set by the monetary authorities and intervention may be necessary to maintain the value chosen.

In the long run the external value of a currency must be related to what it will buy internally, though in the short run there may be a divergence between the exchange rate parity and the purchasing power parity.

Policies to correct a balance of payments deficit include raising interest rates, domestic deflation and devaluation. All of these policies will be effective in restoring balance but will have undesirable side-effects. The effect of a devaluation (and a revaluation) is particularly contentious.

The Balance of Payments accounts consist of current and capital accounts.

Notes

1 The reader who is not thoroughly familiar with demand and supply analysis and the concept of elasticity is recommended to read through Appendix A before proceeding.

Key terms

international trade	111	current account balance	113
domestic trade	111	shift (in demand curve)	114
market clearing prices	112	fixed exchange rates	114
exchange rate	112	flexible (floating) exchange rates	114
demand and supply curves	112	par value (parity)	114
visible trade	113	excess supply of pounds	114
invisible trade	113	excess demand for pounds	115
capital account	113	reserves of foreign currencies	115
balance of payments accounts	113	appreciation	115
balance of trade	113	depreciation	115

Review questions

7.1 Delete whichever is incorrect:
'An increase in foreign sales of Rover cars will increase/decrease/leave unchanged the demand for pounds and increase/decrease/leave unchanged the supply of pounds. This will tend to make the value of the pound float up/down.'

7.2

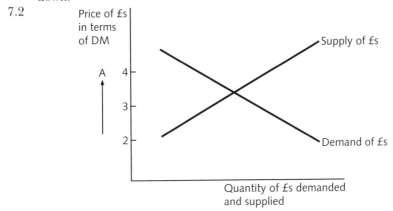

Figure 7.5 The market for sterling

(a) In Fig. 7.5 a movement along the price axis in the direction A represents a depreciation/appreciation in the value of the pound. Delete as appropriate. In what circumstances would one use the terms devaluation or revaluation as opposed to depreciation or appreciation?

    (b) The equilibrium exchange rate is approximately ...

    (c) Under a fixed exchange rate system if the official exchange rate was £1 = DM3.0 this would mean there was an excess demand/excess supply of pounds at the official rate. What would happen as a result of this?

7.3 Assuming that the UK is a net exporter of oil, how would one analyse (in terms of the model in Fig. 7.5) an increase in the price of oil? (Assume the demand for oil is inelastic.)

    Assume now that the UK is a net importer of oil. What would be the effect of a rise in the price of oil? Assume now that the price elasticity of demand for oil is unity (i.e. a 10 per cent price increase causes the quantity demanded to fall by 10 per cent).

7.4 State what the effect of the following would be on the demand for pounds and the supply of pounds. Indicate whether the effect will be shown on the Current Account or the Capital Account of the Balance of Payments.

    (a) The Rover Metro sells well in France.

    (b) A successful sales campaign in Britain for Ford Fiesta cars.

    (c) The London Borough of Ealing decides to raise money by offering bonds for sale to the public, some of which are sold overseas.

    (d) British Embassy staff in Berlin receive a pay increase.

7.5 The basic difference between a fixed exchange rate and a floating exchange rate is:

    (a) under a fixed exchange rate regime the rate at which one currency exchanges for another never changes;

    (b) under a floating exchange rate regime central banks never intervene in the foreign exchange market so they don't need to hold stocks of foreign currencies;

    (c) under a fixed exchange rate the value of a currency is directly fixed to gold;

    (d) only under a fixed exchange rate regime are there declared par values;

    (e) in a floating (or flexible) exchange rate regime the actual rate of exchange varies within a narrow band whereas under a fixed exchange rate regime the rate of exchange does not vary at all.

7.6 Assume that a Rover car sells for £12,500 in the UK and 117,000Fr in France. On which market does Rover make most profit per car sold, if the current exchange rate is £1 = 9Fr?

    If the £ appreciates in value *vis-à-vis* the franc but Rover keeps its French price at 117,000Fr which of the following is true:

    (a) Exporting becomes less profitable to Rover than previously.

    (b) Exporting becomes more profitable to Rover than previously.

7.7 Which of the following policies would, *ceteris paribus*, 'improve' the trade balance (i.e. reduce the size of a trade deficit)?

    (a) raising interest rates;

    (b) reducing employees' National Insurance contribution;

    (c) increasing student grants;

    (d) staging the World Cup in England;

    (e) placing restrictions on convertibility.

7.8 A country records its balance of payments transactions as follows:

Exports of goods	+100
Exports of services	+25

Imports of services	−30
Imports of goods	−105
Interest, profits and dividends (net)	+5
Total inward investment	+50
Outflow of investment	−48

(a) Calculate the 'trade balance' (defined to be visible plus invisible trade).
(b) What does the plus sign on IPD mean?
(c) What is the balance on the current account?
(d) What is the balance on the capital account of the balance of payments? (Explain whether this is a surplus or a deficit and what this implies.)
(e) What accommodating transactions would it have been necessary for the Central Bank to undertake, and what would have happened to the foreign exchange reserves as a result?

7.9 Suppose the demand for British exports is known to be price-inelastic in the short run. What will be the effect of an appreciation in the value of sterling against the German mark (state whether the following are true or false, briefly explaining your reasoning)?

(a) British exporters will benefit from the stronger pound.
(b) German companies selling in Britain will suffer as a result of the fall in the value of the mark.
(c) If British exporters increase their foreign currency prices in line with the rise in the value of sterling then export receipts will fall.
(d) The demand for British exports is likely to be more price-sensitive in the longer run so that exporters who increase their prices in line with the rise in sterling will experience a fall in their export revenues.

Exchange rates, competitiveness and trade flows

8.1 Multilateral exchange rates
8.2 Real exchange rates
8.3 Interpreting movements in the exchange rate
8.4 Competitiveness
8.5 Purchasing power parities
8.6 Trade volume, value and unit value indices
8.7 Does devaluation work?

Preview

This chapter distinguishes between bilateral and multilateral exchange rates and between nominal and real exchange rates. Movements in the exchange rate have an effect on measured competitiveness – other things being equal, a fall in the exchange rate is synonymous with an improvement in competitiveness. This in turn will affect exports and imports in volume terms (quantities) and in value terms (£ million).

8.1 Multilateral exchange rates

The value of sterling – that is, the exchange rate between sterling and other currencies – is of great importance because of its influence on import and export prices and import and export flows. These in turn affect domestic prices, domestic output and hence employment and unemployment. In the last chapter we discussed how the exchange rate was determined in foreign exchange markets by the interaction of the demand for pounds and the supply of pounds. This exchange rate was a **bilateral rate** – the sterling/Deutschemark rate, the sterling/dollar rate, the dollar/Deutschemark rate, the dollar/yen rate and so on. Bilateral exchange rates have the great merit of being easy to understand. The disadvantage of comparing sterling's value with only one other currency, however, is that movements in the bilateral rate tell us as much about what is happening to the other currency as what is happening to sterling. Moreover, a depreciation in the sterling/dollar rate (say from £1 = $1.7 to £1 = $1.6) represents a 'fall in the value of the pound', but only against the dollar. Measured against other currencies the pound may be rising.

Table 8.1 illustrates the movements in the value of sterling measured against a number of other currencies. The value of sterling is expressed as an index with 1990 = 100. A fall in the index represents a depreciation in the value of the pound. As can be seen, when measured against the dollar (column 1) sterling fell in value up until 1994 and then recovered somewhat but was still worth less in 1997 than it was in 1990. When measured against the Deutschemark (column 2) sterling also fell and rose again but by 1997 was worth more than it was in 1990. Against the Japanese yen and the Italian lira the performance was very different. Measured against the yen, the value of sterling in 1997 was only three-quarters of its 1990 value, but measured against the lira it was worth almost a third more.

Rather than comparing the value of sterling against any one specific foreign currency it would be convenient to compare the value of sterling against a basket of other currencies. This is the principle behind a **multilateral exchange rate** where the value of a currency is expressed against a **weighted average** of foreign currencies. A commonly used multilateral exchange rate index is the **Sterling Exchange Rate Index**, which is shown in the last column of Table 8.1. and labelled ERI.

The weights used in a multilateral exchange rate index should reflect the importance in the basket of the currency in question – for example, the US dollar should have a larger weight than the Spanish peseta and the Austrian schilling. An obvious set of weights to use is **trade shares**. That is, the weight attached to a particular currency should reflect the proportion of UK exports which go to the country in question. This is the principle behind the Sterling Exchange Rate Index. The weights in use since February 1995 are shown in Table 8.2.

Table 8.1 The value of sterling compared with other currencies

	US dollar	Deutsche mark	French franc	Japanese yen	Italian lire	ERI
1990	100.0	100.0	100.0	100.0	100.0	100.0
1991	99.0	101.7	102.7	92.3	102.5	100.7
1992	98.9	95.6	96.2	86.9	101.4	96.9
1993	84.0	86.3	87.8	64.8	110.6	88.9
1994	85.8	86.3	87.6	60.8	115.7	89.2
1995	88.3	78.6	81.2	57.6	120.5	84.8
1996	87.4	81.7	82.4	66.0	112.9	86.3
1997	93.5	104.0	104.2	74.8	136.6	104.5

Note: figures are averages for the year, except for 1997 where the June figure is used.
Source: derived from *Financial Statistics*, February 1995 and August 1997.

Table 8.2 Weights used in the Sterling
Exchange Rate Index

Australia	0.48
Austria	1.19
Belgium/Luxembourg	5.39
Canada	1.38
Denmark	1.38
Finland	1.41
France	12.59
Germany	22.49
Greece	0.31
Italy	8.27
Japan	7.00
Netherlands	5.71
New Zealand	0.21
Norway	1.19
Portugal	0.84
Republic of Ireland	3.08
Spain	3.85
Sweden	3.45
Switzerland	3.27
United States	16.49
	100.00

Source: 'Revisions to the calculation of effective
exchange rates' in *Bank of England Quarterly
Bulletin*, February 1995.

Multilateral exchange rates are often referred to as **effective exchange rates** – a rather misleading term since it conjures up the idea of an inflation-adjusted exchange rate but in fact is no such thing. The Sterling Exchange Rate Index was formerly known as the **Effective Exchange Rate for Sterling** – and this title is still sometimes used.

There is a difficulty in interpreting multilateral exchange rates such as the effective exchange rate for sterling since we cannot at any particular point in time measure the *level* of the effective exchange rate. All we can measure is the *movement* in the rate since some arbitrarily chosen point in the past. This is why effective exchange rates are always measured as an index number. The Sterling Exchange Rate Index is shown in this way in Table 8.1. As can be seen, the index fell from 1990 to 1996 and then increased very sharply in 1997.

8.2 Real exchange rates

In the previous section the distinction was drawn between a bilateral exchange rate and a multilateral exchange rate. We now have to make a further distinction – that between **nominal exchange rates** and **real exchange rates**. The concept of a real exchange rate (or **inflation-adjusted exchange rate**) is based on the recognition that relative rates of domestic inflation must in the long run be reflected in changes in nominal exchange rates if these nominal exchange rates are themselves to reflect domestic purchasing power parities. (Refer to section 7.4 to revise purchasing power parities.)

To illustrate this point suppose two countries, Britain and France, have different rates of domestic inflation – say, the annual rate of inflation in France is 10 per cent and that in Britain in zero. Suppose that over a twelve-month period the nominal exchange rate between sterling and the franc – that is, the rate actually paid by dealers in foreign exchange markets – rises from 10 francs = £1 to 11 francs = £1. This, of course, represents a fall in the value of the franc of approximately 10 per cent against sterling in nominal terms. Clearly, however, the movement in nominal rates offsets exactly movements in domestic price levels between the two countries. A bottle of Château Neuf du Pape (a French good) which last year cost 100 francs to produce and sold at £10 in Britain would this year cost 10 per cent more to produce, that is 110 francs, but would still sell at £10 in Britain. Thus the real rate of exchange between the pound and the franc is unchanged.

In summary, it may be helpful to refer to Table 8.3 where the distinction is drawn first between a bilateral and a multilateral rate, and secondly between a nominal and a real rate. As can be seen, this gives us four different types of exchange rate. The first of these – the nominal bilateral rate – is easy to understand but may not be adequate for our purposes. The last of these – the real effective rate

Table 8.3 Summary of different types of exchange rates

Bilateral	Multilateral
nominal	
Easily understood e.g. sterling/dollar rate	Known as 'effective' exchange rate. A weighted average of exchange rates. Example: the Sterling Exchange Rate Index. Cannot measure the *level* of such an index – only *changes* in comparison with some period in the past.
real	
Nominal exchange rate adjusted for differences in the rates of inflation in the countries concerned	Known as 'real effective rate', i.e. a weighted average exchange rate adjusted for the difference between the rate of inflation in Britain and that in the rest of the world.

– may overcome objections to the use of other measures but is rather difficult to understand (and, of course, to measure).

8.3 Interpreting movements in the exchange rate

Movements in some macroeconomic variables have an unambiguous interpretation. For example, an increase in GNP, *ceteris paribus*, is 'a good thing'. An increase in unemployment, or in prices is, *ceteris paribus*, 'a bad thing'. How, therefore, are we to interpret a fall in the exchange rate?

In George Orwell's *Animal Farm* the pigs, when they took control of the farm, wrote a slogan on the barn door: 'Four legs good. Two legs bad.'

In other words, animals who walked on two legs (humans) were bad, others were good. A slogan, you see, was necessary for the other animals who were none-too-bright and could not think things out for themselves. Later on, of course, the pigs began to emulate the behaviour of their former human captors and walked upright on two legs. Then the slogan painted on the barn door was changed: 'Two legs good. Four legs bad.' Few of the animals noticed.

Thus it is with movements in exchange rates. One can point to certain periods in the past (for example, the late 1960s) when a fall in the value of sterling was regarded, if not with horror, then certainly as something to be avoided if at all possible. At other times, for example in the early 1980s, a fall in the value of sterling was something to be encouraged, at least according to the received wisdom as written on the equivalent of the barn door. If, dear reader, we are not to accept uncritically what the pigs tell us then we have to think things out for ourselves.

8.4 Competitiveness

Movements in the exchange rate will clearly have an effect both on **trade prices** and on **trade volumes**. Consider first the effect on the price of UK exports. Assume that exporters set their foreign currency prices by converting sterling prices into a foreign currency price using the exchange rate (this was the behaviour described in Model One in section 7.5). A depreciation in the value of the pound will therefore lead to a fall in the foreign currency price of UK exports – in other words, UK exports become more **competitive**. That is they become cheaper relative to the exports of other countries.

An index which measures competitiveness in this way is shown in Fig. 8.1. It is labelled **relative export prices** and it is defined as the price of UK exports divided by the price of competitors' exports, both measured in a common currency. A fall in the index thus represents an *improvement* in competitiveness. Note that movements in the index measure *changes* in competitiveness. Competitiveness in an absolute sense at any particular point in time cannot be measured by this index.

In section 7.5 we also described a behaviour pattern (labelled as Model Two) in which exporters set their foreign currency prices at a level similar to that of their

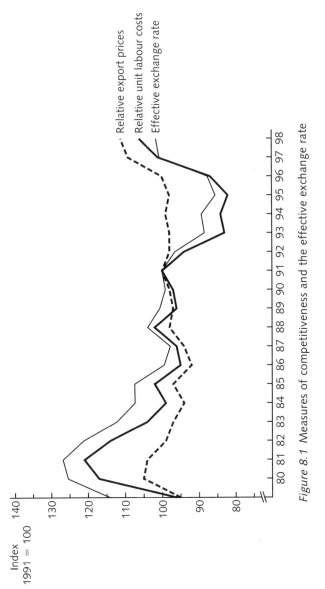

Figure 8.1 Measures of competitiveness and the effective exchange rate

competitors. According to this model of behaviour, even if UK exporters' foreign currency prices remain unchanged following a depreciation of the pound, their export revenues measured in sterling will rise. Hence export sales become more profitable relative to home sales. Thus the **relative profitability of exports** – or rather, movements in this variable – could be used as an indicator of changes in competitiveness. This variable is defined as an index of export prices (of UK goods) divided by an index of prices on the home market (both being measured in a common currency), and it also is one of the standard indices of competitiveness.

There are, of course, other ways of measuring competitiveness. One of these is **relative unit labour costs (RULC)** which is also shown in Fig. 8.1. RULC is defined as an index of unit labour costs in the UK divided by an index of unit labour costs abroad (both in a common currency). Suppose, by way of example, that unit labour costs measured in local currency are constant in both Britain and America. A fall in the value of the pound relative to the dollar will therefore mean that relative unit labour costs *measured in a common currency* will fall. Thus, in Fig. 8.1, a fall in relative unit labour costs indicates an improvement in competitiveness.

In summary, no matter how we choose to measure it, competitiveness will be increased if the pound falls in value. As can be seen, there is a strong correlation between the two measures of competitiveness and the exchange rate, which is also shown in Fig. 8.1. Note the peak of uncompetitiveness in 1980 which corresponds to a very high exchange rate. More recently, note the appreciation in sterling in 1996 which led to a rapid and marked loss of competitiveness.

Clearly, the indices which are conventionally used to measure what we call competitiveness are highly influenced by changes in the nominal exchange rate. Indeed, on the basis of Fig. 8.1 one could go as far as to say that, *ceteris paribus*, movements in the exchange rate lead to equivalent movements in measured competitiveness. An appreciation in the exchange rate is synonymous with a loss of competitiveness.

Suppose competitiveness improves as a result of a fall in the exchange rate. The extent to which export *volumes* rise as a result of this will of course depend upon the relative price elasticity of demand for UK exports and on the extent to which producers respond to the improved relative profitability of exports (that is, the profitability of exports relative to home sales). However, as we mentioned when discussing the J-curve in section 7.5, the improvement in competitiveness brought about by a depreciation of the exchange rate will be partially offset by the resulting rise in import prices. This rise in import prices will tend to raise domestic costs and prices. If this induced rise is significant it will significantly reduce the competitive advantage gained by the initiating fall in the exchange rate.

8.5 Purchasing power parities

The discussion so far has been in terms of movements in nominal exchange rates. These movements in nominal rates may simply be compensating for differences in domestic rates of inflation. The movement in the *real* exchange rate may be less or greater than the movement in the nominal rate. This further complicates an already complicated picture, making it even more difficult to interpret the effects of a fall in the exchange rate and therefore to appraise its desirability.

One possible way out – though not a very satisfactory one – is to try to assess whether the current exchange rate is high or low relative to what it 'ought' to be. Any movement in the exchange rate which moves it towards where it ought to be is therefore a 'good thing'. Our assessment of what the exchange rate ought to be must be based on some notion of an equilibrium rate. One could argue, of course, that the current market rate is the equilibrium rate. In a sense this is true but the logical conclusion to be drawn from this is that the current rate is the correct rate, by definition. Movements up or down have certain effects, but they are neither beneficial nor detrimental, merely neutral. This is a defensible view to hold.

However, we could argue that there is a notion of a 'correct' exchange rate which does make some sense. This is based on the idea of purchasing power parities introduced in section 7.4. The purchasing power parity of a currency is the ratio of the price of a representative basket of goods in country A relative to the price of the same basket of goods in country B. The currency is in equilibrium when the purchasing power parity is equal to the exchange rate parity. This solution to an intractable problem does have an intuitive appeal. In practice, however, estimates of purchasing power parities are calculated only on an infrequent basis, though, of course, lack of data should not deter us if we feel this procedure is fundamentally correct. Comparisons of purchasing power parities and exchange rate parities can sometimes be very revealing. Figure 8.2 shows the relationship between the exchange rate parity and the purchasing power parity of sterling in comparison with the German mark in the period 1976–89. Between 1976 and 1979 both exchange rate parity and purchasing power parity decline. After 1979, however, the e.r.p. rises while the p.p.p. continues to fall. By early 1981 the exchange rate parity is approximately equal to the purchasing power parity. What this means is that, if one were to take £1 and convert it into Deutschemarks, the quantity of goods one could buy in the shops in Germany would have been exactly the same as if one had spent the original £1 in the shops in England.

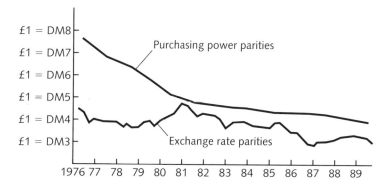

Fig. 8.2 £ versus DM: Exchange rate parity and purchasing power parity

However, it is important to note that one cannot conclude from this that the exchange rate in early 1981 was in some sense 'correct'. As we saw from the earlier Fig. 8.1, the value of sterling was then so high that most commentators would now agree that the pound was 'overvalued' at that time. The implication of this is that purchasing power parity should not be regarded as an infallible indicator of whether a currency is too high or too low relative to some 'correct' value.

8.6 Trade volume, value and unit value indices

The purpose of this section is to introduce some terminology which will probably be encountered in newspapers, textbooks or statistical sources at some time in the future – and would possibly have otherwise been misinterpreted. Most of the confusion surrounds the use of the words 'volume' as in **import volume** and **export volume**. This conjures up a picture of physical quantities of goods, aggregated in some way – so many tonnes of coal plus so many sacks of rice plus so many cars and so on. It is nothing of the sort, of course, because the heterogeneous nature of these goods makes aggregation in anything other than money terms impossible. Thus imports (and exports) are measured initially in **value terms** – so many million pounds' worth of coal plus so many million pounds' worth of rice plus so many million pounds' worth of cars. This gives us a figure for the value of total imports in £ million.

Now, over time the price of these imports (measured in sterling) will change. For example, a fall in the pound or an increase in world prices will tend to increase the price of imports. We can compute an **index of import prices** in a similar way to the way in which we compute an index for domestic prices (the RPI). The price index for imports is sometimes known, somewhat misleadingly, as a **unit value index** or **UVI**. Using such an index of unit values we can adjust the data on the value of imports to take account of changes in the price of imports. The statistical series so derived – which is normally turned into an index number – is known as a **volume index**. The procedure, therefore, is similar to that performed in the National Accounts and explained in section 3.17 when we deflate current price estimates using a price deflator to produce constant price estimates. That is, volume indices for imports and exports are akin to constant price estimates of imports and exports.

8.7 Does devaluation work?

Earlier, in Chapter 7, we distinguished between the terms *depreciation* and *devaluation*. Depreciation, we said, referred to a decrease in a floating exchange rate whereas devaluation referred to a fall in a (nominally fixed) parity. Even though we recognise that a distinction exists we shall here use the terms synonymously. We do so in order to emphasise that a lowering of the exchange rate can be a conscious act of policy designed to bring about certain consequences. That is, a lowering of the exchange rate ('devaluation'), whether a step decrease or a more gradual decline, can be a purposeful act rather than something which just happens as a result of market forces. The purpose of a devaluation is of course to improve competitiveness, thus increasing exports (both in value and volume terms) and reducing imports. In fact, a reduction in imports is not necessary for the devaluation to be considered successful. What is required is that the rise in exports in value terms in the long run outweighs any induced rise in imports in value terms. In short, a devaluation is successful if it improves the balance of trade.

Whether or not a devaluation does in fact improve the trade balance – or could in principle be capable of doing so – is an important policy question. As this chapter illustrates, the question is complex. It is difficult to estimate empirically how trade flows have responded to movements in the exchange rate in the past – hence it is difficult to forecast the likely future response of trade flows to a devaluation in the future.

The crucial issue is whether or not in the long run devaluation produces a sustained improvement in competitiveness. We know (from Fig. 8.1 for instance) that the immediate impact of a devaluation is to increase measured competitiveness. We also know, however, that increased import prices feed through into an increase in the retail price index. This induced rise in domestic prices will reduce the improvement in competitiveness brought about initially by the fall in the nominal exchange rate. In the long run the induced rise in domestic prices and costs may completely eliminate the improvement in competitiveness gained by devaluation. And if there is no long-term improvement in competitiveness, then devaluation cannot improve the balance of trade. If we accept this view, as some economists do, then we must look elsewhere for ways of improving competitiveness, possibly to **supply side improvements** in the labour market and goods market. First, however, in the next chapter we look in more detail at the international monetary system within which exchange rates are determined.

Summary

Bilateral exchange rates measure the value of a currency against a single other currency whereas multilateral exchange rates measure a currency's value against a basket of other currencies. Real exchange rates (or inflation-adjusted exchange rates) take account of movements in the internal purchasing power of currencies.

A rise in the value of a currency is not unambiguously 'a good thing' any more than a fall in a currency is 'a bad thing'. A rise in the exchange rate is normally associated with a loss of competitiveness and this will be bad for exporters.

One way of assessing whether a currency is currently undervalued or overvalued is to compare its current value with its purchasing power parity, since in the long run the exchange rate parity and the purchasing power parity will tend to equality.

A devaluation will increase import prices and hence there will be an induced rise in domestic inflation. But a devaluation is successful in improving the balance of trade if the rise in exports (in value terms) is greater than the induced rise in imports (in value terms).

Key terms

Review questions

8.1 The price elasticity of demand for UK exports is defined as:

$$E_D = \frac{\text{percentage change in quantity of exports bought}}{\text{percentage change in the price (in foreign currency) of UK exports}}$$

If this elasticity were equal to one, which of the following will necessarily result from a 10 per cent fall in the exchange value of the £, assuming exporters change their foreign currency prices by the full extent of the devaluation?

(a) The amount of foreign currency we earn from exporting will rise.

(b) We will have to sell a larger volume of exports to maintain our pre-existing level of export earnings.

(c) Our exports become more competitive so export volume and value will increase.

(d) Export volume will increase but the value of our exports will remain unchanged.

8.2 Suppose a UK exporter sells abroad on markets where the prices charged are determined by local market conditions. Suppose the £ were devalued by 10 per cent. Which of the following statements are true?

(a) The exporter would receive more foreign currency for each item sold.

(b) The exporter would increase his sales volume.

(c) Exporting would become more profitable in comparison with selling on the home market.

8.3 Assume that the government's revenue from North Sea oil is based on the sterling value of the oil exploited. Will an appreciation in the value of the £ reduce/increase/leave unchanged the tax revenue from Petroleum Revenue Tax?

Hint: The oil at the well-head is measured in barrels and its value is denominated in dollars, which then have to be converted to sterling for the purposes of calculating liability for PRT.

8.4 Assume initially that £1 exchanges for \$2 or DM 4. If the value of the DM in terms of dollars rises by
25 per cent (to DM3 = \$2) but the sterling-dollar relationship remains unchanged, what do you expect would happen to the sterling-DM rate? If the sterling-DM rate remained unchanged what would be the best way for a German resident to acquire pounds for spending during her British holiday?

What ensures that the currency relationships are consistent:
(a) arbitrage;
(b) the EU?

8.5 Referring to Table 8.1, which of the following statements are true? Between 1990 and 1995:
(a) The fall in the Sterling Index shows that the pound has fallen against all the major currencies.
(b) The Italian lira fell against the pound.
(c) The pound fell against the Italian lira.
(d) Britain became more competitive *vis-à-vis* West Germany and Japan.
(e) Japanese exports became less competitive.
(f) Italy gained competitiveness *vis-à-vis* Britain.
You may of course wish to qualify your answers or amend the statements above.

8.6 In section 8.2 the distinction was drawn between nominal and real exchange rates. A similar distinction exists, of course, between nominal and real interest rates (i.e. inflation-adjusted interest rates). State which of the following are correct.

The willingness of non-residents to buy UK government securities (in preference to German or American securities) will depend on:
(a) the nominal interest rate offered in London (relative to those overseas);
(b) the real interest rate offered;
(c) the nominal interest rate offered, but investors will also take account of . the likely future movement in the nominal exchange rate;
(d) the nominal interest rate offered, but investors will also take account of the likely future movements in the real exchange rate.

9 The International Monetary System

Preview

The international monetary system is shaped by political imperatives and the history of the system is punctuated by momentous political events. This chapter sketches out a brief history of the international monetary system in the twentieth century. Ostensibly it is a story about the sorts of exchange rate regimes being pursued by trading nations. Look behind the technicalities, however, and you will see that it is a story about power: about great nations, in the ascendancy and in decline, about ideologies, about power blocs, about great men, about political ideals and about war and peace.

9.1 The Gold Standard

Our story starts with an account of the **Gold Standard**. This operated prior to the First World War and for a brief period in the inter-war years when the Chancellor of the Exchequer, Winston Churchill, put Britain back on to the Gold Standard at an exchange rate which, with the benefit of hindsight, we know to have been damagingly high.

As the name implies, the Gold Standard system required the value of each currency to be linked to gold – in theory, linked at an immutably fixed exchange rate. It was a system designed to promote stability in international monetary relations so as to encourage trade between nations. Moreover, it was a system designed to ensure that balance of payments disequilibria would be eliminated in the long run.

To understand how the system worked, recall how, in the nineteenth century when the Gold Standard evolved, that money was backed by gold and other precious metals. The vestiges of this survive today. The bank notes issued by the Bank of England still bear the words: 'I promise to pay the bearer on demand the sum of (five) pounds'. In other words the bearer of a five-pound note in former times would have been entitled to present that note at the Bank of England and receive, in exchange, five pounds' worth of gold. Nowadays the money issued by the Bank of England is **fiat money** – it is not backed by anything.

The fact that money was backed by gold had an important consequence, for it meant that the amount of money issued by the central bank was limited by the amount of precious metals in the bank's vaults. If the central bank suffered a loss of gold, for whatever reason, it would have to reduce the amount of paper money issued.

When countries engage in trade, it is inevitable that at the end of the accounting period some will have a deficit and others will have a surplus – that is, some countries will be 'indebted' to others. Gold was the means of settlement of international indebtedness. The central bank of the deficit country would transfer gold to the central bank of the surplus country. This outflow of gold would force a reduction in the money supply of the deficit country and as a result prices there would fall. The fall in domestic prices would make imports seem comparatively expensive so consumers in the deficit country would switch from buying imports to buying domestically produced goods. Exports, for their part, would become cheaper and export sales would increase. The increase in exports, coupled with a reduction in imports, would reduce the trade deficit and the process would continue until the deficit was eliminated entirely. The reverse of this process would occur in the surplus country – an inflow of gold would increase the money supply, causing prices to rise faster than elsewhere. This would lead to an eventual elimination of the surplus which initiated the flow of gold in the first place. The process is summarised in Table 9.1.

This, at least, was the theory. It is almost certain that the process never worked as smoothly as this model suggests. Even in the nineteenth century the link between money and prices is unlikely to have been as straightforward as was assumed. Moreover, trade flows may not have responded to changes in relative prices in the way that was envisaged.

It was, however, a very neat idea: exchange rates would remain fixed and trade imbalances would be removed by induced changes in relative domestic inflation rates.

Table 9.1 The Gold Standard and the Balance of Payments

Deficit country	Surplus country
Trade deficit	Trade surplus
Outflow of gold ⟶	Inflow of gold
Reduction in money supply	Increase in money supply
Prices fall	Prices rise
Exports cheaper;	Exports more expensive;
home-produced goods cheaper than imports	imports cheaper than home-produced goods
Exports rise; imports fall	Exports fall; imports rise
Trade deficit eliminated	Trade surplus eliminated

Any system – including the Gold Standard – will work reasonably well if conditions are favourable. However, many countries, Britain included, found that when conditions became unfavourable the strain of belonging to such a system was intolerable. This happened in 1931 when the inter-war depression began to bite deeply. The maintenance of the **gold parity** would have necessitated domestic deflation. This would have exacerbated the situation in an already severely depressed domestic economy. Hence Britain left the Gold Standard. The period which followed – up to the outbreak of the Second World War in 1939 – is known by historians as the **Great Depression**. Output fell dramatically, and world trade in particular slumped. In a vain attempt to boost exports, countries devalued their currencies – actions which simply provoked retaliation by other countries. A **beggar thy neighbour** series of competitive devaluations occurred, the net effect of which was to create greater uncertainty, undermining confidence still further.

9.2 Bretton Woods

The Great Depression only really came to an end with the boost to demand caused by rearmament for the Second World War. During the War, once the eventual Allied victory seemed assured, discussions took place about how the post-war world could prevent a recurrence of the monetary chaos of the pre-war decade. Thus it was that a conference took place at Bretton Woods in New Hampshire, USA, in 1944 – attended by men of vision including, incidentally, J. M. Keynes, whose ideas helped posthumously to shape the post-war world. Bretton Woods marks the first major milestone in the recent history of the international monetary system.

The **Bretton Woods System** lasted in a more or less unchanged form from 1944 to 1971. It was a fixed exchange rate system in which the value of a currency was linked to the dollar. The value of the dollar was in turn linked to gold at a fixed rate of $35 an ounce, and for this reason the system is sometimes referred to as the **Gold Exchange Standard**. The fixed exchange rates established at Bretton Woods

– variously referred to as **par values** or **parities** – would be maintained by a system of central bank **intervention**. Central banks undertook not to allow market exchange rates to deviate by more than 1 per cent from the par values that had been established. To this end they held stocks of **intervention currencies**, initially mostly gold, but later any acceptable and available currency which, for reasons to be explained later, meant dollars and sterling. To assist central banks to maintain par values, the **International Monetary Fund** was set up with powers to grant credit, that is, to lend additional supplies of intervention currencies to those central banks that required them from time to time.

Unilateral devaluations (or for that matter, revaluations) were not allowed. However, devaluations were allowed in cases of **'fundamental disequilibrium'** which was defined as a situation in which a balance of payments deficit could not *reasonably* be financed out of reserves, or by borrowing, and could not be corrected by any *reasonable* amount of domestic deflation and unemployment. Note, however, that what could be considered 'reasonable' and what was unreasonable was left undefined.

The Bretton Woods System, initiated in 1944, ushered in a period of unparalleled prosperity. After a brief period of post-war austerity, the 1950s saw a sustained growth of output and of international trade. Harold Macmillan, the British Prime Minister, was legitimately able to claim in a speech in 1957: 'Let's be frank about it; most of our people have never had it so good' – a phrase which he borrowed from the Democratic Party slogan in the US election campaign of 1952. 'You never had it so good.'

The liquidity problem

However, there were flaws in the Bretton Woods system. The dollar was the main intervention currency and its value was pegged to gold. This meant that an increase in the price of gold could only be brought about by a devaluation of the dollar – which was unacceptable. Thus the price of gold remained fixed but the cost of mining and refining gold increased in line with the creeping inflation of the period. Because of this the supply of gold did not expand fast enough to finance the growing volume of world trade. There was, in short, **insufficient liquidity**. Central banks ran short of reserves.

Two options emerged. The first was to increase the amounts central banks could borrow from the IMF. This happened, but did not solve the problem. The second option was for central banks to hold other assets, instead of gold, as reserves. Naturally they chose to use dollars and sterling. This was not simply because these were respected currencies – those of the world's two largest trading nations at the time – but also because dollars and sterling were available in plenty. This in itself was no coincidence, but resulted from the fact that both America and Britain had balance of payments deficits. Had this not been the case dollars and sterling would not have been available for other central banks to hold, no matter how desirable they might have been. This is an important point. If, and only if, America has a balance of payments deficit will there be an excess supply of dollars on foreign exchange markets which foreign central banks can then buy and hold as reserves, to use for intervention.

The confidence problem

However, the fact that dollars (and sterling) were available in abundance made them less desirable. Foreign central banks feared that America's chronic balance-of-payments deficits would force her to devalue the dollar. If this were to happen, central banks holding dollars would suffer a capital loss. Hence central banks became unwilling to hold dollars because they had lost **confidence** in it.

Notice that the problem of confidence and the problem of liquidity are related. The liquidity problem arose because there was insufficient gold. The confidence problem arose because there were too many dollars.

The adjustment problem

In addition to the problems of liquidity and confidence was the problem of **adjustment** – the three together becoming known as the **black trinity**. The adjustment problem arose because certain currencies – the DM, the yen, the French franc – became increasingly undervalued whereas others (the dollar and sterling) became increasingly overvalued. The reasons for this are complex but it is perhaps best explained in terms of **vicious circles** and **virtuous circles**. Germany and Japan enjoyed a virtuous circle. Their exports were cheap, because their currencies were undervalued. The high demand for German and Japanese goods induced high levels of investment which increased labour productivity and helped to keep down wage costs and therefore held down the rate of price inflation, leading to further undervaluation of the exchange rate. America and Britain for their part suffered from a vicious circle. Because their currencies were undervalued their exports were expensive and they therefore failed to sell them in sufficient quantities. In the UK the trade deficit which resulted could only be kept in check by domestic deflation accompanied by high interest rates designed to bolster temporarily the demand for sterling. Both policies affected investment adversely. Productivity growth was therefore slow, inflationary pressure was high, leading to further overvaluation. A circular process of causation.

Of course, the account presented here is a caricature in which many details have been omitted. Moreover, there are some countries who do not fit the general pattern. France, for example, had high rates of domestic inflation but was never afraid to devalue the franc to give herself a competitive advantage. Critics argued that the French did not understand the rules of the game. More probably, with typical French pragmatism, they did understand the rules of the game but they ignored them.

What is clear, with a clarity that only a historical perspective can give us, is that Bretton Woods had no adjustment mechanism. As time went on, currencies became increasingly out of line.

Before the chronological account unfolds we discuss three important features of that period – seigniorage, the Eurodollar market, and SDRs.

9.3 Seigniorage

The United States at the time, and subsequently, enjoyed a unique privilege – that of **seigniorage**. The term relates to the right of kings and princes who historically controlled the minting of the coinage (then the only form of money). Because they made the coins they could take a percentage of the minted bullion and could moreover pay for real resources using money which they themselves created. A distinct advantage. A similar advantage was enjoyed by the USA in the post-war period, for she was able to run chronic balance-of-payments deficits financing those deficits with dollars, money which she herself created. These balance-of-payments deficits resulted partly from deficits on the capital account because Americans were selling dollars in order to buy other currencies which they were then using to purchase assets abroad. Real assets were therefore being acquired and paid for with pieces of paper which could of course be produced at zero cost (in fact, a single piece of paper, a cheque, would have been used rather than cash). As long as other countries are prepared to accept payment *in dollars* for goods which they sell to the US and then *hold* those dollars – either in the vaults of central banks or elsewhere – this advantage will continue to exist. Imagine how nice it would be if you personally could pay for what you buy using money which you created yourself.

9.4 Eurodollars

Where did all those dollars go to? Well, in a geographical sense – and in as much as money can be said to have a physical existence at any point on the earth's surface – many of them went to Europe. And they stayed there to form what came to be known as the **Eurodollar market**. Eurodollars are dollars deposited in banks in Europe. The significance of the market, which grew to be quite large, is that Eurodollars came to be used as a **medium of international exchange** – that is, an international money. These Eurodollars were never converted into other currencies so that those who used them – principally large multinational companies – were completely free from exchange rate risk.

9.5 SDRs

The Eurodollar market flourished because transactions denominated in Eurodollars were free of exchange rate risk. It was a sort of **international money**, the sort of thing in fact that Keynes had called for at the Bretton Woods conference in 1944. His plan was for the IMF to issue an international money called the **banco**. The Keynes Plan was never accepted because it was thought to be too inflationary. Some years later, however, in 1970, the IMF responded to the liquidity problem mentioned earlier, by extending the credit facilities available to central banks. These credit facilities were known as drawing rights and the new facilities were called **Special Drawing Rights** or **SDRs**.

The significance of SDRs is two-fold. First, they are a **reserve asset** used by central banks. That is, central banks can use them as a means of settlement between themselves. This was their original purpose. From 1974 onwards, however, the SDR evolved as a **unit of account**, used by the IMF to denominate its balance of payments financing. To this end the value of the SDR has to be related to other currencies. The SDR was initially related to a basket of sixteen currencies – later reduced to five – the weights of the various currencies in the basket being related to the importance of each country's currency in international trade. Because the SDR was in effect a weighted average of other currencies, this made its value much more stable than a single currency would have been.

It was this feature – the relative stability of the SDR – which made it attractive to non-official users, that is, commercial banks and companies. The SDR therefore became widely used as a unit of account for 'private' transactions – that is, transactions involving private sector banks and companies (as distinct from transactions between central banks).

The use of the SDR to denominate loans and other financial instruments does not of course eliminate entirely the risk of exchange rate fluctuations but it does reduce the risk since the five currencies which now make up the basket – the dollar, mark, French franc, yen and sterling – cannot as a group fluctuate as much as any one of them individually could do. However, although the SDR is important it has not totally taken over the roles (of unit of account and reserve asset) which some believed it might do. There have been no new issues (of SDRs by the IMF) since 1981 and the current total of SDR 21 billion represents only a small part of countries' reserves. Moreover, the private sector's need for liquidity seems to have been met by the eurocurrency markets, especially the Eurodollar market. In the late 1980s, moreover, a new unit of account emerged – the **European Currency Unit** or **ECU**. This too was a basket of currencies rather like the SDR. Its development is discussed more fully below.

9.6 Demonetisation of gold

We left our story with the Bretton Woods system beset by the problems of liquidity, confidence and adjustment. The late 1960s was a frantic time in international monetary relations. In 1964, 1965 and 1966 the UK had balance of payments deficits, financed by borrowing from abroad. In 1967, having built up large debts, the UK 'gave up the long fight to save the pound' and devalued (from $2.80 to $2.40 = £1).

A **domino effect** followed. The weakest currency (sterling) having been knocked down, the next weakest (the dollar) came under attack. The dollar was still linked to gold at this time and therefore a dollar devaluation was equivalent to an increase in the price of gold. Sensing an imminent dollar devaluation, speculators tried to purchase gold, still available at the official price of $35 an ounce. In 1968 America refused in future to sell gold to the free market at the old price of $35 but agreed to stick to $35 for official transactions. The free market price of gold rose rapidly and a two-tier price for gold emerged. Foreign central banks saw this and by 1971 began to demand conversion of their dollars into gold at the official price of $35. The US was technically insolvent, having $10 billion in gold reserves against $50 billion in debts overseas (that is, dollars held overseas).

In August 1971 **gold convertibility** was suspended. The dollar was floated (against gold) and it floated down. Since that time gold has ceased to have any role in international monetary relations. Gold is now just like any other commodity.

9.7 The Smithsonian Agreement: wider margins

What turned out to be a last-ditch attempt to prop up the Bretton Woods system occurred in December 1971. At the Smithsonian Institute in Washington agreement was reached on a new pattern of fixed exchange rates. The significance of the **Smithsonian Agreement**, however, is that it incorporated **wider margins** around these revised par values. Currencies could now fluctuate by up to 2¼ per cent either side of the par values before central bank intervention was necessary (as opposed to 1 per cent under Bretton Woods).

9.8 The Snake

At the same time, and independently, the EEC countries were attempting to link their currencies more closely together, in order to prepare the way for eventual European Monetary Union (EMU). This obviously required narrower, not wider, bands of fluctuation for the European currencies. An elaborate plan was developed whereby the Europeans would keep their currencies close to each other while jointly they would be able to fluctuate more widely *vis-à-vis* the rest of the world. The arrangement – which came to be known as the **Snake** – is illustrated in Fig. 9.1.

An individual European currency was constrained by the skin of the Snake, which was in turn free to wriggle around within the 'tunnel' – the wider margins allowed under the Smithsonian Agreement.

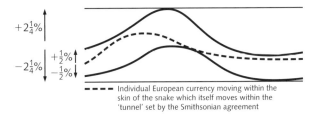

- - - Individual European currency moving within the skin of the snake which itself moves within the 'tunnel' set by the Smithsonian agreement

Figure 9.1 The Snake in a tunnel

Floating

In the event both the Snake and the Smithsonian Agreement collapsed. This was initiated in June 1972 when the pound was officially floated. That is, the Government announced that it would no longer attempt to maintain any particular parity. This heralded the end of the system of fixed exchange rates established 28 years earlier.

In the subsequent months other currencies abandoned fixed parities. Currencies dropped out of the Snake. The transition to a system of floating exchange rates was complete.

9.9 1972 onwards

The floating exchange rates which emerged in 1972 were initially envisaged as a purely temporary phenomenon – a short-term departure from the **adjustable peg** regime which had preceded it. In the event (and with the exception of the European Monetary System) the adjustable peg system has not returned and currencies remain floating. It is, however, worth emphasising that a floating exchange rate does not imply the total absence of intervention on the part of the monetary authorities. 'Managed floating' would be a better description of the policy pursued by many countries. The distinguishing feature of a flexible system, however, is that there is *no declared parity* and (with the exception of the EMS) such policies have characterised the international monetary scene since 1972. In the event flexible systems have coped quite well with the shocks to which the international monetary system has been subjected, most importantly the two oil shocks of 1973–74 and 1979–80 and the associated trade imbalances. One writer comments '. . . it is difficult to envisage how the adjustable peg system could have coped with the scale of this problem, whereas the system of floating rates did.'

9.10 For and against flexible exchange rates

It is worth summarising the main arguments for and against flexible (as opposed to fixed) exchange rates. We do so at this stage so that the reader is better able to judge the merits of the European Monetary System as it currently operates which is, in its essentials, an adjustable peg system. Note, however, that the EMS is seen as a *transitional* stage on the path to full monetary union when individual national currencies will be replaced by a single European currency (discussed more fully below).

The Bretton Woods system, you will recall, suffered from the related problems of liquidity and confidence and the problem of adjustment. These in essence are the inherent problems of any fixed (or adjustable peg) system.

A flexible system in theory does not require intervention on the part of the authorities. Hence there is no need for reserves. In practice, however, even in the absence of a declared par value, the authorities choose to manage the float. That is, they still intervene and this requires that they hold reserves. It would seem reasonable to argue, however, that the amount of reserves required is less under a flexible system. The question of what assets are held as reserves (gold, dollars, SDRs etc.) is of secondary importance.

Adjustment

The liquidity problem is perhaps less important than the problem of adjustment. This is an enormously complex issue. It begs the question as to why, or when, adjustment might be required. 'When currencies get out of line,' is not a helpful answer, because that in turn begs the question of what it means to say that a currency is out of line.

Two or three answers to this question suggest themselves. First, we could have recourse to the notion of purchasing power parity (see section 7.4). According to this view an exchange rate is at its 'correct' level if the *external* value of a currency reflects its *internal* value. In other words, when a representative basket of goods costs the same internally as it does abroad, having converted the price of that basket into foreign currency at the official exchange rate.

A second approach looks at trade imbalances. According to this view, a country with a chronic trade deficit is suffering from an overvalued exchange rate. Depreciation (devaluation) is required to remove the deficit. As we now know, however, this is an overly simplistic view. The effect of a devaluation will depend very much on the elasticities (of demand for exports and imports), on the lags involved, and on the induced effect on domestic inflation.

A third approach looks at *payments* imbalances (as distinct from *trade* imbalances). This approach therefore recognises the fact that trade is not the only thing that affects the demand and supply of a currency on foreign exchange markets. Capital flows (and simple speculation in the short term) may be equally, if not more, important. In the UK the plain fact is that we no longer know the reasons why individual foreign exchange transactions take place. Is a particular transaction financing trade, does it enable the acquisition or disposal of an asset to take place, or is such a transaction undertaken merely in the hope that a capital gain can be made as a result of currency movements? Since the abolition of the **Exchange Equalisation Account** of the Bank of England in 1979 this statistical information is no longer available. It is reasonably clear, however, that in the short term, at least, capital and speculative transactions are very large and may even dominate those transactions related to trade flows.

This illustrates why the adjustment problem is so complex. Not only is the mechanism of achieving adjustment a problem. But also one cannot unambiguously define when adjustment is required. It is not simply a case of saying that when an excess supply of pounds exists sterling is overvalued and should be adjusted downwards because that selling pressure may result mostly from speculative sales. We simply have no way of knowing.

Notwithstanding these points, however, most writers argue that flexible exchange rates 'solve' the problem of adjustment. Flexible rates certainly obscure the problem or more exactly make the responsibility more diffuse. In contrast, under an adjustable peg system the responsibility for choosing a particular par value rests with the policy maker – which in the British context is the Chancellor and/or Prime Minister. In a flexible system there is no par value, so no one has the responsibility, except that diffuse and amorphous mass of individuals known as 'the market'.

A specific problem of adjustable peg systems is that the **burden of adjustment** falls totally on the deficit country. The surplus country cannot be forced to share the burden by revaluing. Under a flexible system the burden of adjustment is borne more equally.

9.11 The European Monetary System

We turn now to the European Monetary System. It has long been realised that the full benefits of economic integration can only be achieved when exchange rate fluctuations have been eliminated, in effect heralding a common currency in Europe. As early as 1949 Jaques Rueff, one the founders of the Community, said: 'L'Europe se fera par la monnaie ou ne se fera pas', which we could perhaps translate into English as 'monetary union is the *sine qua non* of the EU.'

In 1970 the **Werner Report** envisaged four stages by which European Monetary Union was to be achieved (with a target date of 1980). The Snake was the first stage of this process, but, as we have seen, the Snake failed. The idea survived, however, and a new arrangement, retitled the **European Monetary System**, began operations in March 1979.

Essentially an adjustable peg system, the EMS has the following features:

(i) A **parity grid** arrangement establishes a central rate for each currency (against each of the other European currencies).
(ii) The permitted margins of fluctuation are 2¼ per cent (6 per cent for sterling for the brief period when sterling was a member).
(iii) The system uses the European Currency Unit (ECU) in its **divergence indicator**. The ECU is a **composite currency unit** containing specified amounts of the currencies of the member states. In effect, it is a weighted average. The divergence indicator (like an early warning system) is triggered when a currency (say, the French franc) exceeds a pre-specified maximum percentage deviation against its ECU central rate. Intervention (by the Banque de France, say) is then expected to take place.
(iv) There is a pooling of reserves.

9.12 European Monetary Union

European Monetary Union envisages a common currency throughout Europe. The easiest way to think of the consequences of EMU is to consider other examples where different countries share a common currency. This is easy for people living in the UK for the UK comprises four countries – England, Wales, Scotland and Northern Ireland. These countries share a common currency, the pound sterling.

A number of things follow from this. First, the price level and the rate of inflation is approximately the same in all four countries of the UK. More correctly it is only the price level in the **tradeables sector** which is the same for only here does the Law of One Price operate. In the non-tradeables sector – for example, in house and land prices – there is no reason to suppose that prices in Scotland will be the same as those in England. For tradeables, however – cars, computers and cornflakes – arbitrage ensures that the price in Edinburgh is the same as the price in London.

The second thing which follows from a common currency is that the individual countries of the UK do not calculate Balance of Payments accounts either with each other or with the rest of the world. Only the United Kingdom has a balance of payments and that with the rest of the world. The individual countries of the UK, such as Scotland, do not. This follows because the balance of payments relates to *foreign trade*, and foreign trade is defined as a situation where one national currency is exchanged for another. Domestic trade such as that between Scotland and England does not involve an exchange of currencies. Hence, neither trade nor capital flow between these two countries is measured or recorded.

It follows that Scotland on its own can have neither a balance of trade deficit nor a balance of payments deficit with England (nor, of course, a surplus), at least not in a conventional accounting sense. However, it is quite probable that regions or countries sharing the same currency will have an imbalance of trade flows with the other regions with whom they share a currency and that these imbalances will be manifest in other ways – principally in the form of **regional imbalances** in unemployment and activity rates, and especially in income per capita.

Suppose regions A and B share the same currency but that region A has a lower rate of productivity growth. Because productivity growth tends to offset cost-push inflationary forces, region A will *tend* to have a higher rate of cost inflation. This tends to make exports from region A less competitive, resulting in a trade deficit with region B. If the two regions had independent currencies a devaluation of the alpha (region A's currency) could be used to offset the relatively higher rate of inflation there. The magnitude of the devaluation should be such that the *real* exchange rate is restored to its former level. If the two regions share the same currency, however, this offsetting devaluation of the alpha *vis à vis* the beta cannot take place. The imbalance persists.

The problem relates not just to imbalances between regions of the same country, say Scotland and England. Rather, it relates to imbalances between a particular region and the rest of the world. To illustrate, the value of sterling may be at an appropriate level to ensure an approximate balance on trade and payments between *England* and the rest of the world but not at an appropriate level to ensure balance between Scotland and the rest of the world. Because Scotland and England share the same currency, no unique exchange rate can be found which ensures payments balance for both countries. A country which has a higher cost structure, for whatever reason, must compensate for this by having a lower exchange rate. If it cannot have a lower exchange rate this will have a deleterious effect on its economic performance, illustrated by its success in increasing the standard of living of its inhabitants.

Just such an example has been provided by the events following German reunification. Before reunification in 1990 the East German currency, the Ostmark, was worth (at most) 20 per cent of the Deutschemark. When the two countries were reunified the exchange rate chosen between the Ostmark and the Deutschemark was 1:1. At this exchange rate East German industry was hopelessly uncompetitive and within a few months much of it had collapsed. Unemployment, previously a relatively unknown phenomenon, had reached 40 per cent. The *immediate* effect of what is for the East Germans such an overvalued exchange rate is therefore entirely negative. However, the counter argument is that the long-term effect will be to render East German industry more efficient by exposing it to the discipline of market forces at a high exchange rate.

The basic point is this. West German industry can compete very effectively on international markets at what is a relatively highly valued DM. In contrast, East German industry has a much higher cost structure because of the inefficiencies of the former command system of economic planning which produced chronic overmanning. Before reunification East German exports could compete on international markets because higher domestic costs were offset by a low exchange rate. The imposition of a single currency meant that East Germany became a depressed region, at least in the short term.

There are some reasons to suppose that market forces will act in such a way as to even out inequalities in income between different regions. In theory investment should flow to those areas where the potential return is the greatest, and these will generally be areas of capital shortage where there are relatively plentiful supplies of other factors, especially labour. Surplus labour for its part will move from areas of high unemployment to areas where more jobs are available.

9.13 Maastricht: the convergence criteria

The previous section illustrated the problems that would be encountered if a common currency were to be adopted by countries with diverging economic performances, in terms of productivity growth rates and especially inflation rates. In recognition of this and to prepare the way for European Monetary Union, the EU countries agreed to a set of **convergence criteria** at the **Treaty of Maastricht** in 1992. According to the Treaty only those economies which satisfy the criteria will be eligible to participate in the moves towards a single European currency. The timescale for these moves began in 1996–97 and, in theory at least, will culminate in the establishment of a single currency by 1999 at the latest, though by late 1997 this was looking increasingly unlikely. The convergence criteria are set out below.

1 *Inflation.* To be eligible for membership the country's inflation rate should be 'close' to the average rate of the three best-performing members ('close' is interpreted to mean within 1.5 per cent).

2 *Interest rates.* To be eligible for membership, interest rates should be close to the rates in the three best performing countries. Here 'close' is defined explicitly to mean not more than 2 per cent higher. The interest rate in question is that on long-term government bonds.

3 *Budget deficit.* The budget deficit should not exceed 3 per cent of GDP.

4 *Outstanding government debt* (that is, the National Debt). This should not exceed 60 per cent of GDP.

5 *Exchange rate stability in the e.r.m.* For the previous two years the normal margins of fluctuation should not have been exceeded.

Few if any EU members will satisfy these convergence criteria within the agreed timescale. Ironically, the UK satisfies more of the criteria than most other EU countries. The UK does not, however, satisfy the last criterion since sterling has not been a member of the EMS since **Black Wednesday** in September 1992 when the weight of speculative selling pressure forced sterling to abandon its fixed parity against other European currencies and to leave the EMS, since when it has not re-joined.

Summary

The pre-War Gold Standard was superseded in 1944 by the Bretton Woods system of fixed exchange rates. This system suffered from problems of liquidity, confidence and adjustment and eventually broke down in 1972, since when exchange rates worldwide have been floating. However, the currencies of the member states of the European Community (now European Union) have since 1979 been in a fixed exchange rate system known as the European Monetary System (the one notable exception to this being sterling which was forced to leave the EMS in 1992 and has not rejoined). It is intended that EU countries will adopt a common currency by 1999. However, only those EU countries which meet certain convergence criteria will be eligible for membership and by late 1997 it seemed unlikely that the plan would go ahead on schedule.

Notes

1 Partington, I., *Applied Economics of Banking and Finance*, 4th Edn, p. 350.

Key words

Gold Standard	144	'beggar thy neighbour' policies	146
fiat money	145	Bretton Woods system	146
gold parity	146	Gold Exchange Standard	146
Great Depression	146	par values	147

Review questions

9.1 The Japanese and German economies have tended to have trade surpluses for much of the last forty years and therefore their currencies have tended to appreciate. Why therefore don't central banks use these currencies as reserve assets?

9.2 Which of the following are fiduciary currencies?
dollars
gold
SDRs

9.3 Is the ECU a currency or a unit of account or both (or neither)? Does the same apply to the SDR?

International aspects of inflation

Preview

This chapter looks at periods in the past when different countries have experienced simultaneous increases in inflation rates. It investigates these episodes to see if they can shed any light on the nature of the inflationary process.

10.1 Demand pull or cost-push?

Earlier in this book we looked at the Keynesian and monetarist versions of demand-induced inflation and in Chapter 6 we looked at a third explanation – that of cost-push inflation. In this chapter we consider the extent to which any or all of these provide a convincing explanation of inflation rates in an international context.

Figure 10.1 shows the rate of inflation for a number of countries for the period 1978–96. It is clear from this graph that inflation has an international dimension to it – inflation rates tend to rise and fall together. Note particularly the acceleration in inflation which occurred in 1979–80. Following this all countries experienced a fall in inflation rates, but at the end of the 1980s inflation rates started to rise again. In this chapter we shall look at the acceleration in inflation that occurred in 1989 to see if we can infer from it anything about the nature of the inflationary process.

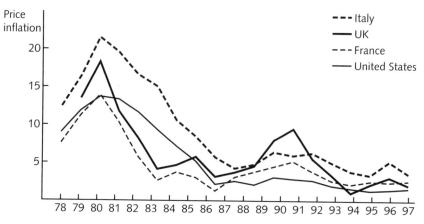

Figure 10.1 Rate of change of consumer prices, 1978–96

10.2 Cost-push inflation

Consider first the cost-push interpretation. The root cause of inflation, according to this view, was **autonomous increases in costs**, and these cost increases fell into two main types: increases in wage costs, and increases in the cost of imports.

The increase in inflation rates experienced by all countries in 1980 and then again in 1989 cannot, without stretching credulity too far, be totally explained by autonomous increases in wage costs. It would be too much of a coincidence to suppose that suddenly and simultaneously workers in all these countries became more forceful in their wage demands, or employers became more submissive in acceding to those demands. Clearly, on its own, this cannot be an adequate explanation of the causes of inflation.

The increase in the cost of imported raw materials seems a more plausible explanation. Table 10.1 shows what was happening to **commodity prices** throughout the period. As can be seen, the fastest rate of increase of commodity prices was in 1979 and 1988. Both of these were years which immediately *preceded* an acceleration in consumer prices in the countries we are studying. Clearly, this increase in commodity prices would appear to be part of the explanation we are seeking. There remains, however, an important unanswered question, namely: Why were some countries more affected by the increase in commodity prices than others? Could it be that some countries are more dependent upon imports – and in particular raw material imports – than others?

Table 10.2 gives some indication of the relative importance of imports in GDP for a number of countries. As can be seen, there is no obvious correlation between dependence on imports and inflation rates. However, the composition of the basket of goods and services which is imported differs from country to country and therefore the impact of rising world prices would also differ from country to country.

Table 10.1 World commodity prices, 1976–89

	Index (1985=100)	% increase
1977	91.5	0.2
1978	99.0	8.2
1979	123.4	24.6
1980	130.8	6.0
1981	121.3	−7.3
1982	108.3	−10.7
1983	114.6	5.8
1984	115.3	0.6
1985	100.0	−13.3
1986	93.9	−6.1
1987	106.5	13.4
1988	135.7	27.4
1989	136.5	0.6

Source: International Financial Statistics Yearbook, 1990.

Table 10.2 Imports as a percentage of GDP (average 1983–89)

UK	27.3
France	22.0
West Germany	28.4
Italy	19.9
USA	10.5
Japan	11.2

Source: International Financial Statistics Yearbook, 1990.

For example, a country might experience a larger than average increase in prices because her basket of imports contains relatively more of those commodities which are increasing in price the fastest.

More importantly, changes in the exchange rate will exacerbate or mitigate the effect of rising world prices. For example, if a country's currency is appreciating this will tend to offset the effect of rising world prices. For instance, commodity prices are by convention measured in dollars. If sterling rises by 10 per cent *vis à vis* the dollar, this will completely offset a 10 per cent rise in the dollar price of imported commodities. In other words the *sterling* price of commodities imported into the UK will not rise at all. Obviously a depreciation of sterling will have the opposite effect.

Table 10.3 shows for each country the net effect of changes in the dollar price of its imports and changes in the exchange rate. That is, for each country it shows movements in import prices *expressed in national currencies*. The differences between

Table 10.3 Movements in import prices (Index of prices expressed in national currencies (1985 = 100) and percentage rate of change in 1989)

	1985	1986	1987	1988	1989	% increase 1988-89
UK	100	109.3	125.1	135.1	130.8	−3.2
West Germany	100	113.9	129.3	133.1	134.0	0.7
Italy	100	105.4	119.6	123.9	126.5	2.1
USA	100	96.6	103.6	108.6	119.4	9.9
Japan	100	85.4	91.9	98.0	101.3	3.4

Source: International Financial Statistics Yearbook, 1990.

Table 10.4 The contribution of imported inflation to the rise in consumer prices in 1989

	Col.1	Col.2	Col.3	Col.4	Col.5
	% increase in import prices (measured in national currencies)	Imports as % of GDP (1989)	'Imported' inflation equals Col.1 times Col.2	Total increase in consumer prices 1989	Residual (inflation caused by domestic factors) Col.4 minus Col.3
UK	−3.2	28.0	−0.9	7.8	8.7
Germany	0.7	28.5	0.2	2.8	2.6
Italy	2.1	19.8	0.4	6.2	5.8
USA	9.9	11.0	1.1	4.8	3.7
Japan	3.4	12.4	0.4	2.3	1.7

countries shown in Table 10.3 therefore reflect movements in exchange rates as well as differences in the size and composition of the import basket.

For the period 1988–89 the table shows that there were considerable differences in the extent to which different countries were affected by rising import prices. Taken together with our measure of the degree of dependence on imports (spending on imports as a percentage of total expenditure), this should give us a rough indication of the contribution which imported inflation made to the overall increase in consumer prices. The results of such an exercise for 1989 are shown in Table 10.4. Column 1 shows the percentage increase in import prices measured in national currencies. As already stated, this will have been affected by movements in the exchange rate as well as movements in the dollar price of imports. Column 2 shows imports as a percentage of GDP in 1989. The product of columns 1 and 2 (shown in column 3) therefore gives a crude measure of 'imported' inflation in 1989 for each country. By comparing this with column 4, which shows the total rise in consumer prices, we can see what proportion of the total rise in consumer prices is 'explained' by imported inflation and the remaining proportion which is therefore attributable to domestic factors (column 5).

The method employed here is fairly rough and ready. One of its principal drawbacks may be that it is unduly sensitive to the exact time period chosen and, had we chosen a different period to study, the results might have been quite different. It does provide us with a valuable indication, however, of the extent to which imported inflation could *potentially* have contributed to the overall increase in consumer prices in 1989. Note that, in this exercise, we cannot evaluate the extent to which imported inflation actually *did* contribute to the overall rise in consumer prices, merely the extent to which it could, potentially, have done so. It is, of course, quite possible that all or part of the increase in import prices was absorbed by manufacturers and retailers and not passed on in the form of higher prices. It is also possible that firms do not base their prices on costs at all – rather, they look at the demand conditions for their product and they charge 'what the market will bear'. If this interpretation of firms' behaviour is correct, then, in a situation where costs are rising, firms would not automatically respond by increasing prices, and the exercise of decomposing the total rise in consumer prices into the 'imported' element and the 'domestic' element is invalid. We shall pick up this point again in section 10.6, when we discuss alternative views on the nature of the mechanism by which inflation is transmitted from one country to another.

Leaving aside this objection for the moment, however, there remains to be explained the residual shown in column 5 of Table 10.4 – which we have described as 'purely domestic inflation'. What determines the strength of these domestic inflationary forces? One possible explanation is that, in the high inflation countries, increases in the cost of living, caused by increases in import prices, provoked high wage demands which led to increases in unit labour costs and hence to wage-push inflation. These countries therefore experienced high rates of price inflation which can be traced *directly* to wage push forces and *ultimately* to import price push forces. In such a situation, economists would call the wage increases the **proximate cause** of inflation, that is, the nearest identifiable cause, even though they recognise it may not be the ultimate cause.

It is unfortunately difficult to test empirically the validity of this seemingly plausible interpretation. The first problem is that it is difficult to determine what constitutes a 'high' wage demand (for the reasons set out in Chapter 6). Secondly, the wage settlements that are actually made will depend to some extent on the willingness of employers, in both the public and private sector, to grant wage increases. This willingness will depend on the rate at which the demand for goods and services is expanding. Thus demand pressures cannot be ignored and any 'explanation' of the causes of inflation which confines itself to cost factors must be at best a partial explanation.

10.3 Demand pull inflation

Could we, however, argue that the increase in inflation which countries experienced in 1980 and again in 1989 was the result of excess demand pressures? Whether we regard aggregate demand as being determined by injections and withdrawals or by the money supply, it seems unlikely that an increase in aggregate demand sufficient to trigger off such an acceleration in the rate of inflation could have occurred *simultaneously* in all those countries at those times. Unless there is some way in which the economies of the world are linked, so that excess demand in one country spills over to other countries, we must regard the level of demand in any particular economy as being determined by the government and the monetary authorities within that country. As such, it is implausible that governments and monetary authorities throughout the Western world should have all decided to create excess aggregate demand at approximately the same point in time. According to this line of reasoning, then (which we shall subsequently qualify in section 10.5), the quickening of inflation in 1980 and 1989 cannot have been initiated by excess demand.

However, even though an expansion of demand may not have initiated the inflation, it may have been responsible for allowing it to proceed. We have seen how some countries managed to keep inflation rates lower than others when faced with comparable amounts of imported inflation (columns 3 and 4 of Table 10.4). We could argue that those countries who were successful in keeping inflation to relatively modest levels may have been those who kept demand in check. Those countries who were not so successful may have been those who allowed demand to increase, thus allowing inflation to proceed and gather momentum.

10.4 A methodological note

It seems quite plausible to argue on *a priori* grounds that the pressure of demand had a significant influence on inflation, though this explanation is quite different from our previous plausible explanation. One of the problems faced in applied economics, and in the social sciences generally, is that one can frequently offer a variety of seemingly plausible interpretations of observed phenomena and it is extremely difficult to decide empirically which is correct. It is not simply a question of having recourse to the empirical evidence, for the empirical evidence itself is often subject to differing interpretations. In other words, there are no 'hard facts'.

However, if we did set out to try to decide empirically which of our explanations remained most plausible when confronted with the evidence, what sort of questions should we ask and what sort of evidence should we look for? The following would appear to be a preliminary list. If we compare a high inflation country such as the UK (in the 1980s) or Italy with a low inflation country such as Germany, then we should ask:

- How severe were the external inflationary pressures facing each economy? To what extent was this the effect of exchange rate changes, which were themselves partly dependent on the level of demand in the economy?
- Did either country show evidence of excess aggregate demand? How could this be measured? Did unemployment rise faster in one country than in the other, and is this symptomatic of insufficient demand, or are other factors more important in determining unemployment rates?

- What was happening to public spending, and to what extent was public spending financed through taxation or through borrowing? What therefore was happening to the growth of the money supply?
- Was the level of wage settlements higher in one country than in the other? Taking account of differences in the rate of productivity growth, did this result in differences in the rate of change of unit labour costs?

We would have to collect data on these things not just for one year but over a number of years, and as such this represents quite a large informational requirement. Even if we had all this information, however, it would not be possible to devise tests which would show conclusively which of our interpretations was correct. Moreover, some epistemologists would argue that it does not necessarily follow that the more information we collect the more certain we can become that one interpretation is correct and the other incorrect.

The essential shortcoming of the empiricist method is illustrated by the story of the empiricist chicken. Every morning the empiricist chicken was fed grain by the farmer. The chicken, being an empiricist, thought 'I do not know for certain whether the farmer is going to kill me or whether he is my friend and is going to keep me as a pet and feed me every morning. But every morning I get more evidence that the second interpretation is correct. Every time that he feeds me increases the probability that the second interpretation is correct and reduces the probability that the first is correct.'

After almost a year the empiricist chicken felt that there was an overwhelming weight of evidence in favour of the second interpretation, that the farmer was going to keep him as a pet. The next day the farmer killed him and had a plump chicken for his dinner.

This cautionary tale is not meant to imply that we should not seek to verify or falsify our theories by an appeal to the evidence. It merely illustrates the difficulty, some might say the impossibility, of so doing. The fact that there is disagreement among economists about the correct interpretation of real world events is in itself evidence of how difficult it is to refute a false hypothesis.

10.5 International monetary forces

In section 10.3 we argued that the level of demand in an economy is determined by the government and the monetary authorities within that country and therefore, since it is implausible that all countries should have decided to expand demand simultaneously, that the cause of the simultaneous increase in inflation rates cannot be attributed to demand pull forces. However, there is a school of thought which argues that, because of the nature of the international monetary system, the economies of the world are *linked* more or less closely together so that an expansion of demand in one country causes demand to be expanded in other countries and that this is how inflation is initiated and transmitted from one country to another.

In theory, excessive monetary expansion in one country can only produce inflation in another country if both countries are linked by a fixed exchange rate. If the exchange rate is immutably fixed, then, in effect, the two countries share the same currency, since a given amount of one currency can always be exchanged for a fixed amount of the other. Floating exchange rates on the other hand act as a sort of 'flexible joint' between the two economies.

International monetarists would argue for example that in the early 1970s a rapid expansion in the *world*'s money supply was caused by an over expansion of the major currency, the dollar. The United States, they would argue, was paying for the Vietnam War with excessive domestic monetary expansion which caused both domestic inflation and balance of payments deficits. Thus the world was flooded with dollars. On international money markets there would thus be an excess supply of dollars and an excess demand for, say, Deutschemarks. In order to prevent the price of Deutschemarks from appreciating against the dollar, the German central bank would have to step in and buy up the excess dollars, paying for them in marks. These marks might be bought by American firms importing German products who would use them to pay German exporters, who would in turn use them to pay their workforce and so on. Thus, there would be a tendency for the domestic money supply in Germany to expand, as a direct result of the expansion of the American money supply. As long as the two economies were linked by a fixed exchange rate, then the larger the American balance of payments deficit with Germany, the greater the tendency for the German money supply to expand. Thus there is a tendency for inflation in one country caused by excessive monetary expansion to generate a sympathetic monetary expansion – and hence inflation – in those countries with which it is linked in a fixed exchange rate system. This tendency will be stronger, the more immutably fixed is the (nominally) fixed exchange rate.

This is not the end of the story, however. The inflationary episodes of 1980 and 1989 were preceded as we have seen by increases in commodity prices worldwide. Although *individual* price increases could have been caused by the action of individual producers it seems plausible to argue that the *general* increase in commodity prices could only have been caused by demand pressure. International monetarists would argue that this demand pressure was associated with an over-expansion of the world money supply through a process such as that described in the previous paragraph.

10.6 The transmission of inflation across national frontiers

The international nature of the inflationary process has been noted and two interpretations of the way in which it passes from one country to another have been described, namely:

- Directly, as a result of rising import prices via a simple cost-push mechanism. Implicit in this explanation is the view that firms base their prices principally on costs. Rising import prices could themselves have been caused either by the actions of individual producers (such as OPEC) or as the result of worldwide demand pressure resulting from a too rapid expansion of the world money supply.
- As a result of the simultaneous over-expansion of the money supplies of various countries, which caused excess demand inflation in these countries. The reason why these monetary expansions occur simultaneously is because of the actions of central banks in trying to preserve a fixed parity in a situation in which an important member of the fixed rate club (often the USA) is allowing rapid monetary growth.

A third interpretation of the way in which inflation crosses national boundaries is to do with a process known as **international price arbitrage**. Assume two countries operate a fixed exchange rate and there are absolutely no restrictions on trade between the two countries, and that they both have the same rate of sales tax. In such a situation, if there are appreciable differences between the price of goods in one country and the price of the same goods in the other country, then it will be profitable to buy up goods in the cheap country for re-sale in the expensive one. To the extent that this process takes place, the effect will be to lower prices in the expensive country and raise prices in the cheap one. In theory, the process would continue until prices of goods in the two countries were equalised, making due allowance for transport costs.

This process of course occurs initially in the **tradeables sector** – those commodities which are or could be traded internationally – but it spreads to the **non-tradeables sector** as a result of pressures in the labour market as workers in the non-tradeables sector seek comparable pay increases with those in the tradeables sector.

The explanations of the way in which inflation spreads from one country to another are, of course, not mutually exclusive. From the standpoint of the policy maker, however, it is vital to know which explanation is closest to reality at any particular point in time, since only then can effective policies be formulated. The fundamental point of disagreement from which these divergent views stem relates to the way in which prices are set. Are prices basically *demand determined* or are they *cost determined*? This was the question with which we began our discussion of inflation back in Chapter 2.

The answer to this key question is of course that both interpretations are correct *a priori*. *A posteriori* – that is, when we look at the evidence – there are some situations in which demand seems to be the principal factor in determining prices, and other situations in which costs seem to play the dominant role.

Summary

At certain times inflation rates can be observed to increase more or less simultaneously in different countries. This suggests that inflationary pressure is spreading from one country to another and may well have a common cause. Notwithstanding this, some countries are better able to contain this inflationary pressure than others.

There are divergent views about the nature of the process whereby inflation spreads from one country to another. These views are predicated upon a particular view of how prices are set in a market economy. To what extent are prices demand determined and to what extent cost determined?

Key terms

Review questions

10.1 Table 10.5 provides data on world commodity prices, food prices from the developed world and the world price of manufactures. Comment on the series. What can you infer about the way in which the prices of these things are determined? What can you infer about 1988 and about 1993?

Table 10.5 Index of commodity prices, world food prices, and world price of manufactures (1994 = 100)

	Minerals, ores & metals	Food, developed countries	Manufactures, world price ($)
1984	89.9	83.7	62.1
1985	86.0	76.2	62.4
1986	81.9	81.5	76.8
1987	96.5	87.9	88.3
1988	141.7	103.3	91.5
1989	133.6	105.2	91.7
1990	119.3	95.1	101.5
1991	102.2	94.2	100.9
1992	99.9	96.4	104.2
1993	85.7	95.2	98.1
1994	100.0	100.0	100.0
1995	119.5	108.1	112.0
1996	105.2	121.3	–

Source: derived from statistical appendix to the *National Institute Economic Review*, 1995Q3 and 1997Q3.

10.2 Classify the following goods and services into tradeables, and non-tradeables – houses, haircuts, hamburgers, postal charges, holidays, clothes.

10.3 Why will inflation in the tradeables sector tend to spread to the non-tradeables sector?

11 Economic growth

Preview

The average rate of growth of the UK economy is between 2 and 2.5 per cent per annum. In some years the economy grows a bit faster and in other years considerably slower. In comparison with our historical experience the growth rate in the post-war period has been acceptable, but in comparison with other advanced economies Britain's growth rate has been poor. Notwithstanding this, however, there have been brief periods of relatively rapid growth, such as the late 1980s. This chapter discusses a number of themes which various writers have put forward to explain Britain's relatively modest rate of economic growth.

11.1 Growth defined

Economic growth can be defined as an increase in real terms, in Gross National Product, or in GNP per capita. In other words, it is an increase in the volume of goods and services the economy produces in a given year. When allowance is made for any increase or decrease in population, the rate of economic growth therefore equates to the change in the average citizen's material **standard of living**. It was not so very many years ago that economic growth was regarded as unequivocally a good thing – something to be pursued and maximised. These certainties have, however, given way in the minds of some people to a more sceptical attitude – indeed, some would now question whether continued economic growth is either possible or desirable. We shall discuss these views in Chapter 12 where we sketch out what could be called 'green' views on these issues. First, however, we shall consider the important question of why the performance of the British economy has been relatively poor in comparison with many of its competitors in the post-war period. We begin in sections 11.2 to 11.6 by considering the period up to the mid-1970s. Subsequent sections discuss the period up to 1997 though many of the themes about Britain's growth performance run through the entire post-war period.

11.2 A methodological note

Table 11.1 gives some comparative growth rates for a number of industrial countries for the period up to the mid-1970s. Clearly, in comparison with other economies, the British economy fared badly in this period. Dozens of different explanations of this apparent failure have been put forward by commentators (both professional and otherwise) – poor management expertise, restrictive practices on the part of trade unions, too much bureaucracy, a work-shy attitude and so on – but the problem with all these 'explanations' is that, although they may possibly contain an element of truth, they are insufficiently precise to merit the status of a scientific hypothesis. This is not to say that economists necessarily act in a more scientific way. In this particular area of enquiry, it is seldom possible to put forward testable hypotheses regarding the importance of any particular factor in promoting economic growth. More precisely it is almost impossible to formulate *refutable* hypotheses about the causes of Britain's poor growth performance.

The major difficulty is that the phenomenon of economic growth is the result of a very complex process, so that any explanation which attributes it to a *single* cause must necessarily be regarded with suspicion. This much is clear, but the difficulty comes in deciding whether any particular factor which has been identified is even a contributory cause and, if so, how important it is.

We shall not attempt to provide a solution to this methodological problem. One notable attempt to assess the quantitative significance of the various factors which

Table 11.1 Real GDP growth: 1951–76 (% per annum)

	UK	France	Germany	Italy	USA	Japan
Average growth rate 1951–76	2.5	4.8	5.5	4.9	3.1	8.5
GDP in 1976 as a multiple of GDP in 1951	1.9	3.2	3.8	3.3	2.2	7.1

Source: OECD National Accounts and CSO quoted in *Economic Progress Report*, July 1978.

could contribute towards economic growth – the work of Denison[1] – has been heavily criticised for its methodological arbitrariness. Indeed, we could argue that such an attempt is doomed to fail since it seeks to discover something which is, in essence, unknowable. The macroeconomy is a social organism whose properties cannot be discovered in the same way as the physicist or the biologist can discover, by experimentation, the properties of the physical world. The social world is different in two important and related respects. First, although experimentation is possible with the macroeconomy (though impractical), *controlled* experimentation is not possible. The essence of a controlled experiment is that all other factors, apart from the one whose influence the experimenter is trying to assess, should be held constant. This is possible under the laboratory conditions where the researcher in the physical sciences operates, but the researcher in the social sciences can never ensure that this condition is fulfilled; that is, the *ceteris paribus* assumption cannot be fulfilled in the real world.

Secondly, in the social sciences the process of experimentation may induce changes in the subject of the study. For example, if the Bank of England wishes to know what the effect will be on the demand for government securities of a 1 per cent rise in interest rates, it can raise interest rates and observe what happens. If the experiment is repeated, however (that is, raising interest rates a further 1 per cent), then the impact on sales of securities may not be the same as in the first experiment. This is because the responsiveness of the demand for government securities to interest rate changes may have been changed by the Bank's previous action. Potential buyers of securities now have a different set of experiences and expectations – they find themselves in a unique situation, just as the previous situation was unique, in the sense that an identical set of conditions had never existed before. Logically, because both situations are unique, one cannot infer anything about the properties of the second situation from experiments conducted in the first.

This is part of the general problem that, in the social sciences, the properties of the systems which the researcher is endeavouring to discover are constantly changing, whereas the laws of nature which the physical scientist investigates are essentially immutable. Thus, the 'law' of gravity is the same when Newton discovered it as it is now – gravitational attraction is 32 feet/second^2 – but social laws change over time. For example, the propensity to save out of aggregate income (the marginal propensity to save or MPS) will change as individuals slowly adjust their behaviour in response to a situation in which the value of savings is eroded by inflation.

In our analysis of the causes of the relatively slow rate of growth of the UK economy in this period we shall not therefore attempt to attribute this slow growth to any single cause. Nor shall we attempt to assess the quantitative significance of any single factor. Because of the sheer complexity of the growth process, economists have tended to concentrate on a few easily observable (and measurable) variables which common sense – sometimes an unreliable guide – tells one are important in promoting economic growth. We shall examine a few of these in the following sections.

11.3 The interaction of demand and supply

The cause of an increase in the output of goods and services of an economy could analytically be broken down into two parts, namely:

- A rise in output attributable to a rise in the **inputs** to the production process of the various factors of production, principally capital and labour.
- A rise in output resulting from the more efficient use of a fixed volume of factor inputs – that is, a rise in **output per unit of input** (or what is sometimes called a rise in **productivity**).

In practice, however, it may be difficult to distinguish between these two. Factor inputs, for example, are not directly observable. The input of the factor **labour** to the production process can be approximated by the number of people in employment multiplied by the number of hours worked. This, however, does not take account of differences in the amount of effort expended, or the skill with which this effort is applied. If one attempts to make allowance for the fact that highly paid skilled labour is more productive than low paid unskilled labour, by measuring labour input in value terms rather than in terms of the number of man-hours worked, then one runs up against the problem of whether wage relativities really do reflect differences in productivity levels, or whether the imperfections of the labour market have a more important determining role.

There are similar difficulties involved in measuring the input of **capital** into the production process. Because capital is a non-homogeneous commodity – that is, a mechanical earth mover is not the same as a capstan lathe – one has to measure capital input in terms of the *value* of capital employed. This raises a number of problems, not the least of which is that a new machine, which may have the same purchase price as an older machine which it is replacing, may be more technically efficient and thus able to produce more output per unit of labour and raw material input. A related problem is that it may be difficult to put a value on the current worth of an item of capital equipment purchased in the past – essentially the question of the rate at which the asset should be **depreciated** for accounting purposes.

There is a further dimension to the problem. An increase in, say, the amount of labour employed in the production process is affected by both the supply of labour and the demand for it. The number of people in employment cannot increase unless there is an increase in the size of the workforce, but part of the increase in the workforce will remain unemployed unless there is also an increase in the demand for labour. Thus, both supply and demand factors affect labour input, and the same could be said of capital input.

In sections 11.3 to 1∤.5 below we examine the importance of capital input (that is, investment) and labour input, though in the light of what has been said above it should be appreciated that both demand and supply factors interact to produce a given amount of factor inputs.

11.4 Investment and economic growth

The idea that investment, by increasing the economy's stock of capital equipment, increases its **productive potential** and hence (potentially) the growth rate, seems self-evidently true. Thus, even though investment is not a *sufficient* condition for growth, and may not even by a *necessary* one, common sense tells us that it is very important. Other things being equal, we could argue that the greater the proportion of current output devoted to productive investment, the greater will be the resultant growth in output. Empirically there is a high correlation between the proportion of current output devoted to investment and growth rates.

Table 11.2 gives some comparative figures for the period up to the mid-1970s and it will be seen that there is a high correlation between the ranking of countries in Table 11.2 and that in Table 11.1; that is, countries which devoted a high proportion of current output to investment tended to have high growth rates. Correlation, of course, is not evidence of causation and it is probable that a **two-way causation** is in operation here since, as we saw in Chapter 3, one of the determinants of the level of investment is itself the rate of growth of output. Therefore, the faster the rate of growth of output, the higher will be the level of induced investment, and thus the growth process tends to be self-sustaining – high levels of investment lead to a growth in output which, in turn, induces higher levels of investment and so on.

11.5 The balance of payments constraint

However, we now have to ask, if investment is so obviously conducive to economic growth, why so little was undertaken in Britain in this period. One widely held view is that the balance of payments formed an effective constraint, preventing the expansion of aggregate demand and thereby the investment that would have followed it. According to this view, the effect of the weak balance of payments was to constrain the British economy to operate within a vicious circle characterised by **stop-go policies** – periods of expansion followed rapidly by periods of deflation made necessary by a crisis in the balance of payments. A low level of investment in comparison with our competitors, and a fixed exchange rate, led to a situation where British exports became increasingly uncompetitive on foreign markets, while, on domestic markets, competition from foreign imports became increasingly

Table 11.2 Fixed investment as a percentage of GDP in major industrialised countries

	UK	France	Germany	Italy	USA	Japan
Average 1950–54	14	18	20	19	17.5	21.5
Average 1970–75	19	24	24	21	17.5	33.5

Source: OECD National Accounts and CSO quoted in *Economic Progress Report*, July 1978.

severe. Thus, there was a continual tendency for the balance of payments to go into deficit, causing a continual run-down of foreign exchange reserves to maintain the fixed parity of the pound. To remove the deficits, imports had to be reduced by deflationary fiscal and monetary measures. These measures – reducing aggregate demand by increasing taxes, cutting public spending and restricting monetary growth – also reduced domestic investment – directly, because investment depends upon the rate of growth of output and, indirectly, because a reduction in monetary growth usually goes hand in hand with high interest rates, and investment, as we saw in Chapter 3, is inversely related to interest rates. At times the authorities actively encouraged high interest rates as a means of attracting foreign capital and hence reducing the balance of payments deficit in the short term. Thus, short-term measures which were necessary to control the balance of payments deficits had an adverse effect on domestic investment and hence, in the long term, on economic growth.

The circular nature of this process cannot be over-emphasised. It is, as we have said, a vicious circle from which it proved extremely difficult to extricate the British economy. In direct contrast to this, countries such as Germany and Japan enjoyed a 'virtuous circle' of high growth rates and a persistent tendency for the balance of payments to go into surplus. Within these 'successful' economies a high rate of expansion of demand, much of which came from export demand, induced a high level of investment, which in turn produced rapid rises in output. Exports, which were initially encouraged by fiscal subsidies and the like, soon gathered their own momentum as the productivity gains derived from investment made exports more cost-competitive on world markets. Thus, the expansion of demand could proceed unhindered by the constant need to check demand in order to check imports. The only constraint on the expansion of demand was a self-imposed one rather than one imposed externally, namely that the growth of demand should not overstretch the economy's capacity to increase output without creating inflationary pressures. The containment of inflation was, of course, made easier by the fact that, to the extent that the exchange rate appreciated – and balance of payments surpluses will always produce this tendency even though it may be checked under a fixed exchange rate regime – the price of imports fell, thus producing a fall in the overall price index.

Since the balance of payments seems to have been the crucial factor in restraining Britain's economic growth in this period, we should perhaps ask why Britain's overseas trading position was so weak, and whether alternative policies might not have eased the constraint that it imposed. There were, of course, a number of relevant factors, but most writers seem agreed that the most important was the **reserve currency role of sterling**. The fact that the pound, alongside the dollar, was used as a reserve (or intervention) currency meant that foreign central banks would hold stocks of pounds and dollars to use in the event of their own currency being in excess supply on currency markets.

Of course, while these overseas sterling balances were being built up this was positively advantageous to Britain, since it allowed her to run balance of payments deficits, paying for them with money created by the Bank of England (known as the right of seigniorage). However, once these overseas sterling balances had accumulated, their existence posed a positive threat since any apparent weakness in the pound would cause foreign holders of sterling to try to sell in order to avoid a capital loss in the event of sterling being devalued.

This selling pressure, of course, exacerbated the trading position of the pound, making a devaluation look still more likely, and therefore further adding to the impetus to sell sterling.

Thus, repeatedly, there was pressure for a sterling devaluation, but, precisely because of the reserve currency role of sterling, the monetary authorities in Britain felt that such a change in par values would be unwise. The par value system, which had worked so well in the post-war period, would, they felt, start to disintegrate if it were seen that one of the key currencies could no longer be relied upon for stability. Britain therefore resorted to alternative policies – domestic deflation to check imports and high interest rates as a means of attracting foreign capital, though this latter policy effectively increased the size of the overseas sterling balances, and hence stored up more trouble for the future. The fixed sterling parity was maintained until 1967, when the pressure for devaluation could no longer be resisted.

It is, of course, impossible to demonstrate conclusively that an alternative policy (such as devaluing earlier) would have been more successful in removing the balance of payments constraint and allowing growth to proceed at a faster rate, though with the benefit of hindsight the majority of writers would probably argue that the policy of protecting the external value of the pound, at the expense of other objectives, was unwise. However, as we saw earlier, devaluation does not automatically bring the balance of payments into equilibrium. Even if the elasticities of demand for imports and exports are favourable, there will be a considerable time lag before the benefits of devaluation become apparent. In the event, the devaluation of the pound in 1967 was to initiate a period of instability in the international monetary system, and five years later the British payments deficit was again so serious that the new parity was abandoned altogether and the pound allowed to float down rapidly.

11.6 Supply constraints: the role of labour supply

Up to this point the explanation for the low growth of the British economy that we have offered has concentrated on the role of *demand* in stimulating the investment needed for economic growth. According to this explanation, the reason for Britain's low growth can be traced to demand mismanagement, and the corollary is that, if alternative policies had been pursued, which had made possible a steady and more rapid expansion of demand, then the level of investment, and therefore growth, would have been higher.

Some writers have tried to explain Britain's low growth in quite different terms, however. For these writers, it was the *supply* of factors – and particularly the supply of labour – which constrained the expansion of the post-war British economy.

According to this line of argument, put forward by economists such as Kindleberger[2] and Kaldor[3], a necessary condition for economic growth is a relatively elastic supply of labour to the manufacturing sector. Countries which hitherto had large agricultural populations were able to satisfy this condition, as the movement of people off the land provided a potential source of recruitment for manufacturing employment. The size of the agricultural workforce in Britain, on the other hand, was already very small in 1945, so that no such source of labour was available. Consequently, so the argument runs, the expansion of the industrial sector was held back by a shortage of manpower.

The effect of this inelastic supply of labour would manifest itself as a tendency for labour markets to become 'tight' as an increasing demand for labour encountered a relatively fixed supply. This would tend to make wages rise, in excess of any rise brought about through changes in productivity, as employers bid against each other for this scarce resource. In this way, a process of wage-push inflation would be initiated. Increased costs would lead to increased prices which, under a fixed exchange rate, would lead to a deterioration in the overseas trading position. That is, exports would become uncompetitive and domestically produced goods would increasingly be unable to compete against imports on the home market, leading to a situation in which deflationary measures would have to be taken to preserve the sterling parity. Thus, the balance of payments again features as a restraining factor on growth, but this time the cause of the difficulties is the overvalued exchange rate which results from the process of wage inflation. The roots of the wage inflation, in turn, can be traced to the inelastic supply of labour to the manufacturing sector.

11.7 The importance of the manufacturing sector

Employment is conventionally classified into one of three sectors: **primary** (mostly agriculture but also including fishing and mining), **secondary** (manufacturing) and **tertiary** (all the service industries). Although this classification is rather crude, it is the one which underlies the foregoing analysis. In this view, the importance of the manufacturing sector in the growth process lies in the fact that it is in this area where most of the increases in productivity can be achieved. Technological advance, which allows a larger volume of output to be obtained from a given volume of inputs, although possible in the primary and tertiary sectors, is much more easily achieved in manufacturing production. Other things being equal, therefore, the larger the size of the secondary sector in relation to the primary and tertiary sector, the larger is the scope for productivity gains, and hence for growth.

Kaldor in 1968 argued that the cause of the slow rate of growth of the UK economy was that the manufacturing sector was too small and the service sector too large. There is a well-known tendency for employment in the tertiary sector to increase as a society evolves from a basically agrarian form to a developed industrial form, and the size of the service sector is an indication of the degree of maturity of the economy. In Kaldor's view, however, Britain was suffering from a **'premature**

maturity' – a large service sector swallowing up resources before a high level of output per head had been achieved. His policy prescription, implemented in the form of a Selective Employment Tax, was to encourage labour to move from the service sector to the manufacturing sector, where the potential productivity increases were greater.

11.8 The importance of marketed output

This theme – an overexpanded service sector depressing the overall growth rate of the economy – was taken up, though in a modified way, in 1975 by Bacon and Eltis[4]. Following Kaldor, they recognised the importance of the manufacturing sector as a source of productivity growth, but they also stressed the fact that manufactures could be exported, whereas the output of the service industry, in general, could not be, so that, if the service sector expanded at the expense of the manufacturing sector, this would necessarily have an adverse effect on the balance of payments.

They also recognised, however, that the classification of manufacturing sector output and service sector output was insufficiently precise, since some service sector output, such as the services of a rock band or a tennis star playing abroad, was sold directly on the market and made a contribution to the balance of payments, while some manufacturing sector output, such as Concorde, could not be sold at a profit and thus represented a drain on resources. They therefore proposed a revised classification – **marketed output** and **non-marketed output** – a classification which corresponds approximately to what most people would understand by the distinction between the private sector and the public sector, though not exactly. British Airways, for instance, formerly a public sector company, produced marketed output since it sold directly to consumers at home and abroad. Virtually all the activities of local government and most of those of central government would, however, be regarded as belonging to the non-market sector.

Bacon and Eltis's basic contention was that people employed in producing non-marketed output, although they themselves do not produce any 'wealth', nevertheless consume the 'wealth' being produced by the market sector. the larger the non-market sector, the larger will be the claims made by the drones on the workers within the hive. If the market sector is too small in relation to the claims being made upon it, then part of those claims will be satisfied from abroad – that is, there will be an increase in imports leading to a balance of payments deficit.

The basic analysis seems fairly sound, though many people would dispute the claim that only people working in the market sector produce wealth. However, whether during this period the poor performance of the British economy relative to our competitors can be ascribed to the excessive size of the non-market sector is basically an empirical question: was the non-market sector in Britain significantly larger than that in other countries at a similar stage of development? Bacon and Eltis presented evidence which purported to show that, first, the non-market sector had expanded rapidly and that, secondly, it was much bigger than in other

Table 11.3 Taxation and government spending as a percentage of GDP – some international comparisons

	1971		1978		1983	
	Tax revenue	*Government spending*	*Tax revenue*	*Government spending*	*Tax revenue*	*Government spending*
Sweden	43	41	51	51	51	52
Netherlands	–	–	45	48	47	52
Belgium	35	33	42	41	44	45
France	35	35	39	41	43	47
W. Germany	37	36	42	42	41	42
Italy	28	32	33	36	41	44
Austria	37	35	42	43	42	43
UK	34	32	33	35	38	39
USA	27	30	29	30	29	33

'Tax revenue' is revenue from direct taxes, indirect taxes and social security contributions as a percentage of GDP.
'Government spending' is current expenditure on goods and services, gross capital formation, current grants and subsidies as a percentage of GDP.
Source: derived from *OECD National Accounts*, detailed tables, Vol. II, 1971–83 (1985 edn).

countries. Their evidence was disputed, however, and a slightly different interpretation of the statistics produced the opposite result – that, although the post-war period saw an expansion of the non-market sector, this sector was no larger in Britain than in comparable countries, and smaller than in some others.

Table 11.3 gives an indication that, according to internationally accepted definitions, the size of the government sector in Britain grew more slowly than in most other comparable countries and that, even before Mrs Thatcher came to power in 1979, Britain had the smallest proportion of output devoted to public spending of any Western European country.

11.9 The deindustrialisation of the British economy

It is convenient at this point to introduce a topic which is closely allied with the discussion of the previous two sections – sometimes called the deindustrialisation debate. The term **deindustrialisation** is a somewhat emotive description of what is alleged to have happened to the manufacturing sector in the UK. Deindustrialisation refers to a process whereby employment in the manufacturing sector falls and there is a decline in the output of the manufacturing sector as a proportion of total output. This is associated with increased import penetration in manufactured goods.

There are a number of specific questions concerning the deindustrialisation debate. Some of these are purely factual questions which can be answered by straightforward inspection of the data. Others are less straightforward. The more important questions are listed below:

- Has the manufacturing sector declined in terms of employment in recent years?
- Has the manufacturing sector declined in terms of its contribution to total output?
- Is the decline in manufacturing peculiar to Britain? If not, is it more pronounced in Britain than elsewhere?
- What trends have been observed in trade in manufactures between countries? Has import penetration increased?
- Is the process of deindustrialisation an undesirable trend which appropriately designed policies could halt and possibly reverse? Alternatively, is deindustrialisation part of a widespread process of structural readjustment, common to all advanced industrial societies which it would be unwise and damaging to attempt to reverse?

As regards employment, it is quite clear that the manufacturing sector has declined in importance. Employment in manufacturing in Britain has fallen from about nine million people in the mid-1960s to about six million in the mid-1980s, falling further to about 4 million by 1996. Not only have the absolute numbers engaged in manufacturing declined but so too has the *percentage* of the workforce as can be seen from Table 11.4, which also presents data for other countries. In the UK in 1970 more than one in three people were engaged in manufacturing. By 1983 this had fallen to less than one in four (and by the mid-1990s it was less than one in five). Careful inspection of Table 11.4 reveals that almost all the countries listed experienced a significant decline in manufacturing employment over the period 1960–86, the exceptions being Japan and, perhaps surprisingly, Italy.

If we compare the decline of manufacturing in the UK with that in other countries then it is apparent that the decline in the UK was somewhat more marked than elsewhere. However, this is mainly because in 1970 the proportion of the workforce engaged in manufacturing in Britain was comparatively large (exceeded only by West Germany). The rate of decline since then has been rapid but by 1983 the proportion of the workforce engaged in manufacturing in Britain was still slightly above the OECD average.

Table 11.4 Employment in manufacturing (percentage of total civilian population)

	1960	1970	1975	1980	1985	1986
Canada	23.7	22.3	20.2	19.7	17.5	17.3
USA	27.1	26.4	22.7	22.1	19.5	19.1
Japan	21.5	27.0	25.8	24.7	25.0	24.7
France	27.5	27.8	27.9	25.8	23.2	22.6
W. Germany	37.0	39.4	35.6	34.3	32.0	32.2
Italy	23.0	27.8	28.2	26.7	23.2	22.9
UK	36.0	34.7	31.0	28.4	23.1	22.5

Source: A. Dunnett, 'The Role of the Exchange Rate in the Decline of UK Manufacturing', in *Royal Bank of Scotland Review*, March 1989.

These figures alone tell us little about the health of the manufacturing sector. Large numbers engaged in manufacturing could reflect low levels of labour productivity. Similarly, a rapid decline in the manufacturing workforce could be evidence of rapidly increasing labour productivity so that the same output – or more output – can now be produced by a much smaller workforce. Alternatively, a declining manufacturing workforce could be evidence of an ailing manufacturing sector with producers falling victim to foreign competition.

In addition to data on employment, therefore, we need to look at data which show manufacturing output as a proportion of total output. This is shown in Table 11.5. As can be seen, the decline in manufacturing output (as a proportion of GDP) is perhaps even more dramatic than the decline in employment. In the United Kingdom in 1960 manufacturing accounted for almost one third of GDP. In 1983 this had shrunk to not much over one-fifth (the figure appears to have stabilised at this level – in 1996 the figure was 21 per cent). However, as we noticed with the employment data, other countries have also experienced a decline. The decline in the UK may be said to have been more marked because the UK manufacturing sector was large in comparison with that in other countries in 1960. Having said this, however, it is clear from careful inspection of Table 11.5 that certain other countries have experienced a more modest decline in manufacturing output – countries such as Japan, France, West Germany and Italy. These countries still retain a comparatively large manufacturing sector.

Before we go on to draw any conclusions from this it is important to point out that over time there will be a change in *relative prices* – that is, the price of manufacturing output relative to the output of the economy generally. The data in Table 11.5 are calculated from the following ratio:

$$\frac{\text{value of manufacturing output}}{\text{value of total output}} \qquad [11.1]$$

Value is equal to price multiplied by quantity. Over time the *price* of manufacturing output will fall relative to the price of output generally because there is more scope for cost-saving technical change in the production of

Table 11.5 Share of manufacturing in GDP* (per cent)

	1960	1970	1975	1980	1985	1986
Canada	23.37	20.4	19.2	18.8	–	–
USA	28.6	25.7	23.4	22.5	20.3	19.9
Japan	33.9	35.9	29.9	30.4	29.8	29.3
France	29.1	28.7	27.4	26.3	22.1	22.2
W. Germany	40.3	38.4	34.5	33.0	31.9	33.1
Italy	28.5	28.9	29.7	30.5	23.8	23.4
UK	32.1	28.1	26.3	23.1	21.3	21.8

* Value added in manufacturing as percentage of current price GDP.
Source: As for Table 11.4.

manufactures than there is in the production of services which are included in total output. For example, many electrical and electronic goods are cheaper now than they were ten years ago, not just relative to other goods and services, but also in absolute terms.

The implication of this is that the ratio shown in [11.1] above should be measured in *current prices* rather than in constant prices. (See section 3.17 for the distinction between current price and constant price data.) It follows that at least part of the decline in the share of manufacturing in GDP is the result of a fall in the price of manufacturing output relative to the price of output generally. For example, suppose in volume terms manufacturing output and total output remained unchanged or – more likely – increased at the same rate. The ratio shown in [11.2] below would therefore remain unchanged:

$$\frac{\text{volume (i.e. quantity) of manufacturing output}}{\text{volume (i.e. quantity) of total output}} \qquad [11.2]$$

In the aggregate, however, we cannot deal with physical quantities because of the heterogeneous nature of the goods involved. All we can measure is *value* (i.e. quantity multiplied by price). If, as we have assumed, the price of manufactures falls relative to prices generally then in *value terms* manufacturing output will decline as a proportion of total output even though in *volume terms* there has been no decline.

This is a complicated index-number problem. It is, however, important to bear in mind when we look at the sort of data shown in Table 11.5. The decline in manufacturing output which it shows is at least partly the result of a fall in the *price* of manufactures relative to other goods and services.

We can now summarise our answers to the first three questions posed at the beginning of this section.

1   The manufacturing sector *has* declined in terms of employment.
2   The manufacturing sector *has* declined in terms of its contribution of total output (though the decline is magnified by the change in relative prices).
3   The decline in manufacturing is not peculiar to Britain. It does, however, appear to have been more rapid than in some other countries with whom we might wish to compare ourselves.

Before we look at the impact this has had on our trade in manufactures with other countries it may be useful to consider a number of possible interpretations of why these changes have occurred.

One explanation which has been put forward to explain the decline of the manufacturing sector is that this simply reflects a change in the **pattern of demand**. As society becomes richer, it is said, it increases its demand for services at the expense of manufactured goods. However, it is known that the pattern of demand in all countries at a similar stage of development is approximately the same, so that such an explanation cannot be reconciled with the much smaller decline in the importance of the manufacturing sector experienced by some countries who are as rich as or a good deal richer than the UK.

Moreover, the notion that as society becomes richer it increases its demand for services at the expense of manufactured goods is only partly correct, since the increased demand for a service often manifests itself as an increased demand for goods. For example, people no longer send their clothes to the laundry to be cleaned – they buy a washing-machine and perform the service for themselves at home. When just a few people were rich and most people were poor, the rich could afford to employ servants to perform services. Now the relative cost of servants is too high (you simply cannot get the staff these days) so that the rich, unless they are very rich, can no longer afford to employ them and hence their demand for services is satisfied by the purchase of various labour-saving devices which can be used for the **home production** of services.

A different interpretation of the fall in manufacturing employment is that the manufacturing sector is experiencing an increase in labour productivity, so that the same (or increased) output can be produced with less labour. This is undoubtedly true, but the rate of growth of labour productivity is usually reckoned to be somewhat lower in Britain than in other countries. Such an interpretation, therefore, cannot readily be reconciled with the fact that countries with a more rapid growth of labour productivity – Japan, Germany – have not experienced a similar decline in manufacturing employment.

These interpretations, then, are clearly inadequate, and the only interpretation which seems plausible is that the demand for the output of the manufacturing sector in Britain does not increase as fast as it does in other countries. We should be careful to distinguish here, however, between the demand for manufactured goods and the demand for *domestically produced* manufactured goods. It seems that, in the UK, a fair proportion of any increase in demand is satisfied by an increase in imports – that is, the propensity to import in the UK seems quite high, so that any increase in demand does not necessarily create very much demand for the domestic manufacturing industry.

The result is that import penetration has been marked. In other words, foreign manufacturers have penetrated the UK market for manufactured goods, ousting domestic producers. This, coupled with a slow growth of UK exports of manufactures, has led to the decline in manufacturing output we have observed.

Although this is a plausible hypothesis, and one which has received widespread popular support, the evidence to back it up is not clear cut. Table 11.6 gives some estimates of the propensity to import manufactured goods. This shows the proportion of the domestic demand for manufactures which is accounted for by imports. As can be seen, this rose everywhere in the period 1970–80 as economies became more open, a process which is continuing. It is clear from the table that the propensity to import is related to size – the Netherlands, for example, is a much more open economy than the United States. However, the table also shows that in the UK the propensity to import manufactures is smaller than that in Germany or Italy. Overall, what the table highlights is the disparity in the degree of openness of economies – Japan and the USA are comparatively 'closed' economies whereas Germany and Canada are 'open'.

Table 11.6 Imports of manufactures (% of domestic demand for manufactures)

	1970	1980	Average annual growth 1970–80 (%)	1983
Canada	27.4	31.4	1.4	34
USA	5.6	9.3	5.3	10
Japan	4.7	5.8	2.0	5.5
France	16.2	23.3	3.7	24.5
W. Germany	19.3	31.4	5.0	36
Italy	16.2	32.0	7.0	33.5
Netherlands	51.5	61.7	1.8	68
UK	16.2	28.2	5.7	31

Source: Economic Progress Report, June–July 1985.

Import propensities for manufactures can only present a partial picture of course. The performance of *exports* of manufactures is also relevant. In short, one should look at the manufacturing *trade balance*. Allegedly it is here that we find the most convincing evidence that deindustrialisation in the UK has proceeded at a pace faster than that in other countries. The data show that the manufacturing trade balance which historically has always shown a surplus has slipped inexorably into deficit. The first deficit was recorded in 1983.

The fact that the UK's receipts from exports of manufactures is no longer sufficient to pay for our imports of manufactures does indeed seem a disturbing trend. We should put this in context, however. As Table 11.7 shows, countries which have a deficit on manufactured trade – such as the UK, Canada and Norway – tend to have a surplus of approximately the same order of magnitude in trade in other goods and services. Similarly, the large surpluses on manufactured trade in Japan, West Germany and Italy have to be seen in the context of the large deficits which these countries have in trade in other goods and services.

It should be noted also that, with the exception of the United States, the countries shown in Table 11.7 which have a deficit on manufactured trade – namely Canada, Norway, the Netherlands and the UK – were all energy producers. There may well be some causal relationship at work here, whereby oil exports displace an equivalent amount of non-oil exports. The causal mechanism which allegedly brings this about can be sketched as follows. First, assume that for the country in question the balance on capital account is zero. With no net capital flows it follows that the balance of trade will tend towards equilibrium given a floating exchange rate and a few more assumptions.[5] A deficit on one sector of the trade account must therefore be offset by an equivalent surplus on the rest of the trade account if the balance of trade is to be in overall equilibrium. Although, roughly speaking, this tends to be borne out by the data in Table 11.7, the precise nature of the forces which cause this to happen is uncertain. Induced movements in the exchange rate are partly responsible, as are deflationary or reflationary actions taken by the government to restore a balance of trade equilibrium.

Table 11.7 Trade balances as a percentage of total imports

		1973–79 average	1980	1984	1986	1987
Canada	A	−19.6	−13.9	−10.6	−13.7	−14.8
	B	+20.0	+21.0	+25.5	+17.2	+17.6
USA	A	+4.7	+7.0	−20.1	−32.0	−27.1
	B	−10.3	−14.2	−7.2	−0.4	−3.2
Japan	A	+67.5	+61.0	+72.5	+89.1	+75.0
	B	−63.6	−67.1	−51.5	−38.9	−32.4
France	A	+9.1	+4.5	+8.1	+1.3	−1.9
	B	−9.2	−11.8	−10.1	+3.7	+3.1
W. Germany	A	+39.7	+27.5	+31.7	+36.8	+35.7
	B	−28.3	−29.3	−22.4	−15.5	14.8
Italy	A	+24.5	+15.6	+23.6	+21.4	+15.5
	B	−26.1	−25.9	−31.6	−19.3	−16.7
UK	A	+9.9	+6.4	−7.6	−8.0	−7.9
	B	−13.2	+3.4	+6.9	+5.0	+4.4

A – Manufacturing trade balance
B – Balance on other goods and services
Source: as for Table 11.6.

We have not as yet attempted to provide an answer to the final set of questions posed at the beginning of this section. Nor shall we, for the issues involved are too complex for simplistic answers. We shall, however, sketch out the main lines which the debate has followed.

On the one hand, there are those who argue that the decline in manufacturing in the UK is not a cause for concern. They point quite correctly to the fact that a similar decline has occurred elsewhere. This is a worldwide **process of structural readjustment**, they argue, the speed of which is dictated not by the policies of national governments but by market forces. The market ensures that countries specialise in producing those goods and services in which they have a **comparative advantage**. The fact that at one time Britain had a comparative advantage in producing, say, textiles does not mean that she will retain that advantage forever. When she loses it the subsequent decline in the UK textile industry cannot be prevented. Protectionism can only serve to slow down a historical inevitability. Thus it is with any activity which is subject to market forces. There is nothing sacrosanct about manufacturing, they argue. If Britain's manufacturing sector declines then the resources thus freed can be more profitably employed in some other activity.

In contrast, there are those who argue that the manufacturing sector, though not sacrosanct, is especially important to the future prosperity of the economy. The manufacturing sector is important not just for the employment it brings but for its contribution to the balance of trade. It is argued that the service sector on its own is not capable of earning the foreign exchange necessary to pay for our manufactured imports. There are three reasons for this. First, many services are by their nature not tradeable – that is, they cannot be traded internationally. Some can – such as tourism, insurance, banking and civil aviation and shipping – but things such as retailing and distribution clearly cannot.

Secondly, it is argued that the potential for raising productivity is greater in manufacturing than it is in the service sector. Although in some parts of the service sector – for example, in retailing and in financial services – very substantial increases in productivity continue to be made, the scope for raising productivity is limited in those sectors in which the performance of a personal service is an intrinsic part of the activity – health care and education spring immediately to mind.

Finally, it is argued that the service sector, though large in terms of domestic employment, is small in terms of its contribution to foreign exchange earnings. Thus it would take a very large expansion of invisible earnings to make up for a further small decline in trade in manufactures. This, it is said, is unlikely to be achieved. When we look at the evidence in support of this view, however, we find, perhaps surprisingly, that a rather dramatic decline in the importance of manufactured exports has been accompanied by an equally dramatic increase in receipts from invisibles.

Figure 11.1 shows the contribution made to our foreign exchange receipts by manufactures, by oil and by the major categories of invisibles. As can be seen, throughout the 1970s manufacturing was by far the most important source of foreign exchange, contributing on average over 45 per cent of total credits on the current account of the balance of payments. Between 1978 and 1981, however, the importance of manufactured exports declined dramatically, so that by 1984 manufactures contributed less than 32 per cent of the total. The decline in the share of manufactures was associated with an increase in receipts from two other sources. One was oil whose contribution reached a peak in 1985 and declined thereafter. The second was that category of invisibles known as interest, profits and dividends (IPDs). Other invisibles such as shipping and tourism declined slightly in importance. As can be seen in Fig. 11.1 the increase in importance of IPDs over the period 1977–82 almost exactly mirrored the decline in manufactures. Although the share of manufactures increased steadily in the second half of the 1980s, its contribution to foreign exchange receipts is still no larger than that from IPDs. The growth in IPDs results primarily from increased overseas lending by UK banks.

It is difficult to appraise the significance of the increased importance of IPDs. There is, however, a widely held view that it is complacent to assume that a further expansion of such banking activity as a source of foreign exchange is possible or desirable. Many writers do not relish the prospect of the British economy's becoming so heavily dependent on invisible earnings such as these.

When one also considers the decline in the production of North Sea oil, the prospect for the British economy, in this pessimistic analysis, seems poor. Unless the performance of the manufacturing sector can be improved, and the trade deficit on manufactures eliminated, this analysis envisages a scenario in which the British economy will continue to be balance-of-payments constrained. Domestic demand will have to be held in check in order to restrain the growth of manufactured imports.

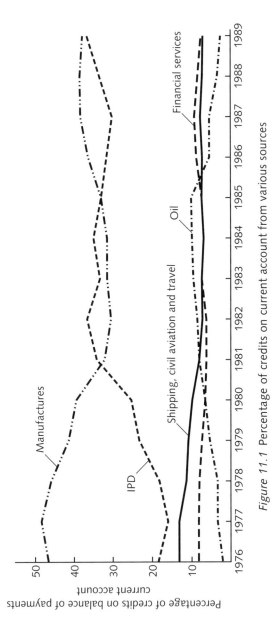

Figure 11.1 Percentage of credits on current account from various sources

11.10 Growth in the 1980s and 1990s

The period since 1979 can be divided into three distinct phases. The first four years of Mrs Thatcher's government (1979-82) were years of deep recession. As can be seen from the first column of Table 11.8, the economy peaked in 1979. It was not until 1983 that the economy regained the level of output achieved in 1979. The performance of the manufacturing sector taken separately (and shown in column 3 of Table 11.8) was even worse. It took ten years (up until 1988) to reattain the level of output reached in 1978.

Throughout this period, of course, unemployment rose at a very rapid rate, the rise only being checked when the economy started expanding again in 1984-85. The recession in the British economy, and the consequent rise in unemployment, was part of a world-wide phenomenon. It was, however, more severe in the UK than elsewhere. The relatively poor performance of the British economy in comparison with that of other countries can be ascribed to two sets of factors. The first relates to those factors we have identified in sections 11.2 to 11.9 of this chapter. The second set of factors relates to the policies which were pursued by the government in the UK at the time. It is difficult to quantify the relative contribution of these two sets of factors to Britain's poor performance – or at least it is not possible to do so in a way with which all economists would agree. However, using econometric models (described later in Chapter 15) it is possible to give a very

Table 11.8 Output (GDP) and manufacturing output 1978–1996

	GDP at constant prices (index 1990 = 100)	Rate of growth of real GDP	Output of the manufacturing sector (index 1990 = 100)
1978	76.4	3.4	90.8
1979	78.5	2.7	90.6
1980	76.9	−2.2	82.8
1981	76.0	−1.3	77.7
1982	77.4	1.7	77.6
1983	80.3	3.7	79.2
1984	81.9	2.4	82.2
1985	85.2	3.5	84.5
1986	88.6	4.4	85.7
1987	92.7	4.8	89.7
1988	97.3	5.0	96.3
1989	99.4	2.2	100.1
1990	100.0	0.4	100.0
1991	97.9	−2.0	95.0
1992	97.4	−0.5	94.9
1993	99.6	2.1	96.3
1994	104.0	3.8	100.8
1995	106.9	2.5	102.5
1996	109.5	2.1	102.8

Source: derived from *UK National Accounts*, 1997, Table 1.6.

approximate estimate. One such study, conducted by the National Institute for Economic and Social Research in 1985[6], concluded that in the first half of the 1980s about half of the **output gap** – that is, the difference between what could have been produced and what was produced – was attributable to the world recession, with the other half being attributable to government policies.

As can be seen from Table 11.8, however, the second half of the 1980s saw the British economy expanding rapidly. Indeed, during this phase the rate of growth of the UK economy compared favourably with that of other European countries. Much of this was merely a catching-up process of course and some of the increased output consisted of what has been dubbed 'candyfloss'. Nevertheless, during this period there were substantial gains.

As we now know, however, this second phase was short lived. Tax cuts in the 1988 Budget exacerbated the situation in an already overheated economy. The balance of payments deficit became very large and the rate of inflation again rose to over 10 per cent per annum. Draconian deflationary measures were introduced to counteract this which had the effect of creating a recession as deep as that ten years earlier. In the early 1990s the level of unemployment, an indicator of economic activity, was again approaching three million.

After 1992, however, (and as can be seen most easily from column 2 of Table 11.8) the UK economy achieved a steadier rate of growth. Overall, however, the UK economy remains a relatively slow-growing economy. The implication of this is that living standards in other countries will over time tend to outstrip those in the UK. This is discussed in the next chapter.

Summary

A country's rate of growth gives an indication of the rate of increase in the material standard of living of its citizens. In the post-war period the rate of growth of the UK economy has been rather low in comparison with that of other advanced countries. No single factor or group of factors can explain this. In attempting an explanation, however, one can approach the question either from the demand side or the supply side – though the two approaches interact. One explanation points to the low level of productive investment in the UK, caused by the failure of the economy to expand in a steady manner.

In the 1970s many writers saw the UK economy as being trapped within a vicious circle of low investment, low growth of productivity and output, and recurrent balance of payments crises. The key to this vicious circle lay in the fixed exchange rate and the status of sterling as a reserve currency. However, after 1972 the pound was floated so that in theory at least the balance of payments constraint was removed. The period after 1979 was characterised by a policy-induced recession which lasted until 1983. In the period 1986-88 the economy expanded rapidly – too rapidly as it turned out – and another recession followed which lasted until the end of 1992. Thereafter, the economy expanded, assisted by the rapid depreciation of sterling following Black Wednesday in September

1992. There is, however, no evidence of any major improvement in the UK's growth performance.

A recurrent theme is the poor performance of the manufacturing sector. Less than one person in five is now employed in manufacturing which compares with one person in three in the early 1960s. However several other countries have experienced similar declines and some writers argue that there is nothing particularly special about manufacturing, though others point to its vital role as an earner of foreign exchange and focus for productivity gains.

Notes

1 Denison, E. F. (1967) *Why Growth Rates Differ*: Brookings Institution.
2 Kindleberger, C. P. (1967) *Europe's Postwar Growth: the Role of Labour Supply*: Harvard University Press.
3 Kaldor, N. (1968) *Causes of the Slow Rate of Economic Growth of the United Kingdom*: Cambridge University Press.
4 Bacon, R. and Eltis, W. (1975) *Britain's Economic Problem: Too Few Producers*: Macmillan.
5 Some rather crucial – and controversial – assumptions are in fact required, which the reader may care to try to work out for him or herself, as an exercise. One could start by thinking about elasticities.
6 This was an unpublished simulation exercise conducted with the NIESR model.

Key terms

standard of living	170	reserve currency role of sterling	175
inputs (to the production process)	173	primary, secondary, tertiary sectors	177
output per unit of input	173	premature maturity	177
productivity	173	marketed and non-marketed output	178
labour	173	deindustrialisation	179
capital	173	pattern of demand	182
depreciation	173	home production	183
productive potential	174	process of structural readjustment	185
two-way causation	174	comparative advantage	185
stop-go policies	174	output gap	189

Review questions

11.1 The term 'economic growth' refers to an increase in:
    (a) GNP;
    (b) GDP per capita;
    (c) GDP per person employed;
    (d) GNP per unit of capital employed;
    (e) GNP or GDP.

11.2 Which of the following statements are correct?
   (a) A high rate of growth of output increases expenditure on new plant and machinery to meet the anticipated future rise in demand.
   (b) A high level of investment spending (on fixed capital formation) leads to an increase in output. It is sufficient condition for economic growth.
   (c) Investment is a necessary condition for economic growth.

11.3 'If interest rates in the United Kingdom rise, direct investment will fall but portfolio investment will increase.' Explain this paradox (i.e. explain the difference between *direct* investment and *portfolio* investment).

11.4 'If they suffer an unexpected fall in sales, manufacturers are forced to invest in stocks and cut other investment.' Explain this paradox. Useful concepts: inventory investment, fixed capital formation.

11.5 A reflationary policy will increase demand. This may not, however, increase output because:
   (a) things might be too expensive for people to buy;
   (b) the increased demand may be dissipated in higher prices;
   (c) people's wants may already be satisfied;
   (d) the increased demand may all go overseas, resulting in increased import penetration.

11.6 Give examples of goods or services which are:
   (a) marketable and tradeable;
   (b) non-marketable and non-tradeable;
   (c) marketable and non-tradeable;
   (d) non-marketable and tradeable.

11.7 Can you give examples of goods or services which are:
   (a) produced in the public sector but are marketable;
   (b) produced in the private sector but are non-marketable.

11.8 What does crowding-out imply about the magnitude of the government spending multiplier?

12 The standard of living

12.1 International comparisons of living standards
12.2 Net Material Product
12.3 The Limits to Growth
12.4 The social limits to growth

Preview

This chapter looks at the difficulties in using GNP to compare the standard of living in different countries. It then investigates the 'green critique' that continued exponential growth is impossible given the finite nature of the earth's resources. Finally, it considers the view that there are social limits to growth which makes the process of economic growth largely self-defeating.

12.1 International comparisons of living standards

In conventional analysis the primary yardstick by which the success of an economy is judged is Gross National Product – or rather the rate of growth of Gross National Product. In this section we use this yardstick to make comparisons between a number of different European economies. In particular, we compare the UK with three other European economies – France, Italy and Germany. Two of these, France and Italy, are approximately the same size in terms of population as the UK. The third, Germany, has since reunification in 1981 been considerably larger, and hence GNP is significantly greater.

A major problem which arises in making international comparisons of GNP is to do with exchange rates. Countries calculate their GNP in their own currencies – France in francs, Italy in lire, and so on. These estimates have to be converted into a common unit of measurement before comparisons can be made. It would seem to be fairly straightforward to convert currencies using market exchange rates, but, as we shall see, this may produce misleading results.

First, consider estimates of GNP for 1996 for the four economies derived by converting national currencies into dollars at current exchange rates. These are shown in Table 12.1.

Note that, according to these estimates, GDP in Italy was greater than that in the UK (when this first happened it was referred to in Italy as 'il sorpasso' (overtaking) and that the output of the UK economy was just less than half that of the German economy.

However, these estimates use market exchange rates to convert national currencies to dollars. These market exchange rates may not reflect differences in the price level in different countries. A conversion factor which does reflect differences in the domestic purchasing power of a currency is the so-called **purchasing power parity** which we encountered earlier. Estimates of purchasing power parities are available and these can differ quite markedly from exchange rate parities. Table 12.2 shows estimates of both purchasing power parities and exchange rate parities for the mark, franc, lira and pound (all relative to the US dollar).

In principle, the ratio of the purchasing power parity to the exchange rate parity should produce the estimates of **comparative price levels** shown in Table 12.3. In practice, there are slight differences due to differences in timing. Moreover, it should be appreciated that the estimates of purchasing power parities are rather 'soft' pieces of data (in contrast to the figures for exchange rates which

Table 12.1 Gross Domestic Product for 1996 at current prices and exchange rates (billions of US dollars)

	GDP	As % of German level
Germany	2353	100
France	1540	65
Italy	1207	51
UK	1145	49

Source: OECD *Main Economic Indicators*, August 1997.
Note: the estimates mostly refer to Gross *Domestic* Product rather than Gross *National* Product but for our present purposes there is no significant difference between these two measures.

Table 12.2 Purchasing power parities and exchange rate parities (1996) (relative to US dollar)

	ppp	erp
German mark	2.05	1.53
French franc	6.57	5.21
Italian lira	1629	1513
Pound sterling	0.678	0.594

Source: OECD *Main Economic Indicators*, November 1996 and August 1997.

are 'hard' data). Table 12.3 also shows estimates of comparative price levels for a selection of other countries which will assist in interpreting what is meant by the concept. As can be seen, for the visitor from the United States (or indeed from Britain) prices are very cheap in Mexico and in Turkey and expensive in Switzerland and Japan – in other words the exchange rates for these countries do not adequately reflect differences in domestic price levels.

If we convert the various national estimates of GDP to dollars, taking into account the comparative price levels shown in Table 12.3, we arrive at the revised estimates of GDP in dollars shown in Table 12.4.

Compare these with the estimates shown in Table 12.1. It appears that the performance of the Italian and UK economies was somewhat better in comparison with France and Germany than appeared to be the case from the original estimates. Note, however, that the UK economy still ranks in fourth place with a GDP slightly less than that of Italy.

Table 12.3 Comparative price levels for GDP (1996)

Germany	120
France	113
Italy	93
UK	93
Mexico	39
Japan	141
Denmark	131
Portugal	71
Switzerland	148
Turkey	42

Source: OECD *Main Economic Indicators*, August 1997. These comparative price levels are defined as the ratio of purchasing power parities to exchange rates.

Table 12.4 Comparisons of GDP for 1996 taking into account differences in price levels (billions of US dollars)

	GDP	*As % of German level*
Germany	1929	100
France	1363	70
Italy	1299	67
UK	1232	64

Source: derived from OECD *Main Economic Indicators*, August 1997.

12.2 Net Material Product

The early 1990s saw the official end of CMEA (the Council for Mutual Economic Assistance), otherwise known as COMECON. The Eastern European countries which had formerly made up this alliance – Bulgaria, Czechoslovakia, GDR, Hungary, Poland, Romania, USSR, and Yugoslavia – began the process of perestroika, abandoning the command systems they had used to plan their economies for the past 50 years, creating a vacuum into which they hoped market forces would flow, delivering the goods and services which the people wanted. As part of this process of restructuring (**perestroika**) their economies became more open (**glasnost**). It was natural therefore that commentators wished to have some sort of measure of the standard of living in these countries.

There are two major difficulties involved in making such an assessment. The first is to do with exchange rates. We saw in the previous section that market exchange rates do not always adequately reflect purchasing power parities. In comparing COMECON countries with the West this problem existed *a fortiori* because the exchange rates involved were not market exchange rates at all. Rather, the value of their currencies was held at an artificially high level *vis à vis* Western currencies by controlling the volume of foreign exchange transactions which took place. In other words, the currencies were **non-convertible**, and the official exchange rates bore no relation to the values they would have had if they had been determined by market forces.

The second problem arises because the COMECON countries did not in general calculate the statistic we call Gross National Product. Rather, they calculated **Net Material Product** (**NMP**) which differs from GNP in two respects. First – and this is a minor point – the statistic is calculated net of the depreciation of the capital stock used up in production. In this respect it corresponds to what Western economists call NNP (Net National Product). Much more importantly, however, Material Product related only to *physical goods*. It left out all of the services which make up the major fraction of GNP in advanced Western countries, though it should be pointed out that the service sector of these countries was much smaller than that in Western economies, as Table 12.5 shows.

Table 12.5 Sector shares in COMECON countries (1984–85)

	Primary	*Secondary*	*Tertiary*
Bulgaria	18.5	67.6	13.5
Czechoslovakia	8.8	71.1	20.5
GDR	8.3	84.3	10.5
Hungary	20.6	44.7	34.7
Poland	18.1	60.4	21.5
Romania	15.5	69.8	14.7
USSR	19.9	56.7	23.4
Yugoslavia	14.4	48.4 (inc. mines)	37.2

Table 12.6 Estimates of GNP in COMECON countries

	GNP[1] US$ bn	GNP per capita US$	GNP[2] US$ bn	GNP per capita US$
Bulgaria	45.0	5284	24.3	2700
Czechoslovakia	117.0	7500	77.0	5000
GDR	176.0	10 602	115.0	6900
Hungary	60.0	5660	20.4	1927
Poland	175.0	4630	63.2[3]	1711
Romania	56.8	2500	50.7	2434
USSR	1650.0	5800	1093.0	3922
Yugoslavia	49.0	2120	43.1	1889

1 *Source*: Barclays Bank: estimates relate to 1985–87.
2 *Source*: Lloyds Bank: estimates relate to 1984–85.
3 Net Material Product, 1984.

The implication of this is that NMP could in no way be equated with GNP. Since there were no official estimates of GNP, Western economists had to make up their own estimates and these of course differed widely depending on what assumptions were made, as Table 12.6 shows.

12.3 The Limits to Growth

The previous sections illustrated some of the difficulties involved in obtaining reliable estimates of Gross Product. However, they were predicated on the assumption that Gross Product was in some sense a meaningful indicator of the standard of living. GNP was a maximand because a greater output of goods and services meant a higher standard of living. Growth was good. The faster an economy grew, the better.

The idea that economic growth could unequivocally be regarded as beneficial was a belief which was held almost universally in the period which followed the Second World War. More recently, however, increasing numbers of people have begun to question the validity of such a belief. There are essentially two aspects to such a debate. First, is continued economic growth *possible* given the physical constraints of our planet? And second, is economic growth *desirable* in the sense that the benefits that it provides clearly outweigh the costs?

The question of whether continued economic growth was possible came to the forefront with the publication of the Meadows[1] study, *The Limits to Growth*, in 1972. The question with which they were concerned was as follows: given the finite nature of the earth's resources and its capacity for absorbing waste, what would be the effect of continued **exponential economic growth**? Now, of course, if one poses the question in this form, the answer is immediately obvious. Whether growth is proceeding exponentially at 1 per cent a year or 20 per cent a year, the absolute increase in output becomes larger every year. Given the finite nature of resources, there must therefore come a time when all those resources are used up and economic growth comes to a halt. Indeed, not only economic growth would cease but our whole way of life, built on the profligate use of non-renewable resources, would cease to be possible. One notable feature of exponentially growing systems is the suddenness with which catastrophic changes occur. Consider the well-known example of a pond in which there grows a lily doubling in size every seven days. (Mathematicians will know that this is equal to an exponential growth of 10 per cent per day.) Suppose that after one year the lily completely covers the pond. How long did it take for the pond to be half covered?

The answer is, of course, 51 weeks. Now, if one considers the finite limits of the pond to be the analogue of the finite resources of the planet earth, one can appreciate the suddenness with which the catastrophe occurs. Moreover, even when the dangers of exhaustion of natural resources become apparent, society may be unable to amend its resource-using behaviour in time to prevent catastrophe.

The forecasts presented by Meadows suggest that, within the next century, mankind faces a three-fold dilemma. First, there is the problem caused by the impending exhaustion of the worlds's **non-renewable natural resources**. Secondly, they predict, the **pollution** problem will become so acute that the capacity of the physical environment for self-cleaning and re-generation will be exhausted. Thirdly, the worldwide **population** explosion will reach a point where the human species will destroy itself through sheer weight of numbers. As these various trends interact there then follows a decline in world population because of pollution and the shortage of food and natural resources. The physical and psychological stress caused by crowding will cause further population collapse from war, disease and social strife. Those few who remain will be able to enjoy only a very meagre existence as they pick over the detritus of the former industrial age.

Such models have, of course, been criticised for being unnecessarily alarmist. Predictions of impending disaster following the exhaustion of natural resources are not exclusively a twentieth-century phenomenon. The Industrial Revolution in England in fact provoked a similar response from some people, who predicted then that world coal reserves were rapidly approaching exhaustion. Moreover, the critics of the **Doomsday Models** claim that these predictions fail to take account of the workings of the **price system** as a device by which impending exhaustion of resources tends to reduce their usage slowly and in advance.

Let us examine briefly the role of the price mechanism in limiting the usage of scarce natural resources. As resources become scarce their price tends to rise relative to those resources which remain in plentiful supply. This causes both consumers and producers to reduce their usage of the scarce resource.

Suppose, for example, that world supplies of aluminium were approaching exhaustion. The price of aluminium would therefore rise and goods containing this metal would also rise in price. Consumers would therefore amend their consumption behaviour and buy less of those products with a high aluminium content. This in itself would tend to reduce the demand for aluminium, but such **substitution in consumption**, as it is called, would be reinforced by **substitution in production**. Those manufacturers who were producing goods with high aluminium content would find that their sales would be reduced as a result of the high prices they found it necessary to charge for their goods. Producers would therefore search for substitute materials which would do the task formerly performed by the aluminium component. Substitutes such as stainless steel, copper, plastics or wood might be suitable, depending upon circumstances. Manufacturers would therefore reduce their demand for aluminium. The scarcer aluminium became, the more it would increase in price and the greater would be the incentive to economise on its use through substitution in consumption and in production. It is important to note, moreover, that this economising on the use of a scarce raw material takes place automatically through the workings of the price mechanism, without the need for any governmental or supra-national intervention.

It is, however, possible to criticise this line of argument. The readjustment in the rates of depletion of the various resources is brought about by a change in *relative prices*. But it is essentially a readjustment rather than an overall reduction which occurs, since the reduction in the rate of usage of aluminium brings about an increase in the rate of usage of substitutes – stainless steel, copper and so on. Thus, the prices of these substitutes will rise as they, in turn, become scarce, and a *general* increase in the price of raw materials ensues, as general shortages develop. A cost-push inflation thus results. Because of the high price of raw materials it becomes economic to exploit the more marginal oilfields, to mine the poorer quality coal lying deeper in the ground and to farm the more marginal land. Improvements in technology may enable the higher real costs of production to be more than offset – the record so far shows that, by and large, this has occurred – but if this ceases to happen then increased production costs will result in a reduction in the amount of goods that consumers can afford to purchase; that is, the standard of living generally will decline. The age of plenty gives way to the age of scarcity.

The key point is that the price mechanism does effectively limit the demand for a scarce commodity, through a change in relative prices, provided only a few commodities are in short supply. But, if there are *widespread* shortages, a rise in the price level (or inflation) occurs rather than a change in relative prices. This does not necessarily limit demand, since the overall level of demand is determined by other factors.

Thus, it could be surmised that, when commodity prices worldwide have risen rapidly, this is in part the result of resource shortages. The spectre of an international struggle for resources, forecast in the Doomsday Models, may already be upon us, and this signals the end of the era of rapid and continued increases in living standards which seemed, since the beginning of the Industrial Revolution, to be the natural order of things.

12.4 The social limits to growth[2]

In the previous section we asked whether there might not be some physical limits to the extent to which the industrial society can actually continue to increase the welfare of its citizens. We now turn to a more fundamental appraisal of the nature of economic growth and ask whether, in fact, an increase in a country's GNP, conventionally defined, really is synonymous with an improvement in its citizens' standard of life.

On a fairly simple level this is equivalent to asking whether the increased output of goods and services that constitutes economic growth has not been of an unbalanced nature, producing primarily an increase in those goods and services which, though they may give short-term pleasure, do not produce long-term satisfaction. On a more fundamental level, however, we should ask whether the idea of increasing human happiness through economic growth may not prove self-defeating.

Social scarcity

As societies develop they pass through the stage of being able to supply all the biological necessities for existence. When consumption rises beyond this level, then consumption takes on an increasingly *social* as well as an individual aspect. That is, the satisfaction that individuals derive from consumption depends not just on their own consumption levels, but on the consumption levels of others as well. For example, the satisfaction to be derived from owning a car depends to a large extent on the number of other people that own cars and therefore the level of congestion that they create. The level of other people's consumption may be a more important determinant of the satisfaction to be derived from car ownership than the purely private characteristics of the car – its speed, its comfort and so on. What the individual enjoys consuming is not the car itself but the personal transportation services it offers – and the quality of these services will have a social aspect as well as the purely technical one. Even if the value which the individual attaches to their car derives not from its value in use but from its value as a status symbol, a means of displaying their affluence, then this too will have a social aspect since the degree of status which the car conveys depends not on its size, speed or cost in absolute terms, but on its size, speed or cost relative to their neighbour's car. It follows, therefore, that economic growth, even if it enables every household to own a better car or to become a two-, three- or even four-car household, does not necessarily increase the wellbeing of the individual, since this is dependent not just on their own consumption but on the consumption levels of others as well.

The self-defeating nature of economic growth does not spring simply from the congestion problem cited above, but is derived from the fundamental observation that economic growth, though it may be able to reduce the amount of physical scarcity, cannot reduce the amount of **social scarcity**. Certain goods and facilities from which individuals derive satisfaction are subject to absolute limitations in supply. The availability of these so-called **positional goods** is not increased by economic growth, no matter how rapid. Thus, even though physical congestion might be reduced (temporarily) by building more roads, social congestion cannot be reduced. For example, satisfaction is derived from employment in a high status job. The greater the responsibility involved, the higher the status and the more benefit the individual derives from it. But individuals can only increase their status in society if they move up the ladder – in other words, if they move nearer the top of the heap. It is not possible for all individuals simultaneously to improve their status, since status depends upon their relative position in the hierarchy. Employment prospects, in other words, are subject to social scarcity.

There are many other examples of positional goods whose availability is fixed, either because of physical scarcity or social scarcity. Country cottages in quiet rural surroundings are clearly positional goods, access to which is determined by one's position in the income distribution. The supply of such commodities is not merely fixed but shrinking, in the sense that the increased demand for the available supply of cottages reduces the quality of the 'quiet rural surroundings' of those that do exist, thereby further reducing the availability and increasing the price of cottages in 'unspoilt' surroundings.

Foreign travel is another example of a positional good – a service which, at one time, was only available to the rich, but is now so cheap that it is available to all. But the increased availability of travel, made possible by technical progress and economic growth, has at the same time reduced the value of it. When travel was only available to the rich it was 'worth doing'. Now our attitude to it can be summed up by '. . . it's not worth going there. Everybody goes there . . .'

Air travel in particular, which has resulted in the mass migration of individuals across the globe, has had a two-fold effect. First, people are no longer going to the place they thought they were going to, but a place which has changed simply because they are there; and secondly, the influx of people to the more remote corners of the world has had a corrupting influence on the host society, reducing everything to the lowest common denominator of the Coke can, the Big Mac and the digital wristwatch. The multinational mentality is one of increasing sameness.

Positional and material goods

The value of positional goods derives from the element of social scarcity embodied in them. They are in fixed supply and the access which any individual has to these positional goods depends on their position in the distribution of income. The value of so-called **material goods**, on the other hand, is not dependent on their scarcity – thus, to a starving man, food has an absolute value which is unaffected by other considerations. The supply of material goods is not fixed but will increase in line with output per head (assuming that raw material shortages can be overcome by improvements in technology). If we assume that individual preferences for positional *vis-à-vis* material output remain constant as income rises, then the fixity of supply of positional goods means that their price will rise relative to the price of material goods; that is, the more that economic growth provides an increasing supply of material goods, the less highly will these goods be valued. Positional goods become more highly valued, but their supply cannot be increased. The things that are valued most are precisely those goods that economic growth cannot provide.

Public goods, private goods and externalities

The concepts of **public goods** and **externalities** will extend our understanding of the foregoing analysis. Public goods, in the sense in which the term is being used here, need not be produced in the public sector. In fact, they may not be produced at all. For example, a river or the air in a city comes within the economist's definition of a public good. The distinguishing characteristics of public goods are that they are **non-excludable** and **non-rival**. A pure private good is excludable in the sense that the seller can determine who shall enjoy the benefits of the good or service being offered. This means that the seller can exclude from consuming the good or service those people who do not pay for it. In this sense, defence-of-the-realm is a pure public good since individuals who cheat by not paying their taxes cannot be excluded from enjoying the benefits of being defended.

Defence is also non-rival in the sense that the benefits which an individual derives from it do not detract from the benefits which his or her neighbour derives from it. On the other hand, a pure private good such as a glass of beer is a rival good – if I drink it then no one else can drink it. Fig. 12.1 may clarify the point.

Pure private goods are both rival and excludable. Things such as food, houses, cinema seats, cars and haircuts are all pure private goods. **Pure public goods**, which are both non-rival and non-excludable, are things such as defence and radio and TV broadcasts. It is interesting to note, however, that although TV broadcasts are, by their nature, non-excludable (in the sense that anyone with a TV set can enjoy the benefits of them) attempts are often made to use the legal system to make them excludable – to receive broadcasts without first purchasing a licence is illegal. Because of the nature of the good, however, such laws are difficult to enforce.

A great many goods are, however, neither pure public goods nor pure private goods in the sense that the extent to which they possess the elements of rivalness or non-excludability depends upon the conditions of use. Roads, for example, become a rival good when the level of use reaches the stage where journey times are increased by congestion. They are typically non-excludable, but there are also instances where they are excludable – for example, toll roads. Public parks may be excludable (for example, Woburn Safari Park) or non-excludable (for example, the

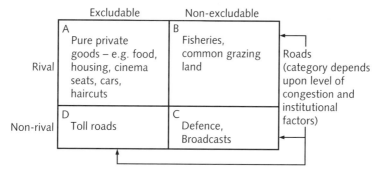

Figure 12.1 Excludability and rivalness

Lake District National Park). Like roads, they become rival goods only when they become so crowded that the presence or the activities of one group of people detracts from the enjoyment that other people derive from them. This may be at quite a low level of use if people go to national parks in search of seclusion and solitude. When the activities of one person or group affect the enjoyment or benefit which another person or group can derive from a given situation, then *externalities* are said to exist. For example, suppose that one group of people enjoys water-skiing. The noise of the power boats annoys other people who come to the area in search of peace and quiet. It therefore reduces their enjoyment. In this instance, the water-skiers are said to impose **external costs** or externalities on the other holiday-makers. They impose costs on the environment for which they do not have to pay.

In this respect the national park is a public good in as much as it is non-excludable. As is the case with many public goods, the extent to which any one individual has rights is ill-defined by the law. In order to limit the use made by individuals of the public good, the state (or, in this case, the National Park Authority) has to use the legal system to define more exactly what activities will be permitted in the park (in other words, to what the property rights of the individual extend).

The reluctant collectivism

We have seen how the satisfaction which an individual derives from the consumption of a public good is often affected by the activities of others. Individuals, by their behaviour, impose externalities on others. The existence of externalities was at one time treated by economists as a special case. It is now clear, however, that externalities affect the vast majority of consumption and production activities. Modern man, living in an industrial, urban society, affects his fellow man in almost everything he does. Many of these externalities are trivial, some are beneficial or positive (such as the enjoyment you may derive from contemplating your neighbour's well-kept flower garden). But many are **negative externalities** – the smoke from your neighbour's bonfire or the unpleasant habits of his dog, the noise of passing traffic or aircraft, the smoke from a chimney or the litter that adorns your favourite beauty spot. All of these things affect the individual's standard of living in a negative way. Moreover, it is clear that economic growth which increases everyone's income does not reduce the extent of these negative externalities. Only if the individual's income grows faster than that of his fellow men (in other words, if he moves up the income distribution) is he able to avoid these externalities by moving to a more expensive house further away from his neighbour's bonfire and dog, and from the noise of traffic.

Given the pervasiveness of externalities it is difficult for economic growth to increase the standard of living of the average citizen since so many of the goods from which they derive utility are positional goods, which are in fixed supply. If individuals move up the income distribution they can improve their access to these positional goods but, by definition, it is impossible for the average citizen to move up the income distribution.

The only conceivable way of increasing average living standards is to attempt to limit the amount of externalities. In other words, to limit the freedom of individuals by imposing restrictions on their right to pollute the environment with noise or smoke, and by imposing heavy penalties on those who are guilty of creating such externalities. Thus, the freedom of the individual is constrained and the role of the state is increased. Societies move reluctantly towards increasing state intervention.

In summary, the ability of a market economy to bring about real and sustained improvements in the welfare of its citizens is constrained by social scarcity, the need for public goods and the existence of externalities. Goods which by their nature are public goods cannot be produced efficiently by the market. As societies become more urbanised and industrialised, so the demand for such goods increases and so therefore does the role of the state. This same urbanisation makes the problem of externalities more acute and, again, the logical response of a democratic society is, however reluctantly, to increase governmental controls. Thus, we see that the rationale for state intervention is based not on political dogma, but on necessity.

There is an opposing view, however, which deprecates the expansion of state activity which has taken place in the post-war era. The public sector, according to this view, has grown too large. In the following chapter, after a discussion of some technical matters, we consider this view.

Summary

GNP (or more likely GNP per capita) is used to compare the standard of living in different countries. To this end estimates measured in local currencies have to be converted into a common currency. The use of market exchange rates for this purpose is sometimes inappropriate since the market exchange rate may not reflect the domestic purchasing power of the currency concerned.

The countries of the former Soviet bloc did not use GNP – rather, they used Net Material Product which just measured the output of physical goods and ignored the output of services.

Some writers question whether the exponential growth of GNP is sustainable. The earliest such study, *The Limits to Growth*, warned that the negative feedback from pollution and the exhaustion of natural resources would produce periodic crises. Other writers have stressed that the welfare of each individual is dependent not just on private consumption possibilities but also on the activities of other customers and producers. Embedded in this is the notion of society and the idea that the wellbeing of society affects the wellbeing of the individual. This therefore leads to the conclusion that the state has both rights and responsibilities in such things as the provision of public goods and the control of externalities.

Notes

1 Meadows, D. *et al.* (1972) *The Limits to Growth*: Earth Island.
2 The title is taken from Hirsch, F. (1977) *The Social Limits to Growth*: Routledge,
Kegan & Paul, on which this section is based.

Key terms

Review questions

12.1 On the basis of the estimates shown in Table 12.4 would it be approximately
correct to say that the standard of living in Britain was only about 65 per cent
of the German level?
12.2 It is difficult to get a reliable estimate of the growth rate of GNP for Russia,
though it has become easier for the Czech Republic and Poland. Why is that?
12.3 The price system works automatically to limit the use of resources as they
become scarce. This occurs through *substitution in consumption* and *substitution
in production*. Explain what this means.
12.4 Does the supply of positional goods increase more rapidly in a high growth
economy than in a low growth economy?

Public
Spending

13.1   Flow of funds analysis
13.2   The Public Sector Borrowing Requirement
13.3   Should the PSBR be reduced?
13.4   The impact on the money supply
13.5   Government borrowing and the effect on interest rates
13.6   Is public spending bad for the economy?
13.7   Flow of Funds: New Cambridge

Preview

We saw in Chapter 5 that public spending is financed partly through taxation and partly through borrowing. In this chapter we shall consider how the government borrows to finance its spending and what impact this has on the economy.

13.1 Flow of funds analysis

To illustrate the way in which the government borrows funds to finance (part of) its spending, we will use so-called **flow of funds** analysis. Initially, to demonstrate the principles involved we distinguish just three sectors, within or between which all financial transactions take place. This sectoral analysis is shown in Table 13.1.

The **private sector** comprises both households and firms. The **public sector** includes central government, local government and public sector corporations (nationalised industries) such as the Post Office. The **overseas sector** comprises all non-resident persons, companies and institutions. Each sector has both income and expenditure, and if expenditure exceeds income that sector is said to have a **financial deficit**, which means that it is becoming indebted to one or both of the other sectors – that is, it is accumulating debts payable to the other sectors. This indebtedness takes the form of currency, bonds, loans, and so on depending upon the sectors involved. In contrast, if the sector has a **financial surplus**, income exceeding expenditure, then the sector as a whole is acquiring financial assets which constitute **claims** on other sectors.

Table 13.1 The financial surplus or deficit of the private, public and overseas sectors (1996)

Sector	Income	Expenditure	Financial surplus or deficit (£bn)	Types of asset involved
Private (i.e. households plus companies)	Households' incomes plus corporate income	Spending by households; current and capital spending by firms	34.7 (surplus)	Individuals hold National Savings certificates, local authority bonds and currency. Financial institutions and companies hold Treasury Bills and other government securities.
Public (i.e. central and local government plus nationalised industries)	Income from taxation (income tax, VAT etc.) plus public corporations' income from sales to public	Total spending on defence, NHS etc.; current and capital spending by public corporations	33.6 (deficit)	Central government sells Treasury Bills, other government securities and National Savings certificates. Local authorities and public corporations issue bonds; Bank of England issues notes and coin.
Overseas (i.e. non-resident persons, companies and institutions)	Income received by foreign companies exporting to Britain	Expenditure by foreigners on buying British exports etc.	0.4 (surplus)	Sales of government securities overseas; also some local authority and public corporation debt. Change in reserves of foreign currency.

Using an alternative nomenclature, a sector with a financial surplus is said to have a positive **net acquisition of financial assets** (**NAFA**). A negative NAFA on the other hand corresponds to a financial deficit. To summarise:

if income > expenditure, the sector has a financial surplus and a positive NAFA
if expenditure > income, the sector has a financial deficit and a negative NAFA

For the three sectors taken together, deficits should exactly cancel out surpluses so that (apart from a residual error) the overall NAFA should be equal to zero. Table 13.1 incorporates some illustrative figures for 1996 from which it can be calculated that the residual error was about £1.5 billion (34.7 + 0.4 − 33.6).

In 1996 the private sector had a surplus of £34.7 billion. It was acquiring financial assets (claims on other sectors). The public sector in contrast had a deficit of £33.6 billion because its expenditure exceeded its income. This deficit meant that it was building up debts with other sectors (principally the private sector in the UK). The overseas sector had a surplus of £0.4 bn. The financial surplus of the overseas sector is equal to the current balance in the balance of payments accounts (you can check this in Table 7.2). Finally, it should be emphasised that this analysis illustrates *net* flows of funds between the three sectors – the total or gross amount of borrowing and lending between the three sectors is, of course, much larger than this.

Table 13.2 gives a more detailed breakdown. Here, seven sectors are distinguished. The private sector is disaggregated into the personal, corporate and financial sectors, and the public sector is broken down into central government, local authorities and public corporations, Note that each sector has a financial deficit or surplus which is determined, as before, by the difference between its income and its expenditure. In Table 13.2, however, this is shown to be equal to the difference between the sector's current 'saving' (i.e. the excess of income over current expenditure) and its investment expenditure. In 1996, for example, the personal sector (that is, households) had an excess of income over current expenditure of £64.2 billion. This was more than sufficient to finance the £31.7 billion of investment spending undertaken (which was mostly fixed capital formation, principally on house purchase). This then left them with a substantial financial surplus. To summarise:

income minus current expenditure = 'saving'
'saving' minus investment spending = financial deficit/surplus = NAFA

Table 13.2 illustrates sectoral balances for two very different years. The salient feature of 1989 is the large private sector deficit, as households and (particularly) companies spent large amounts on investment. Most of the finance for this came from overseas (the overseas sector was in surplus). Moreover, the public sector was also in surplus. In 1996 the situation was quite different. The salient feature here is the large public sector deficit of £33.6 billion, financed mostly by borrowing from the private sector (especially the personal sector).

Table 13.2 Financial surplus or deficit: analysis by sector (£ billion)

	1989	1996
Private sector		
1 Personal sector		
Saving	23.6	64.2
less investment[1]	−27.3	−31.7
financial surplus/deficit	−4.4	32.5
2 Industrial and commercial companies		
Saving	30.9	67.9
less investment[1]	−55.4	−64.3
financial surplus/deficit	−24.5	3.5
3 Financial companies and institutions[2]		
Saving	18.5	5.2
less investment[1]	−14.8	−6.5
financial surplus/deficit	3.7	−1.3
Public sector		
4 Public corporations		
Saving	5.4	2.5
less investment[1]	−3.9	−1.0
financial surplus	1.5	1.5
5 Central government		
Saving	11.9	−23.4
less investment[1]	−6.6	−12.8
financial surplus/deficit	5.3	−36.2
6 Local authorities		
Saving	1.5	3.2
less investment[1]	−2.2	−2.0
financial surplus/deficit	−0.7	1.2
Overseas sector		
financial surplus	19.1	0.4
Financial surplus or deficit:		
(minus = deficit; plus = surplus)		
Private sector	−25.3	+34.7
Public sector	+6.1	−33.6
Overseas sector	+19.1	+0.4

1 'Investment' includes gross domestic fixed capital formation, the increase in the value of stocks and work in progress, and capital transfers.
2 'Financial companies and institutions' are life assurance and pension funds.
Source: *UK National Accounts*, 1990 and 1996, Table 11.1.
Note: in the 1997 Blue Book Table 11.1 is incorrect. The page showing the sector summary for 1996 is in fact the summary for 1995. The figures which are shown for 1995 are for 1994 and so on. The figures for 1996 are actually the ones labelled as those for 1992.
   The Blue Book costs £32.50 plus £2.50 handling charge.

In the 1980s attention had been focused on the public sector deficit and the Government strove to reduce and eliminate this deficit. As we can see, by 1989 they had succeeded in doing so. However, as we now know with the benefit of hindsight, the UK economy in 1989 was expanding far too fast. It was the last stages of the **Lawson boom** which were to produce such high inflation and such large balance of payments deficits, making it necessary to savagely deflate the economy in 1990 which in turn produced a slump in output and a rapid rise in unemployment. The fiscal reflation necessary to pull the economy out of this recession necessitated large public sector deficits, which remained into the mid-1990s and beyond.

13.2 The Public Sector Borrowing Requirement

The financial deficit of the public sector is financed by borrowing from various sources. The total borrowing of the public sector, the so-called **Public Sector Borrowing Requirement** (**PSBR**), depends upon the **public sector financial deficit** (**PSFD**) but the two things are not exactly equal. For example, in 1996 the PSFD was £33.6bn but the PSBR was only £24.9bn. There are a number of reasons why the two figures are not the same. One of the more important is the item known as the **accruals adjustment**. If, for example, tax payments fall due but are not in fact received by the Inland Revenue then the government will have to borrow additional funds necessary to finance its expenditure. In addition, in the 1980s **privatisation proceeds** totalling many billions of pounds were received which were not treated as income (that is, they did not reduce the financial deficit) but did reduce the borrowing requirement. This continued into the 1990s but on a smaller scale.

13.3 Should the PSBR be reduced?

As we saw earlier, the public sector financial deficit is related to the Public Sector Borrowing Requirement and this in turn is related to the size of the National Debt (which is the accumulated borrowing requirement). Other things being equal, the larger the public sector deficit the larger will be the borrowing requirement and the larger will the National Debt become.

With the upsurge of monetarist thinking in the 1970s, it became fashionable to concentrate attention on these totals. The PSBR in particular became a key statistic in macroeconomic management during the Thatcher years. Moreover, in 1992 at Maastricht the control of the PSBR and the National Debt became enshrined as part of the accepted wisdom and, as two of the key **convergence criteria** for monetary union, they remain there to this day. However, many economists are unhappy about the importance attached to the PSBR and the National Debt. As early as 1944 in a classic work Abba Lerner had written:[1]

The size of the national debt (when held by citizens of the country) is a matter of almost no significance beside the importance of maintaining full employment. The national debt is not a burden on posterity because if posterity pays the debt it will be paying it to the same posterity that will be alive at the time when the payment is made. The national debt is not a burden on the nation because every cent in interest or repayment that is collected from the citizens as taxpayers to meet the debt service is received by the citizens as government bondholders. The national debt is not a sign of national poverty any more than the certificates of ownership of government bonds are a sign of national wealth – the two amounts exactly cancel out in any measure of the national wealth. Just as increasing the national debt does not make the nation poorer, so repaying the national debt does not make the nation richer. It is not true that the national debt 'must be repaid sometime' any more than it is true that all the banks must call in all their debts and repay their depositors on some catastrophic day or that all firms and corporations will have to be dissolved some day to repay the obligations to the individuals who invested in them. Every individual buyer of government bonds must be able to get his money when it is due, but another lender can take his place when this happens (if the individual should not wish to renew his loan) and the national debt can continue – just as the forest can go on forever even though every tree in it must ultimately fall.

Abba Lerner

Note, however, that this only applies if the debt is held by the citizens of the country. If debt is sold *externally* (that is, to non-residents) then this may indeed represent a burden for future generations in the sense that redeeming this debt or paying interest charges on it will constitute a drain on the balance of payments. However, apart from a small percentage held overseas (about 13 per cent in

Table 13.3 Distribution of sterling national debt: end of March 1996 (£ billion; percentage of market holdings in italics)

	£ bn	%
Market holdings		
Public corporations and local authorities	5.3	*1.6*
Banking sector	26.8	*8.2*
Building societies	7.8	*2.4*
Insurance companies and pension funds	155.2	*47.5*
Overseas residents	43.3	*13.2*
Individuals and private trusts	57.9	*17.7*
Other (including residual)	30.9	*9.4*
equals Total market holdings	327.2	*100.0*
Official holdings	45.7	
Total sterling debt	372.9	

Source: Bank of England Quarterly Bulletin, November 1996.

1996) Britain's national debt is, in fact, held internally. Table 13.3 shows the distribution of the national debt in 1996.

Note, also, that for Lerner in 1944 the significance of the National Debt was its importance in maintaining full employment. In a recession, government tax revenue falls as fewer people are employed and company profits are lower. Government expenditure, on the other hand, tends to rise as expenditure on unemployment benefit and social security increases. The gap between government receipts and payments therefore widens automatically, leading to a corresponding rise in the borrowing requirement. However, the effect of the budget deficit is to increase the overall level of demand, above what it would otherwise have been. This helps to offset the effects of the recession, since it helps to maintain the level of demand, thus preventing demand-deficient unemployment. The Keynesians, of course, would go further than this. In a recession, they argue, not only should the government *allow* the PSBR to increase but is should actively engineer such an increase by *deliberately* increasing public spending and reducing taxes, thereby boosting demand. To try to reduce the PSBR in a recession is the opposite of what is required.

Given that public sector borrowing is not in itself a bad thing, how therefore can one explain the preoccupation with the size of the PSBR which was so prevalent in the Thatcher years in Britain and which features prominently in the Maastricht convergence criteria? The first possible explanation stems from the view that 'the government of a country must keep to the fiscal principles appropriate to a grocery store'.[2] In other words, they should follow Mr Micawber's philosophy of keeping their expenditure within their income.

> Annual income twenty pounds, annual expenditure nineteen ninety-six, result happiness. Annual income twenty pounds, annual expenditure twenty pounds ought and six, result misery.
>
> Mr Micawber in Charles Dickens' *David Copperfield*

Although this view is quite clearly incorrect – for the government at least, and arguably for individuals and companies as well – it is deeply ingrained within out consciousness. Children learn that they cannot spend more than they are given in pocket money. Since their income consists of the cash they are given at the beginning of the week, they soon come to understand the benefits of thrift and financial responsibility and the seemingly absolute necessity of keeping expenditure within the limits of income. If companies accepted this maxim, however, they would find it very difficult to expand. Since they could not borrow to finance their investment, they would be limited to whatever funds they could generate internally. If individuals accepted this view they would never take out bank loans or mortgages and they would never buy on credit. In short, they would never *borrow*. Neither, therefore, would anyone lend, since for every borrower there has to be a corresponding lender. No one's consumption would exceed his or her income. Usury would not exist.

Leaving aside the question of whether people would feel more righteous as a result of this, they would certainly feel, and be, very much poorer since the economy would collapse. Any economic activity beyond subsistence agriculture would come to a halt.

Although the prejudice against public sector borrowing is mostly irrational and can be explained in terms of the ethical position mentioned above, there are two more reasons for it which have more substance. The first is connected with the view that government spending financed by borrowing can lead to an undesirable increase in the money supply. The second – and related – reason is that a high level of public borrowing pushes up interest rates and is responsible for displacing or **crowding out** the private sector investment that would otherwise have taken place. We shall deal with each of these in turn.

13.4 The impact on the money supply

We saw earlier in section 4.5 that the impact on the money supply of the sale of public sector debt depended crucially upon whether the debt was being sold to the banking sector or to the non-bank private sector. Certain types of public sector debt (e.g. Treasury Bills) were regarded by the banks as assets which were sufficiently liquid so as to be a very good substitute for cash. If the banks bought Treasury Bills, therefore, the amount of liquid assets they held would remain unchanged (since they would now have less cash but more Treasury Bills), so that they would not have to curtail their lending. In fact, they could *increase* their lending, since the public spending, which was being undertaken by the funds so generated, would *increase* their holdings of liquid assets. Thus, the net effect of public spending financed by selling Treasury Bills *to banks* was to increase the money supply. The same effect would not occur if public sector debt was sold to the *non-bank* private sector since, in this case, banks would suffer a reduction in their holdings of liquid assets when purchasers of

Table 13.4 Financing of the PSBR (£bn)

	1995	1996
PSBR	35.1	24.9
financed by sales of debt to:		
Non-bank, non-building society private sector	28.3	25.4
of which:		
other financial institutions	20.6	20.0
industrial and commercial companies	0.9	−0.1
personal sector	6.8	5.4
Banks and building societies	6.2	−7.3
Overseas sector	0.6	6.8

Source: UK National Accounts 1996, Table 11.14.

Treasury Bills drew cheques on their bank accounts in favour of the Bank of England.

In some years in the 1970s, a large PSBR resulted in substantial sales of debt to the banking sector. In the 1980s the PSBR was progressively reduced to such an extent that by 1989 it had become negative – a **Public Sector Debt Repayment (PSDR)** rather than a PSBR. In the 1990s, however, the PSBR in the UK again became quite large but for the most part this was financed by selling government debt to the non-bank private sector. Table 13.4 presents some illustrative figures for 1995 and 1996.

In any case, it is doubtful whether in practice there is any strict relationship between so-called **unfunded** public sector borrowing and monetary growth ('unfunded' borrowing is that part which is financed by selling short-term debt, such as Treasury Bills, to the banks). Kaldor[3], for example, had pointed out that empirically there is no statistically significant relationship between changes in the money stock and unfunded public sector borrowing, even though in an accounting sense the two things may be related.

13.5 Government borrowing and the effect on interest rates

It is sometimes argued that, even when the Bank of England is successful in financing the borrowing requirement by off-loading government debt on the non-bank private sector, this has only been achieved at the cost of increases in interest rates which have had a discouraging effect on private sector investment. This is part of what, in the 1980s, was called the crowding-out hypothesis, and in the 1930s was known as the **Treasury view**.

In the depression of the 1930s Keynes was advocating budget deficits to boost demand and thereby raise output and employment. The conventional wisdom of the time took the opposite view, that the government should pursue 'sound' financial policies, which meant balancing the budget. According to this view, which came to be known as 'the Treasury view', expansionary fiscal policies would not raise output and employment because extra public spending would lead to a fall in output in the private sector as firms became starved of resources. The modern counterpart of this Treasury view is the crowding-out hypothesis – high levels of public spending result in a large borrowing requirement. This forces up interest rates, which depresses private sector investment and hence output falls in the private sector.

In the UK context there is, however, no empirical support for this hypothesis. The notion that high rates of interest result from high levels of government borrowing has no empirical basis. In fact, in the 1990s the reverse has been true. In the early 1990s the PSBR was at an historically low level but interest rates were very high. After 1992 the PSBR increased dramatically and interest rates came down, equally dramatically.

13.6 Is public spending bad for the economy?

Many commentators have argued that the preoccupation with the PSBR has simply been used as an excuse by those who wish to reduce the role of the state in the economy and that it is based on some fairly shaky analysis, of which the crowding-out hypothesis is the best example. This can be illustrated with the **production possibility frontier** shown in Fig. 13.1.

Imagine a hypothetical closed economy which is currently operating at full capacity. Suppose that, if all the economy's productive resources were devoted to producing private sector output, the maximum amount available would be Oy as in Fig. 13.1. Similarly, if all resources were devoted to public sector output, the amount available would be Ox. The line joining point y with point x is known as a *production possibility frontier*. It shows combinations of private sector and public sector output that are available with a given state of technology. Output levels beyond this frontier are not attainable unless the productive potential of the economy is enhanced, perhaps by an improvement in technology or more factors of production becoming available.

Consider a point such as A on the frontier. Since we are already on the frontier, public sector output can only be increased at the expense of private sector output. Increased public spending will take us to a point such as B, in which case the extra public spending will have displaced or 'crowded out' a certain amount of private sector spending. The cost to society of the extra public sector output has been the private sector output foregone. Economists term this the **opportunity cost** of the extra public sector output. It is the real cost to society of this extra output.

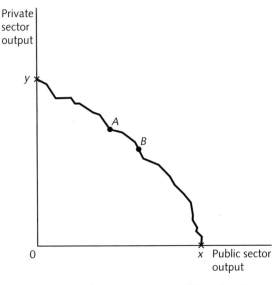

Figure 13.1 The production possibility frontier

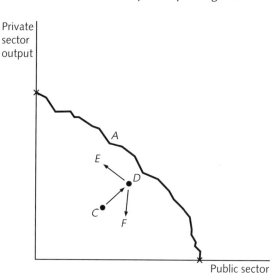

Figure 13.2 Crowding out or crowding in?

In such a situation society should choose the point on the production possibility curve it deems optimal, choosing more public sector output and less private sector output or *vice versa*. This choice should be expressed through the democratic process, however imperfect that process may be. On the assumptions that we have made, it follows quite logically that increased public sector output can only be achieved at the expense of less private sector output, that is, a form of crowding out occurs.

It should be noted, however, that, although output levels *beyond* the frontier are impossible to attain, output levels *within* the frontier, such as point C in Fig. 13.2, are quite probable. At point C the economy is operating at less than full capacity, that is, there exist unemployed resources of capital and labour in the economy. Suppose we now increase public spending. There is no reason why private sector output should suffer as a result – in fact, the reverse seems intuitively more likely, that the increased demand in the economy will induce an increase in output in the private sector. Thus public spending has **crowded in** rather than crowded out private sector output.

What of the reverse situation, when we start at a point such as D and reduce public spending in an attempt to increase private sector output? Will the economy move to a point such as E (for Enterprise) or F (for Failure)? Consider the two scenarios.

E for enterprise

Because the government is spending less, its borrowing requirement is reduced. Personal sector savings, which previously were lent to the government, are now channelled to private sector firms, who as a result increase their expenditure on fixed capital formation. Lower public spending enables taxes to be reduced, resulting in a rise in disposable income and hence a rise in consumption spending. The private sector responds by increasing output, which has been made possible by the increased investment it has undertaken.

F for failure

The cut in public spending will cause some firms, who previously sold to the public sector, to experience a fall in demand. Some public sector workers will suffer a fall in income as a result of pay restraint or redundancy. These groups thus cut their spending. Since spending and incomes fall, tax revenues fall, leading to an *increase* in the borrowing requirement. In an attempt to 'get back on course' public spending is cut still more, deepening the recession. The decline is cumulative.

On the face of it both these scenarios seem plausible but, on closer inspection, we see that the first is seriously flawed because it ignores the influence of demand. A reduction in the budget deficit will reduce the overall level of demand. If demand falls, supply is most unlikely to rise – in fact, it is likely to fall too because supply or output is basically **demand determined**. The gap left by the reduced public spending will not necessarily be filled because, although Nature abhors a vacuum and rushes in to fill it up, there is no such general tendency in the economies of complex industrial societies.

We should note, however, that this view – that the level of output is demand determined – is not universally accepted. The so-called **supply-siders** of the monetarist school argue that much greater attention should be paid to the factors which shape the decisions of individual workers and firms as regards what they produce and sell. One such influence would be the rewards available from work, and here they argue that a cut in tax rates will encourage greater effort and enterprise and thus boost output. We examine the views of the supply-siders in the next chapter.

13.7 Flow of Funds: New Cambridge

The concept of the flow of funds between sectors gives us a useful insight into the structure of the economy and changes that may be occurring. This section discusses an approach, based on flow of funds analysis, which for convenience we shall label the New Cambridge approach. The term originates from the late 1970s when a group of Keynesian economists working in Cambridge, England, became identified with this type of analysis (the word 'new' was to distinguish them from the Cambridge View – a version of the Quantity Theory of Money developed in the 1920s).

The analysis starts with an identity:

injections = withdrawals [13.1]

or

$$G + X + I = T + M + S \qquad\qquad [13.2]$$

In equilibrium, injections equal withdrawals. That is, the flow of spending being injected into the economy is matched by an exactly equal flow of spending leaking out of the economy. Although the nature of equilibrium is complex, and disequilibrium situations are at least a theoretical possibility, nevertheless in accounting terms the economy is in equilibrium, always. In other words, equation 13.1 above is true by definition.

In equation 13.2 we define injections to the economy to be equal to the sum of government spending, exports and investment spending. Similarly, withdrawals are defined to be the sum of tax revenue, spending on imports, and saving. We already know of course that $(G - T)$ is the budget deficit (or surplus). Similarly, we know that $(X - M)$ is the trade surplus or deficit. Finally, $(I - S)$ is the surplus of investment spending over saving. In other words, it is the level of investment spending which is not financed by domestic saving.

A number of things follow from these accounting identities. In effect we have three pairs of variables:

$$(G - T)\,(X - M)\text{ and }(I - S)$$

If one of these pairs were zero (say, $I = S$ so that $(I - S) = 0$ for example) then it follows that the other two pairs must be equal (though opposite in sign). By rearranging equation [13.2] we find that:

$$(G - T) = (X - M) \qquad\qquad [13.3]$$

In other words, if domestic savings are just sufficient to finance investment spending by firms (that is, if $S = I$) then it follows that the budget deficit must be reflected in an equal sized trade deficit. It also follows of course that a budget surplus will have its counterpart in a trade surplus of equal magnitude.

When the New Cambridge view came to prominence it was presented in this way. That is, it was claimed that in the 1970s in Britain savings and investment had been approximately equal so that one would expect to observe – and in fact did observe – an approximate equality between the budget deficit and the trade deficit.

In the late 1980s the situation had changed somewhat but it was still of course possible to analyse it in terms of the accounting identities set out above. In the latter half of the 1980s the UK economy was characterised by three features:

(i)   a substantial decline in the savings ratio (personal savings as a percentage of personal disposable income declined from about 13.5 per cent in 1980 to about 4.2 per cent in 1988);

(ii) a substantial trade imbalance peaking at £19bn in 1989 or nearly 5 per cent of GDP;

(iii) the elimination of Budget deficits, so that the Budget was approximately in balance.

In terms of the framework established above we would therefore expect to find, with G approximately equal to T, that:

$$(M - X) = (I - S) \qquad [13.4]$$

When we inspect the data for the UK for the late 1980s this is of course what we do find. In other words, the trade deficit $(M - X)$ has its counterpart in a net inflow of investment funds from abroad $(I - S)$. That is, a Capital Account surplus. In other words, within the UK total saving (S) was insufficient to finance investment expenditure (I). This investment expenditure must therefore have been financed by the savings of non-residents. These non-residents were for the most part Japanese and German households and firms, for in those countries there was an excess of domestic saving over domestic investment. Moreover, in Japan and Germany there was – as we would expect – a trade surplus. Thus the accounting identities established above hold for Japan and Germany also.

In the mid-1990s the situation had changed completely but the accounting identities we have noted still held true – they must have done since they are identities. In 1996 the current account of the balance of payments $(M - X)$ was almost in balance. It therefore follows that the public sector deficit $(G - T)$ must have been matched by a private sector surplus $(S - I)$ of an equivalent amount. This is exactly what happened, as can be confirmed by looking back at Table 13.1.

Evaluation

The analysis presented above is, in a sense, tautological since it is based on an identity – that is, something which is true by definition. There are two major shortcomings with this analysis, however.

First, it tells us nothing about the *mechanism* which brings about the result. For example, suppose that as in 1996 the trade account is in balance (that is, $X - M = 0$) and that we find by inspecting the data that the public sector deficit is indeed matched, as our theory predicts, by an equal-sized private sector surplus of domestic savings over investment. The theory does not explain how this equality between $(G - T)$ and $(S - I)$ is brought about. Which of the four variables responds – G, T, S or I? And to what other variables do they respond – interest rates, inflation rates, the exchange rate or what? The 'theory' tells us nothing about the underlying mechanisms which produce the statistical result we observe.

Summary

Flow of funds analysis measures the net flow of loanable funds between various sectors. At the broadest level of aggregation we can distinguish three sectors – the private sector (comprising households and firms), the public sector (comprising central and local government and nationalised industries), and the overseas sector (comprising all non-resident households, firms and governments). Since deficits must have their counterpart in corresponding surpluses elsewhere, the net acquisition of financial assets for the three sectors taken together is zero.

Attention is often focused on the public sector financial deficit and its analogue, the public sector borrowing requirement. EU governments must keep public borrowing below a certain level if they wish to meet Maastricht criteria for membership of the European Single Currency. The rationale for this has to do with the supposed impact which high public borrowing has on interest rates, though there is no empirical basis for this view.

Flow of funds analysis is an accounting identity. It follows therefore that, if one of the three sectors is in balance, the surplus in one of the remaining sectors must be identically equal to the deficit in the other. However, the analysis tells us nothing about the causal mechanism whereby this is achieved.

Notes

1 Lerner, A.P. (1944) *The Economics of Control*.
2 The phrase is taken from Lerner (1944) (*op. cit*). Lerner could not possibly have foreseen that one day a grocer's daughter would control the economic policy of Britain!
3 See Kaldor, N. (1982) 'Evidence to Treasury and Civil Service Committee' in *The Scourge of Monetarism*: OUP.

Key terms

Review questions

13.1 The following table gives some information on the financial surplus or deficit of the private, public and overseas sectors in 1988, 1989 and 1996 in the United Kingdom (in £bn).

	1988	1989	1996
Private sector	−20.2	−25.3	+34.7
Public sector	?	+6.1	−33.6
Overseas sector	+15.1	?	+0.4
Residual error	−1.7	+0.1	

(a) What was the size of the public sector's surplus or deficit in 1988?
(b) What was the overseas sector's surplus or deficit in 1989?
(c) Does the positive sign for the overseas sector in 1996 indicate that the current account was in surplus or in deficit?

13.2 Which of the following will result from a positive PSBR:
(a) the National Debt will increase;
(b) interest rates will rise;
(c) demand will be higher than if there had been no public sector borrowing;
(d) private sector borrowing will fall;
(e) the ratio of the National Debt to GDP will rise (one of the Maastricht criteria).

13.3 Suppose that asset sales (such as British Gas in 1987) raise about £6bn. Which of the following are true:
(a) The PSFD was £6bn less than it would have been if there had been no asset sales.
(b) The PSBR was £6bn less than it would have been without the asset sales.
(c) This allows the Chancellor to cut taxation by £6bn and still achieve his target for the PSBR.

14 The real wage debate and supply-side economics

Preview

In the 1980s critics of Keynesian orthodoxy proposed a revolutionary method of modelling the way in which people form their expectations of future inflation rates. This Rational Expectations hypothesis provided an intellectual justification for much of the policy making that went on in the 1980s and its legacy survives today. Demand management along traditional Keynesian lines is no longer the accepted wisdom. A more eclectic approach incorporating supply-side policies characterises policy making in the second half of the 1990s.

14.1 A historical perspective

There is no new thing under the sun. Or, at least, so it must appear to those who observe the waxing and waning of economic ideas. In the depression years of the 1930s Keynes argued that demand could and should be expanded to reduce unemployment. The classical economists resisted, arguing in favour of balanced budgets and action to reduce wages. Neither side can be said to have won the intellectual argument at the time; rather the reflation that occurred in the late 1930s resulted from rearmament. In the post-war era Keynesian economics held sway. It was the **conventional wisdom**. Perhaps as a result of Keynesian policies, or perhaps coincidentally, the 1950s and 1960s were a period of unprecedented growth and prosperity. By the mid 1970s, however, the conventional wisdom was under attack. By 1980 Keynesian economics was in the wilderness. The Western economies, and Britain in particular, were in deep recession with unemployment reaching levels which had not been seen since the 1930s, while influential economists, with the ear of the government, argued that unemployment could not be reduced by reflation. This view was popularly labelled 'monetarist' though it was rather different from the old style monetarism of Milton Friedman with its emphasis on the money supply as a determinant of aggregate demand. New-style monetarism was the absolute negation · of the Keynesian belief that demand management was capable of raising output and reducing unemployment. The new monetarism argued that the government was powerless to reduce unemployment. The wheel had come full circle.

The first part of the attack on Keynesianism came with the so-called crowding-out hypothesis which we discussed in the previous chapter. The essence of this hypothesis was that the government was incapable of raising demand because any increase in government spending would displace an equivalent amount of private investment spending. Although it is too simplistic to say that the crowding-out hypothesis was disproved, it is certainly true to say that it lost support in the 1980s as a mass of empirical evidence built up against it. In the meantime, however, a much more sophisticated and damaging critique of Keynesian views was being developed. This critique was based on a rather esoteric piece of theory called the **rational expectations hypothesis** but this theory gave a new impetus to the debate about the causes of unemployment. Thus, in the mid 1980s, the stage was set for a replay of the debate which had taken place in the 1930s. This time it was called the **real wage debate**. It centred around the question of whether unemployment was the result of real wages being too high. Had workers priced themselves out of jobs and would unemployment fall if workers accepted lower real wages? Would an expansion of demand engineered by the government succeed in reducing unemployment or would it merely lead to wage inflation without any impact on employment levels?

14.2 Rational expectations

An important aspect of the real wage debate was concerned with the way in which expectations (of future price changes) were formed. In the late 1970s and early 1980s a novel – some would say revolutionary – way of modelling expectations was increasingly discussed by economists. This was the so-called Rational Expectations hypothesis (REH or simply RE). This hypothesis had a major impact on the debate about labour market dynamics.

Economic agents – that is, firms, consumers, employers, trade union negotiators and so on – necessarily have expectations about certain key economic variables. For example, firms will have some view about their sales revenue next year. Consumers will have some view about what their incomes are likely to be in three years' time, and so on. A key variable about which economic agents form expectations, however, is the price level. In other words, all economic agents have some view about future inflation rates. These expectations will influence the decisions they take in the present about things such as the level of wage settlements. Those decisions themselves will, in turn, influence future events – for example, the actual rate of increase of wage costs will influence the rate of increase of prices.

Before the 1980s, economists had traditionally modelled expectations in a backward-looking way. In other words, economic agents were assumed to base their expectations of the future on what had happened in the recent past. For example, if the rate of inflation in the current year was known to be 3 per cent then, in the absence of any information to the contrary, the economic agent will expect the rate of inflation next year to be 3 per cent as well. On the face of it this seems sensible. But imagine a situation in which the rate of inflation is falling from, say, 5 per cent two years ago to 4 per cent last year, to 3 per cent this year. If inflation really does continue to fall, but economic agents still base their expectations on the most recently experienced actual rate of inflation, they will tend to overpredict the rate of inflation for next year (they will predict 3 per cent, whereas the actual rate next year will turn out to be lower). More importantly, expectations formed in this way cannot pick up turning points – that is, if the rate of inflation in the past has been on a rising trend, but the government and monetary authorities take action to reduce it, economic agents' expectations about the rate of inflation will be much higher than the rate which actually occurs.

Modelling the formation of expectations in this way therefore presupposes a degree of irrationality – agents always get it wrong. Let us suppose, the advocates of RE argue, that we make the opposite assumption, namely that economic agents are *rational* in the sense that they get it right, or, at least, that on average they get it right. To be able to do so, of course, economic agents would need to have in their minds some model of the economy which could, on average, correctly forecast inflation (and other key economic variables). Critics of RE point out that this requirement will not be fulfilled. Not even the best informed group of economic forecasters can correctly predict the future, so the man in the street, they argue, cannot possibly hope to do so. In reply, the advocates of RE argue that to assume rationality (in the sense used here) on the part of economic agents is no more implausible than to assume the sort of irrationality implied by modelling expectations in a backward-looking way. Moreover, and this is a vital distinction, the Rational Expectations Hypothesis does not assume that economic agents forecast correctly. Rather it assumes that *on average* they forecast correctly, or more exactly that on average the expectations of economic agents will be the same as those generated by a correct model of the economy.

14.3 The implications of RE for policy

On the face of it, the REH seems to be a fairly minor piece of theory – perhaps a little implausible but definitely innocuous. It seems to be policy-neutral in the sense that it does not appear to strengthen or weaken the case for any particular policy stance. It is surprising to find therefore that the REH has provoked so much controversy among economists, being heralded by some as the most important theoretical advance in the economic theory in a generation while others have treated it with disdain and derision.

There are probably two reasons for the popularity – if that is the right word – of RE. The first and least important is a technical one; namely, that for those engaged in producing forecasts from economic models (which we discuss in Chapter 15) RE appears to offer a neat way of producing consistent forecasts. More importantly, however, when RE is combined with a certain view of the labour market, it appears to offer a theoretical justification for the sort of policy stance which right-wing governments like to adopt. That is, RE provides radical right-wing governments (such as that of the former Prime Minister, Mrs Thatcher) with a justification for eschewing any sort of reflationary actions to reduce unemployment since it forms a vital part of an analysis which concludes that such reflationary policies are ineffective and damaging. If the REH is true, and if the labour market works in the way that monetarists believe, then expansionary fiscal and monetary policies cannot alleviate unemployment. Reflation brings inflation without any increase in real output. Demand management, in a Keynesian sense, is dead and the way is open for 'supply-side' policies – 'making markets work better'. Thus RE is the missing link which the opponents of Keynesianism have been seeking. It may, like the missing link in the evolutionary debate, turn out to have been a fraud.

14.4 The dynamics of labour market adjustment

Suppose we accept (as monetarists do) that the labour market can be modelled by the sort of demand and supply analysis illustrated in Fig. 14.1. (The monetarist view of the labour market was sketched out in Chapter 5 and it may be helpful to re-read that. It is important to recall also that the demand curve for labour is the marginal revenue product curve which is explained in section 5.7.) Note in Fig. 14.1 that both the demand for labour and the supply of labour depend upon the real wage (W/P). Figure 14.1 illustrates a situation of long-run equilibrium. In equilibrium the market *clears* in the sense that the level of real wages is just sufficient to ensure that the demand for labour and the supply of labour are equal. Thus there is no involuntary unemployment. All those who wish to work can find a job.

A long-run equilibrium situation such as this is not particularly interesting since equilibrium is defined in such a way that the problem we are studying is defined out of existence. The problem we are interested in is that of unemployment. If the labour market is in equilibrium then by definition unemployment cannot exist.

We also noted, in section 5.5, an important corollary of this argument, namely that expansionary monetary and fiscal policies could not in the long run move the level of employment away from its **natural level**. Hence, the level of *unemployment* also remained at its natural level in the long run. In summary, unemployment could not, in the long run, be reduced by monetary and fiscal expansion.

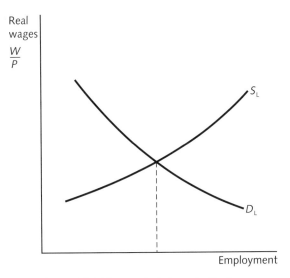

Figure 14.1 The market clears in the long run

As Keynes is said to have remarked, however, in the long run we are all dead. We live here and now in the short run, in a world in which markets do not necessarily clear. Is it possible, in this short run, for expansionary policies to increase employment?

If this question can be answered in the affirmative then the possibility of reducing unemployment by stimulating demand is proved. In fairness, to reduce unemployment *permanently* it might be necessary to keep on applying successive stimuli to demand, and this might result in accelerating inflation, but the ability of governments to reduce unemployment – if they wish to do so – is demonstrated. It would then become clear that a high level of unemployment reflected the fact that the government had taken the conscious decision not to expand demand and thereby reduce unemployment, since it gave a higher priority to reducing inflation and avoiding balance of payments difficulties than to reducing unemployment. This is an intellectually defensible, if somewhat callous, position but it is not one which is likely to appeal to the hearts and minds of the electorate. A certain amount of disquiet and unease might result, even in the minds of the policy-makers themselves, if it were recognised that the well-being of the employed majority was being purchased at the expense of the unemployed minority. How much simpler to argue that even in the short run it was *impossible* to reduce unemployment by stimulating demand.

This is where rational expectations enter the analysis. Deviations from the long-run equilibrium depicted in Fig. 14.1 can only be achieved if there is some divergence between the **actual real wage** and the **expected real wage**. If such divergences are impossible then deviations away from the natural level of employment are also impossible, even in the short run.

To illustrate this, consider Fig. 14.2 where the vertical axis measures both actual real wages and expected real wages. Assume that the demand for labour is a

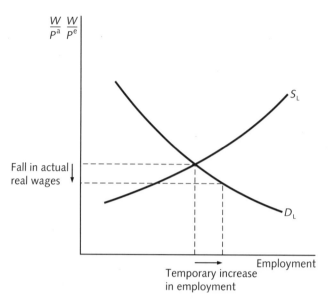

Figure 14.2 A temporary increase in employment

function of *actual* real wages (money wages deflated by the actual price index) whereas the supply of labour is a function of *expected* real wages (money wages deflated by the expected price index). If the expected price index is the same as the actual price index (i.e. $P^e = P^a$) then the market stays in equilibrium. If, however, actual and expected prices diverge it is possible for disequilibrium situations to arise. This implies that the level of employment could deviate from its natural level. The scope for discretionary fiscal policy to reduce unemployment therefore depends upon the ability of the authorities to generate such disequilibria.

For example, suppose wages are rising at 10 per cent per annum and prices are also expected to rise at the same rate. Expected real wages (W/P^e) thus remain unchanged so there is no change in the amount of labour supplied. Suppose, however, that prices actually rise by 12 per cent. Actual real wages thus fall, leading to an increase in the demand for labour. This is illustrated in Fig. 14.2 where a movement down the demand curve for labour results in a temporary increase in employment. Notice, however, that this will only occur if the authorities generate an actual rate of inflation which is different from the expected rate of inflation. If the suppliers of labour form their expectations in a rational way – that is, if on average: $P^e = P^a$, then such deviations away from long-run equilibria will not occur. This is because the rate of inflation which actually occurs will always be fully – and correctly – anticipated by workers. Thus expected real wages are equal to actual real wages: $W/P^e = W/P^a$ and deviations from the natural level of employment cannot occur even in the short run.

This analysis of labour market dynamics has very important implications for policy. First, if the analysis is correct it implies that the only way for the government to reduce unemployment permanently is to keep generating surprises, by producing an actual rate of inflation which is higher than the expected rate. After a while it would become more and more difficult to surprise people, since the surprises would be anticipated. The expected rate of inflation would equal the actual rate. Expected and actual real wages would therefore remain unaffected by expansionary fiscal and monetary policies. Such policies would result only in higher and higher rates of inflation, as the authorities strove ineffectually to generate surprises and there would be no effect on employment even in the short run.

In addition to demonstrating that reflationary policies do not reduce unemployment, the REH also implies, of course, that deflationary policies do not increase unemployment. Suppose the government deflates the economy to reduce inflation. If the ensuing fall in the rate of inflation is fully anticipated by all economic agents, then expected and actual real wages will remain unchanged. Inflation will be brought down painlessly. The transition from a high rate of inflation to a low rate of inflation is accomplished without the need to go through a high-unemployment period of transition in which economic agents gradually adjust their expectations – and hence their wage demands – to the lower rate of inflation.

14.5 Rational expectations and monetary policy

The emphasis which this analysis puts on expectations explains the thinking behind the monetary policy carried out in Britain in the 1980s. This was the so-called **Medium Term Financial Strategy**, the essence of which was the announcement of a target rate of growth for the money stock. Economic agents, it was claimed, would take note of the projected fall in the growth of the money supply and would anticipate that a fall in the rate of inflation would result. They would therefore adjust their behaviour accordingly – in particular, they would moderate their wage demands. The resulting fall in wage inflation would help reduce price inflation (though the prime mover was the reduction in monetary growth) and this would confirm that agents' expectations had been correct.

It seems incredible now that anyone could ever have believed that economic agents in the real world would behave in the way that this theory supposed. In the event the monetary authorities consistently failed to reach their pre-set monetary targets, so that expectations were generated that the authorities would in future miss their monetary targets, which were thus effectively ignored. Even if the authorities had met their monetary targets it was becoming increasingly apparent by the mid-1980s that the power of the money supply statistics to predict the rate of inflation was very poor. The Medium Term Financial Strategy faded away.

14.6 RE: an assessment

We saw in section 14.3 how a monetarist view of the labour market, when combined with RE, could be used to support the notion that reflation would not reduce unemployment. Such a conclusion was anathema to Keynesian economists who were thus initially highly critical of RE and regarded it as sophistry. The Keynesian attack was somewhat misplaced, however, since the critical part of the analysis was not RE itself but rather the monetarist view of the workings of the labour market. Forward-looking expectations could in fact form part of a Keynesian model of the economy and by the mid-1980s some Keynesian macro-models had indeed incorporated such a feature.

RE is now acknowledged as a significant innovation in economic analysis. It has done little to increase our understanding of macroeconomic behaviour, however, since the propositions of the REH are so difficult to prove empirically – or rather to disprove. On a simplistic level the REH is obviously incorrect. What little evidence there is from surveys (of people's price expectations) shows quite clearly that people do not on average guess the future rate of price inflation correctly. On a more sophisticated level, however, it seems sensible to acknowledge that people do anticipate future changes in economic variables, and that their expectations are based on quite complex models of the causal links within the economy – though these models are implicit rather than explicit.

The real wage debate remains unresolved. If the labour market does indeed function in the way that monetarists believe, then it is a logical possibility that reflation could lead to an increase in both prices and wages which would leave real wages and the level of employment essentially unchanged. The crucial question is whether the labour market really can be modelled in the way that monetarists believe.

14.7 The legacy: policy in the 1990s

As the 1990s wore on, the debate between the monetarists and the Keynesians became less and less intense. Policy became more eclectic and pragmatic, owing less to highfalutin theory and more to practical realities. By 1997, however, with the change of government it was clear that the debate had produced a long-term legacy. The incoming Labour government would not reverse the policies of its Conservative predecessors. They would not revert to old-style Keynesianism with its emphasis on demand management as the principal tool with which to control the economy and improve its performance. Rather, they would continue with the policy that had evolved during the Conservative years – that of improving the supply side of the economy, with particular emphasis on improving the skills of the labour force through education and training.

14.8 Supply-side economics

As we have seen, the rational expectations revolution (so-called) made governments question whether demand management in a Keynesian sense was sufficient to bring about the goals of low inflation, low unemployment and rapid economic growth. Some time during the 1970s the phrase **supply-side economics** emerged. The supply-siders argued that demand management at the macro level was relatively ineffective. What was needed was a policy at the micro level to improve the competitive efficiency of markets. In particular, attention was directed towards the labour market. Incentives could be improved, it was argued, both for those in work and those currently out of work.

14.9 Taxation and incentives

The supply-siders argued that high rates of income tax represented a disincentive to work effort. If taxes were reduced people would work harder and the economy would become more productive. Unemployment would also be reduced since those who had previously been discouraged from working by high marginal tax rates and had registered as unemployed would now re-enter employment.

To assess the validity of this analysis we need first to distinguish between the **marginal rate of income tax** and the **average rate** of income tax. The average tax rate is the proportion of total income paid in tax. The marginal tax rate is the proportion of any *additional* income paid in tax. For all taxpayers the marginal rate of tax is higher than the average rate of tax because of the presence of initial allowances and also because, for those on higher incomes, marginal tax rates rise as income rises. Marginal tax rates tend to receive more public attention and discussion than average tax rates simply because they are more apparent. Most people know what their marginal tax rate is. Relatively few will know what their average tax rate is.

Two groups of individuals are subject to high marginal tax rates – those on very high incomes and, paradoxically, those on very low incomes. For some people on low incomes it is now recognised that the **marginal rate of deduction** – similar to the marginal 'tax' rate – effectively exceeds 100 per cent. This is because of the withdrawal of certain **means-tested cash benefits** which results when such people experience a small increase in pre-tax income. For such people a **poverty trap** exists because attempts to increase their income make them worse off. This is an unintended consequence of the tax and benefit system which is obviously undesirable but is difficult to avoid if a means-tested system of benefits is employed together with a tax system which extends downwards to encompass those on comparatively small incomes.

In contrast, the high marginal tax rate paid by those on high incomes is an intentional feature of any progressive tax system. Taxation is linked to ability to pay. When the Conservative Government took office in 1979 the top rate of income tax was 83 per cent (or 98 per cent if you include the investment income surcharge). In their first budget in June 1979 this was reduced to 60 per cent. This was widely regarded as a sensible reduction since most of those on high money incomes were able to arrange their affairs so as to avoid such high rates of deduction. In subsequent Budgets the top marginal rate (now called the higher rate) was reduced progressively to 40 per cent.

Is there a distinctive effect which results from high taxes and, in particular, from high marginal rates of income tax? It is not possible to give a definitive answer to this question since the outcome depends on the strength of the so-called **income and substitution effects** which result from the change in relative prices brought about by the imposition of a tax. Taxes change the terms of the trade-off between labour and leisure, reducing the reward for a given amount of labour. Since leisure is pleasant and labour unpleasant, it is argued that at the margin individuals will opt for more leisure since the opportunity cost of an hour spent in leisure (the net income forgone) has been reduced by taxation. Thus, the higher the marginal rate of tax the greater the disincentive effect. This is known as the *substitution effect* since individuals substitute leisure for labour at the margin because of the change in relative prices.

It could equally well be argued, of course, that taxes on income *encourage* rather than discourage work effort. Suppose one's objective is to secure a given amount of post-tax income. The higher the tax rate the higher the level of pre-tax income necessary to secure it. Thus the higher the tax rate the greater the incentive effect. This is called the *income effect*.

It is well known to economists that a change in relative prices (such as that produced by taxes) produces both a substitution effect and an income effect. *A priori*, we cannot say which of the two effects will be the stronger; therefore we cannot say with certainty what the effect of taxation will be on work effort and incentives. What can be said in criticism of this approach is that many people do not typically have the option of substituting labour for leisure at the margin since their hours of work are fixed. Moreover, it may not be correct to equate work effort with hours spent working. A more telling point is that pecuniary rewards, either pre-tax or post-tax, are not necessarily closely related to work effort.

Moreover, a more fundamental objection is that, although most people are motivated by money to a greater or lesser extent, almost no one would claim that money is the only thing that motivates them in their work. Status, intellectual interest, contributing to the well-being of others, companionship and comradeship, meeting other people or simply 'getting out of the house' are all aspects of working which, for most people, provide an important incentive in addition to the pecuniary one. Moreover, these non-pecuniary incentives are obviously present to a greater degree for highly paid and therefore highly taxed workers like doctors and company executives than they are for low-paid workers such as office cleaners.

Numerous studies by economists have tried to assess empirically whether taxes on income do have a disincentive effect. In principle, there are two ways of finding an answer to this question. Either one can simply put the question to a sample of people in a questionnaire or an interview, or one can make inferences from past behaviour. The first method is open to the objection that people's behaviour and their perception of that behaviour do not necessarily coincide. What people say they do and what they actually do are two different things. More importantly, the researcher can perhaps unwittingly slant the question asked in such a way as to elicit the answer he or she wishes to receive. It is very difficult not to 'lead' the interviewee into a particular response, no matter how objective and unbiased the interviewer tries to be. For example, suppose a group of company executives were asked the following questions:

1   Does the fact that you pay high marginal tax rates discourage you from working longer hours or from taking a more stressful but better paid job?
2   Does the fact that you pay high marginal tax rates mean that you don't put as much effort into your job as you could do?

Although the two questions are trying to shed light on the same basic issue, namely whether or not taxes have a disincentive effect, respondents are more likely to reply 'No' to the second question than to the first.

An alternative method is to make inferences from past behaviour by applying statistical techniques to macroeconomic data. Although this method is more 'objective' in the sense that it uses data derived from what people have actually done as opposed to what they say they would do, it suffers from the usual objection that it is difficult to prove or disprove any proposition in the social sciences by statistical means. Statistical studies in this area have often been built around the **Laffer curve**, a relationship noted by the American economist Art Laffer. In the folklore of economics, Laffer is said to have drawn the relationship shown here as Fig. 14.3 on the back of a cigarette packet. He observed that total revenue from income taxes would be zero if the tax rate was zero; but total tax revenue would also be zero if tax rates were 100 per cent since in this case there would be no incentive for people to work (for money income) and hence the tax base would be zero. He further pointed out that there must be some relationship joining these two points. Attempts have been made to estimate this relationship since its shape tells us something about the disincentive effect of taxation.

Up to point A in Fig. 14.3 tax revenue increases proportionately with the tax rate. We can interpret this as implying that there is no disincentive effect up to this point. Between point A and point B there is evidence of a disincentive effect since tax revenue increases less than proportionately with the tax rate. Beyond point B

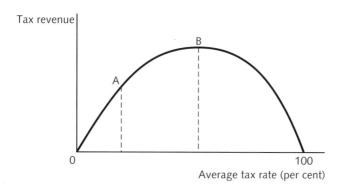

Figure 14.3 The Laffer curve

further increases in the tax rate succeed only in reducing tax revenue, which indicates a very pronounced disincentive effect. In this range the substitution effect dominates the income effect.

Clearly, it would not make sense to operate the economy beyond point B. What is perhaps less clear is that the peak of the curve at B is an optimum only if the objective is to maximise tax revenue. However, it is not necessarily true that the economy should never be operated beyond point A. Indeed, one might be prepared to put up with a small disincentive effect and trade this off against the benefits to be derived from higher tax revenue.

The crucial question regarding the Laffer curve, however, is whether the data support the hypothesis that the relationship between tax revenue and tax rates is similar to the one illustrated in Fig. 14.3. In other words, is the relationship linear (as it is up to point A) or is it non-linear (as it is beyond A)? A linear relationship suggests there is no disincentive effect whereas a non-linear relationship suggests there is. The evidence appears inconclusive. While some researchers[1] claim to have found evidence of non-linearity, the present author found that data for the UK economy for the period 1972–85 were consistent only with a linear relationship between the average tax rate and tax revenue. There was no statistically significant evidence of non-linearity.

14.10 Taxation and incentives: policy implications

The policy implications of the above analysis are not as straightforward as might at first have been supposed. In practice, policy-makers have a number of objectives, one of which is concerned with the distribution of income (though the Conservative Government in Britain has given this low priority). The tax instrument affects the amount of tax revenue raised and therefore, *ceteris paribus*, affects the amount of public expenditure which can be undertaken. But the way in which the tax instrument is wielded also affects the **distribution of income**. It may also, if there are disincentive effects, affect the level of that income and output. It follows therefore that a policy which may produce a small stimulus to output at the cost of a relatively major shift in the distribution of income away from the poorer section of society is not necessarily a preferred policy. There may be a trade-off between the twin objectives of what we might call economic **efficiency** (maximising output) and **equity** (the distribution of income). The hypothesis that such a trade-off exists is, however, based on the notion that taxation in some sense has a deadening effect on incentives and that income and output would be increased if taxation were to be reduced.

We have to be careful to distinguish here between two quite distinct ideas. One is the notion that output would be increased if taxation in general were to be reduced. The other is that output would be increased if the **balance of taxation** were shifted from direct to indirect taxation. **Direct taxes** are taxes on earnings, such as income tax and National Insurance contributions. **Indirect taxes** are taxes on spending, such as value added tax, customs and excise duties and other specific taxes such as car tax. The argument that taxation reduces incentives relates, of course, only to direct taxes. Taxes on expenditure cannot have a disincentive effect on work effort and therefore if the burden of taxation is shifted towards indirect taxes this should, it is argued, reduce the overall disincentive effect. The Conservative Government which took office in Britain in 1979 brought about a significant shift in the balance of personal taxation, as Table 14.1 shows. As a result of the 1979 Budget the share of tax revenue obtained from indirect taxes jumped from about 36 per cent to 43 per cent and it remains at over 40 percent.

Unfortunately, indirect taxes tend to be regressive in the sense that people on low incomes pay a larger proportion of their income in tax than people on high incomes. This results from the fact that people on low incomes spend proportionately more of their incomes on highly taxed items such as tobacco. Even before the balance of taxation shifted towards indirect taxation, a number of studies had shown that the weak progressivity of the direct tax system is offset almost completely by the regressivity of the indirect tax system. The net effect of the tax system in the UK is to leave the distribution of post-tax incomes more or less unchanged. It is only the system of cash payments (such as social security benefits) and income-in-kind (such as free school meals) which leads to any substantial redistribution of income. Figure 14.4 gives a broad indication of the effect on income distribution of various forms of governmental intervention.

A further indication is given in Table 14.2 where four definitions of income are used. These are explained in Fig. 14.5. As can be seen from Table 14.2, the effect of the system of indirect taxes is to *reduce* the share of the bottom quintile (from 7.9 per cent to 6.9 per cent) and *increase* the share of the top quintile (from 40 per cent to 43 per cent). Most surprising of all perhaps is the Gini coefficient shown in the last line of Table 14.2. The Gini coefficient for post-tax income is 37, which compares with a coefficient of 36 for gross income. In other words the net effect of the tax system in 1995-96 was to *increase* the inequalities in income.

Table 14.1 Percentage of total taxation derived from various sources

	1976	1981	1992
Taxes on persons			
Direct taxes	39	30	30
Social security contributions[1]	19	17	18
	58	47	48
Indirect taxes	36	43	41
Community Charge	–	–	4
Taxes on companies	5	9	7

1 Including employer's contribution.
Source: Taxes and Social Security Contributions: an international comparison 1982–92, *Economic Trends*, January 1995.

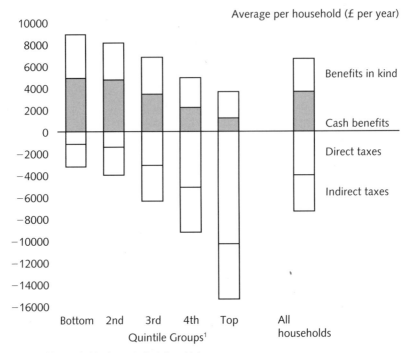

1 Households are ranked by their equivalised disposable income.

Figure 14.4 Summary of the effects of taxes and benefits on all households, 1995–96

Table 14.2 Percentage shares of total household income and Gini coefficients, 1995–96

	Original income	Gross income	Disposable income	Post-tax income
Quintile group				
bottom	2.6	7.4	7.9	6.9
2nd	7.0	11.0	12.0	12.0
3rd	15.0	16.0	17.0	16.0
4th	25.0	23.0	23.0	23.0
top	50.0	43.0	40.0	43.0
All households	100.0	100.0	100.0	100.0
Decile group				
bottom	1.1	3.2	3.2	2.5
top	32.0	27.0	25.0	27.0
Gini coefficient[1] (per cent)	52.0	36.0	33.0	37.0

1 The Gini coefficient is a measure of the dispersion of income which takes account of all the values in the distribution. A completely equal distribution of income would produce a Gini coefficient of zero.
Source: 'The effects of taxes and benefits upon household income', 1995–96 in *Economic Trends*, March 1997.

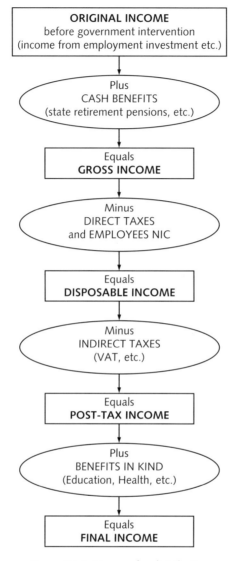

Figure 14.5 Stages of redistribution

14.11 Incentives for the out-of-work

Although the social security system is the most effective way of redistributing income, it is argued that an unfortunate side-effect is to produce disincentives for those currently out of work. In Britain the two major elements of the income-maintenance programme for those of working age (other than the chronically sick and disabled) are the Jobseeker's Allowance (formerly known as unemployment benefit) and social security benefit. The objective of these cash payments is to raise the incomes of those out of work to some minimum acceptable level. The advocates of supply-side economics argue, however, that such payments have an undesirable effect on the labour market since they lead people to choose longer spells out of work than would otherwise be the case. Rather than being forced to accept the first low-paid job that comes along the unemployed can be more discerning and can afford to spend longer periods looking for more attractive jobs. As already noted, the fact that those who qualify for social security benefit also qualify for other means-tested benefits (such as free school meals) creates a poverty trap. Those previously unemployed who take a low-paid job can find themselves worse off in employment than they were when unemployed. It is argued that a relatively generous income-maintenance programme will lead to higher recorded unemployment levels. In terms of what has been said earlier, the natural level of unemployment will be higher, the higher is the level of social security and unemployment benefits relative to wages. If one's only objective is to reduce recorded unemployment it therefore follows that a policy which makes it less attractive to be unemployed (such as cutting unemployment benefit) will, *ceteris paribus*, reduce recorded unemployment. Such a policy, however, conflicts directly with the purpose of the income maintenance programme, which is to provide a safety-net for those whose incomes would otherwise be unacceptably low. Such a policy may also bring about a reduction in recorded unemployment without bringing any 'real' change in unemployment levels. This takes us back to a point we made in section Chapter 5, namely that the official statistics may underestimate the 'true' level of unemployment.

14.12 Making the labour market work better

In addition to increasing the incentive to work, supply-side policies aim to remove the rigidities in the labour market which prevent it operating like the neo-classical model. In this model prices adjust rapidly so as to equate demand and supply. The market clears. There is no stickiness. Economic agents respond to price signals and information is costless.

Whether the labour market could ever operate like the neo-classical model is open to question. What is certain is that supply-siders believe that the existence of trade unions can introduce rigidities which hinder the smooth operation of market forces. They therefore advocate that measures should be taken to curb the power of the trade unions. Advocates of supply-side policies also call for further legislation to change the institutional framework within which the labour market operates. For example, various statutes enacted in the past to protect employees from unfair dismissal and to provide compensation for redundancy may now have the effect of discouraging potential employers from taking on new workers because the cost of dismissing such workers, once hired, is so high.

The repeal of such statutes, it is argued, would increase the willingness of employers to recruit new workers. Supply-siders also advocate the abolition of **Wages Councils** which were established to raise wages in the lowest-paid occupations. These Wages Councils, it is argued, keep wages artificially high and therefore reduce the level of employment in such occupations. For similar reasons supply-siders also oppose the introduction of a national **minimum wage**, arguing that it would result in higher levels of unemployment.

Summary

The dynamics of labour market adjustment depends crucially on the way in which economic agents form their expectations of future price changes. Before the Rational Expectations revolution economists modelled expectations in a backward-looking way, which implied that economic agents consistently overpredicted or underpredicted the actual rate of inflation and did not learn from their mistakes. The REH assumes the opposite – that economic agents do not make systematic errors in predicting future inflation rates. When combined with a monetarist interpretation of the labour market, the REH can be used to show that expansionary policies cannot reduce unemployment, even in the short run.

As a tool for reducing unemployment, demand management along traditional Keynesian lines is thus shown to be ineffective, and the way is opened up for supply-side policies. When applied to the labour market, these take the form of policies designed to improve incentives and reduce disincentives, through changes in the tax and social security systems.

Notes

1   See, for example: Beenstock, M., (October 1979) 'Taxation and incentives in the UK', *Lloyds Bank Review* (134). Beenstock, however, used total tax revenue rather than revenue from direct taxes or revenue from direct personal taxes. My estimate, using NIESR data, related revenue from direct personal taxes to the average tax rate. The estimated equations were:

$$REV = 13.1 + 285.3T \quad R^2 = 0.625$$
$$(2.4) \quad (9.2)$$

$$REV = -18.2 + 638.2T - 982.3T^2 \quad R^2 = 0.620$$
$$(-0.3) \quad (1.1) \quad (-0.6)$$

The fact that the coefficient on T^2 is statistically insignificant suggests a linear relationship rather than a non-linear one.

Key terms

Review questions

14.1 Which of the following statements best describes the concept of 'rationality' embodied in rational expectations:
(a) Economic agents always forecast the future correctly.
(b) People anticipate future events. On average their expectations are correct.
(c) Economic agents base their expectations of the future on past events.
(d) People's expectations of price inflation next year are correct.

14.2 Suppose it could be shown that the relationship between tax revenue and the average (direct personal) tax rate was non-linear (as it is between points A and B in Fig. 14.3). Which of the following are necessarily true:
(a) This is evidence that taxes have a disincentive effect.
(b) If tax rates were lowered, tax revenue would rise.
(c) If tax rates were lowered, tax revenue would fall.

14.3 Classify the following taxes into direct or indirect tax:
(a) Income tax;
(b) Capital gains tax;
(c) Value added tax;
(d) Vehicle excise duty;
(e) Council tax.

14.4 Figure 14.4 shows the impact of indirect taxes, direct taxes, cash benefits and benefits in kind. Which of these four measures is the most regressive and which is the most progressive?

14.5 Which of the following are valid arguments for not making the tax system more progressive:
(a) It will encourage the growth of the black economy.
(b) People have already reached the limit of their taxable capacity.
(c) It will further encourage evasion.
(d) People are more aware of income taxes than they are of taxes on spending. Therefore they resent them more.

15 The formulation and implementation of economic policies

Preview

This chapter looks at how the policy-maker combines instruments so as to produce a beneficial effect on the various targets of economic policy. It considers the nature of economic forecasting models and how to assess the accuracy of those models and the forecasts that emanate from them. Finally, it considers whether active intervention in the economy, in the form of fine-tuning, can be counterproductive.

15.1 The objectives of macroeconomic policy

The preceding chapters of this book have discussed in detail the major objectives of macroeconomic policy. These can be restated as follows:

- The rate of growth of real output should be as high as possible.
- The rate of inflation should be as low as possible.
- The level of unemployment should be as low as possible.

239

- Balance of payments deficits should not be allowed to become so large that they make other objectives more difficult to achieve.

Not everyone would agree with the way in which these four objectives have been specified, nor the way in which they have been ranked, but there would be general agreement that, when we are considering inflation, for example, less is better than more; and that when we are considering economic growth, more is better than less. To these four major macroeconomic objectives we could add many others: to achieve a reduction in regional disparities in income and employment; to ensure that the standard of the public services – education, health etc. – is as high as possible; to achieve an acceptable distribution of income among the members of society, and so on.

15.2 The balance between public and private spending

To a large extent, however, political opinions colour one's attitudes towards these issues. One of the major areas of disagreement between left and right wing parties is the balance between public and private spending. This is a disagreement both about ends and about the means by which these ends should be achieved.

In as much as a high level of consumption of, for example, health care and education is accepted as a desirable end, the dispute between left and right is about the means by which that high level of consumption should be brought about – should these services be provided publicly or should the individual purchase them for himself? But in as much as the high level of public expenditure determines the degree of influence of the State on the lives of its citizens, the debate over the extent to which the State should provide these services is also a debate about the desirability of increased public expenditure as an end in itself.

The public provision of these services is also an egalitarian measure, however, providing **income-in-kind** for all members of society and therefore leading to a more equal distribution of income. Increased public expenditure on these services will therefore tend to find more support from those who advocate a more equal distribution of income. In this sense increased public expenditure is a means towards the end of a greater equality, and in this case there is disagreement as to the desirability of that end.

15.3 Conflicts in objectives

As we saw earlier, each of the four major objectives – economic growth, the control of inflation and of employment, and the avoidance of balance of payments deficits – would be more or less universally accepted as desirable when considered separately. The problem is that these four objectives are often in **conflict** so that an improvement in one of them can only be achieved at the expense of one or more of the others. For example, a reduction in unemployment can normally be achieved by stimulating aggregate demand (for example, by cutting income tax). But this same increase in aggregate demand will also increase the demand for imports and thus may lead to a trade deficit. Moreover, any increase in aggregate demand will increase demand-inflationary pressures and may increase the rate of inflation. In a similar way, measures which are taken to remove a trade deficit – measures such as domestic deflation and higher interest rates, may have an adverse long-term effect on economic growth since they discourage investment.

15.4 The instruments of economic policy

Faced with these (often conflicting) objectives, the policy-maker has a variety of instruments available. These can be classified as either **fiscal instruments**, or **monetary instruments** or **direct controls**. Fiscal policy, which emanates from the Treasury and is normally the subject of the annual Budget, consists of changes in taxation (of all forms) and in all forms of public spending. Monetary policy, which emanates from the Bank of England, which is a separate institution from the Treasury, consists of changes in interest rates and in the growth of the money supply. The term 'direct controls' covers the remaining policy instruments – for example, direct controls on wages or import controls.

In the UK it is the Chancellor of the Exchequer who is the policy-maker with overriding control over these instruments. This is despite the fact that, in theory at least, the Central Bank has a degree of independence in determining monetary policy, and indeed in 1997 was given nominal independence in setting interest rates and other monetary instruments.

15.5 Targets and instruments

Each of the instruments which the policy-makers have at their disposal will have an impact on more than one of the objectives, or **target variables** as we shall call them. For example, an increase in public spending may reduce unemployment, but at the same time it may increase imports and the rate of inflation. The pressure on the balance of payments can be eased by using a second instrument, such as raising interest rates, to encourage an inflow of short-term capital. This, however, may discourage firms from investing (in fixed capital formation), in which case a third instrument, such as a tax-cut, may be required to boost demand for domestic output, and so encourage investment spending.

Clearly, the macroeconomy is a very complex set of inter-relationships between variables. We could say that ultimately a change in any one of our instrument variables will affect all the other variables in the system. An economic policy can be defined as a set of changes (many of them zero) in all of the instruments that the policy-maker has at his disposal. The question is, how should the policy-maker go about formulating an economic policy so as to bring about the best possible outcome in the economy?

15.6 Constructing an economic model

There are several stages in the formulation of an economic policy. The first stage – and the essential prerequisite – is to have some idea about the way the economy works. These ideas can be formalised in terms of an **economic model** which will take the form of a set of equations which describe the inter-relationships between the variables in the system. These inter-relationships can be visually represented by means of a flow-chart such as that shown in Fig. 15.1, where the direction of the arrows between the boxes represents the direction of causation between variables. For example, the exchange rate affects import prices, which, in turn, affect the volume of imports. This, in turn, affects the current trade balance. Import prices are also affected by foreign prices and by the overall domestic price index and so on. Note that this flow chart is not meant to be a faithful reproduction of the equations of the Treasury model. In the same way that the map of the London Underground simplifies and distorts for the sake of clarity, so this classic 'map' of the Treasury model is an attempt to represent hundreds of behavioural equations in a visual form which is capable of being understood.

The variables within the model can be sub-divided into two main groups, as follows:

1 **Exogenous variables** affect other variables in the system, but are not themselves affected by what is happening within the system.
2 **Endogenous variables**, on the other hand, both affect and are affected by other variables in the model. In Fig. 15.1 all the endogenous variables are shown in *boxes* and the exogenous variables in *circles*.

The endogenous variables can be further sub-divided into the main *target variables* (shown with thick lines) and the remaining *intermediate variables*.

The exogenous variables can also be sub-divided into two subsets. Those exogenous variables which are under the control of the policy-maker are the *instruments*; for example, indirect tax rates and, arguably, the exchange rate. The remaining exogenous variables, such as the level of world trade, which clearly affects the values of the endogenous variables in the system but over which the policy-maker has no control, are known as *predetermined variables*. The nature of the relationships between any two variables can then be estimated by applying a statistical technique such as regression analysis to data collected in previous years. We say that the 'parameters of the equations are estimated.'

15.7 Forecasting and the formulation of economic policy

The second stage in the process of economic policy formulation is to use the model to forecast the future levels of the target variables. Because of the way the model is structured, the values of the exogenous variables determine the values of all the other variables in the system. Once the forecaster has fixed the values of these

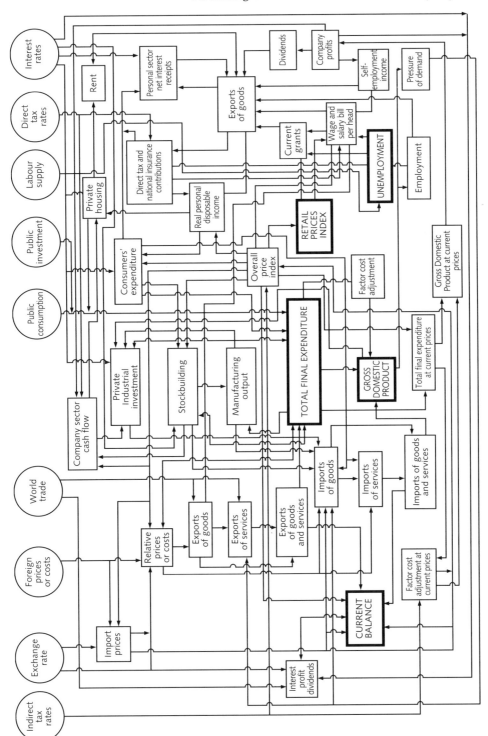

Figure 15.1 Flow chart of the Treasury Macroeconomic model *Source: HM Treasury Macroeconomic Technical Manual, 1978.*

exogenous variables the model can then be used to work out the values of all the endogenous variables and, in particular, the target variables. Typically, initially the values of the instruments will be set at their current levels (indicating no change in policy). The predetermined variables will have to be forecast separately, or some other forecast of their values used.

The process of policy formation starts with this initial forecast. The forecast values of the target variables represent the forecaster's best estimate of what is likely to happen in the economy in, say, twelve months' time, if current policies are unchanged. The values of the target variables are inspected and if, as usually happens, they appear unsatisfactory in the sense that, for example, the predicted rate of inflation is higher than we would like it to be, then the model is used to investigate the probable effects of changing one or more of the instruments. For example, the effect of reducing income tax by two pence in the pound can be predicted by setting the tax rate at this new lower level, while leaving all the other exogenous variables unchanged, and using the model to predict the new levels of the target variables. Normally, some of the targets will be better and some worse than previously.

In this way a series of laboratory experiments or **simulations** can be conducted, whose purpose is to investigate the effects on the targets of changes in our instruments. Since, in the real macroeconomy, experimentation is impractical and controlled experimentation is impossible, these simulations, made possible by advances in statistical techniques, but more importantly by the advent of the computer, fulfil a vital role. To quote from the Treasury itself: 'The Treasury model is used extensively for estimating the effects of possible policy changes: along with forecasting, this is the model's major use.'[1]

Several different policies can be tried out by conducting several simulation exercises. In this way the policy-maker can find out which policies produce an acceptable set of solution values for the target variables. Several acceptable sets will probably present themselves and the policy-maker can then pick what he regards as the 'best' solution.

It should be made clear that the simulation exercises themselves cannot tell the policy-maker what is the 'best' attainable set of solution values and it therefore cannot tell him what is the 'best' policy to pursue. To understand the reason for this, consider the hypothetical forecast outcomes of two policies A and B, where A involves a lower level of public spending than B. The results are shown in Table 15.1.

Clearly, one cannot say that policy A produces a better result than policy B or that B produces a better result than A. Only if one specifies the relative importance which one attaches to the various objectives can one begin to talk of one policy being superior to another. For example, if one decided that the overriding objective was to maximise the rate of growth, then B is apparently more effective in achieving this. Things may not be quite as simple as they appear, however, since the effect of B *may* be to produce a lower rate of growth in the long term than A. Suppose, in this hypothetical example, that the forecasted state of the economy after 30 months was as shown in Table 15.2.

Table 15.1 Hypothetical outcomes of two policies

	State of economy after 12 months	
	if policy A followed (lower public spending)	if policy B followed (higher public spending)
Growth	2%	2½%
Inflation	4%	10%
Unemployment	2.8 m.	1 m.
Trade balance	£1 bn deficit	£3 bn deficit

Table 15.2 Hypothetical outcomes of two policies

	State of economy after 30 months	
	if policy A followed (lower public spending)	if policy B followed (higher public spending)
Growth	2.2%	2%
Inflation	4%	8%
Unemployment	2.7 m.	2.1 m.
Trade balance	surplus of £1 bn	deficit of £3 bn

The policy-maker then has to choose between a policy which produces relatively rapid growth for a short time but at high costs in terms of inflation and the balance of trade (policy B) and a policy which produces a higher rate of sustained growth but at a high cost in terms of unemployment (policy A). Thus the policy-maker not only has to decide on his priorities but also on his time preferences. The policy-maker's time horizon may be relatively short, particularly when faced with a general election. Myopia, it is said, is the price we pay for democracy.

15.8 The implementation of economic policy

Let us assume that, for whatever reasons, the policy-maker has decided upon his best policy. The implementation of this policy then involves setting the values of the instruments at the levels that the simulation indicates are required. This may or may not be straightforward but, in any event, it will take some time to achieve. Particular difficulties may be experienced if a reduction in public spending is called for.

The actual outcome of the chosen policy in the real world will not, of course, be exactly the same as the outcome predicted in the simulation exercises. In other words, the forecasts will be wrong. Of this the forecasters can be certain. The only thing that is uncertain is by how much they will be wrong, and in what direction.

There are various reasons why the actual outcome will not be the same as the predicted outcome. Many of these are what could be called errors of technique. For example, the parameters of the model – the numbers in the equations – may have been incorrectly estimated either because of poor statistical technique or because of inaccurate data used in the estimation procedure. Worse still, the structure of the model may be wrong. For example, the model may have missed out some vital element from an equation or the paradigm within which the model is constructed may be incorrect. Finally, since forecasting is not a completely mechanistic procedure, it involves the exercise of judgement which may, at times, be faulty.

Apart from the errors of technique there remain more fundamental reasons why the actual outcome will not be the same as the predicted outcome. First, the economy of the real world is subject to **random shocks** which cannot be predicted. Events such as war in the Middle East, a dock strike or an exceptionally hard winter will all affect the target variables and, although it may be possible to assign probabilities to the occurrence of these events, this is of little practical value to the forecaster.

Secondly, there is a problem which lies at the heart of econometric forecasting – that of **structural change**. The equations embodied within the model represent a more or less accurate description of the supposed structural relationships which existed in the real world during the period in which the data were collected. There is no reason to suppose, however, that the structural relationships in the real world will continue to hold in that future period to which our forecast relates. Indeed, there is every reason to suppose that the parameters will change over time, sometimes quite rapidly, and this effectively removes the statistical justification from our forecasting procedure. For example, the propensity to save out of income may, for all practical purposes, have remained constant for a long period. Suppose that, during this period, we collected data on savings and income and the constancy of the ratio between the two may have lulled us into a belief that our 'law' of savings behaviour, which we had 'discovered', was true for all time. But, unlike the laws of physics, the relationships between variables in the social world are not immutable, so that the forecasting process which implicitly assumes a constancy in social behaviour is based on shaky foundations.

15.9 The accuracy of economic forecasts

One question which immediately arises is, how accurate are such forecasts? Unfortunately, it is not possible to give a sensible answer to the question posed in this form since all forecasts are based on assumptions, which are rarely correct. The assumption most commonly adopted is that of **unchanged policies**. If a change does occur – for example, in the rate of income tax in the period to which the forecast relates – then, even if the *model* from which the forecast is derived is completely correct, the *forecast* will still turn out to be wrong. It is therefore important to distinguish between **forecast error** and **model error**. An example will make this point clearer.

Imagine that a model predicts that the rate of inflation for a particular year will be 8 per cent, and that this prediction is based on the assumption of *unchanged policies*. Suppose, however, that there is an increase in VAT and, if this change had been incorporated into the simulation, the model would have predicted a rate of inflation of 4 per cent. If the actual rate of inflation turns out to be 5 per cent, what is the size of the error, and is it an overprediction or an underprediction? The forecast error is calculated as '**actual minus predicted**', so it would appear to be $5 - 8 = -3$ (that is, an *overprediction* of 3. However, if the correct assumption had been incorporated into the model, the error would have been $5 - 4 = +1$ (that is, an *underprediction* of 1). In this example, therefore, we could say that the forecast error is -3 but the model error is $+1$.

15.10 Estimating the equations of a model

Before we look at some estimates of the predictive accuracy of one particular econometric model, it will be useful to consider how the equations of such a model are estimated. Suppose, for illustrative purposes, that we wish to estimate an export function of the form:

$$X = a + bW \qquad \qquad [15.1]$$

where X is UK exports, W is world trade and a and b are the **parameters** of the equation – the numbers whose values we wish to estimate. In practice, an export function would be more complicated than this, since other explanatory variables apart from world trade – such as the exchange rate – would affect exports. The advantage of this simplified version, however, is that we can illustrate the relationship on a two-dimensional graph. Moreover, this export function can be treated independently of the rest of the model since here exports are a function of an *exogenous* variable only. It would not be so straightforward to deal with an import equation such as:

$$M = f(Yd) \qquad \qquad [15.2]$$

where M is imports and Yd is disposable income, since both these variables are *endogenous* and hence both have to be forecast together, using the model rather than a single equation.

Suppose that we have a series of observations on UK exports and world trade as in Table 15.3 and Fig. 15.2. The period 1969-78 has been selected for expositional convenience and we can see from Fig. 15.2 that there is a relationship between the two variables which is approximately linear. Thus we can legitimately represent this relationship by an equation of the form:

$$X = a + bW \qquad \qquad [15.1 \text{ repeated}]$$

However, we wish to know how good this equation is and we will use **predictive accuracy** as an indicator of this. The equation can be used to 'forecast' the level of

Table 15.3 UK exports and world trade, 1969–78

		X	W
	1969	17 614	257.1
X = UK exports	1970	19 351	294.6
(millions of US dollars)	1971	22 333	329.0
	1972	24 345	284.9
W = World trade	1973	30 659	534.9
(billions of US dollars)	1974	38 881	785.2
	1975	44 523	814.0
	1976	46 696	922.9
	1977	58 205	1000.3
	1978	71 705	1229.6

Source: International Financial Statistics.

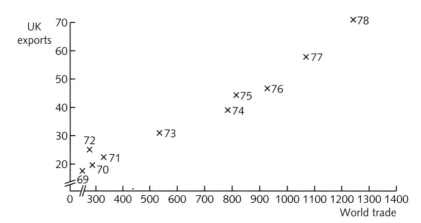

Figure 15.2 Exports and world trade

exports in 1978 and compare the forecast value with the actual value – which in this example is known already.

We could use *all* of the data to estimate the relationship. The line which provides that best fit[3] to the set of points for 1969-78 is:

$$X = 5329 + 49.3W$$

Such an equation would underpredict the level of exports in 1978. In fact, the predicted or forecast level of exports in 1978 is:

$$5329 + 49.3 (1229.6) = 65\,948$$

The *forecast error* is therefore the actual level of exports in 1978 minus the predicted level:

$$71\,705 - 65\,948 = 5757$$

This is known as an **ex post forecast error** since the forecast was derived from an equation, the parameters of which were estimated when the actual level of exports was already known.

By comparison, an **ex ante forecast** is one which predicts into the future using an equation estimated from past data. In this example, if we omitted the last observation and estimated the parameters using data for the period 1969-77 only (as opposed to 1969–78), then the line which best fits this set of points is:

$$X = 7468 + 44.5W$$

If we assume that the value of the exogenous variable is known, having been derived independently from some completely accurate forecasting procedure, we can plug this value into the equation and, therefore, the ex ante forecast of exports in 1978 is:

$$7468 + 44.5\,(1229.6) = 62\,185$$

and the ex ante forecast error is:

$$71\,705 - 62\,185 = 9520$$

This is illustrated in Fig. 15.3. Note that the inclusion of the observation for 1978 has the effect of rotating the fitted line slightly in an anti-clockwise direction. Note also that, as we would expect, the ex post forecast error is smaller than the ex ante forecast error. Since this is generally true, it is therefore important, in assessing the accuracy of forecasts, to know whether ex post or ex ante forecasts are being discussed.

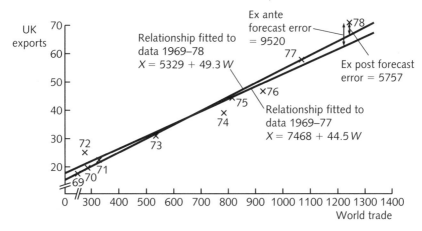

Figure 15.3 The fitted line depends on which observations are included

15.11 Decomposition of forecast errors

An ex ante forecast (that is, a prediction of the future using past data) can be broken down into four parts, as follows:

- **Exogenous variable error**. We noted above that the ex ante forecast of exports was *conditional* upon the value of the exogenous variable world trade. We assumed that the correct value of this was known. In practice, of course, when ex ante forecasts are made of the future, the exogenous variables have to be forecast first and these forecasts will themselves be subject to error. Any error in the forecast of the exogenous variable feeds through into an error in the forecast of other endogenous variables in the model. The error which results from the use of an incorrect value for the exogenous variable such as world trade is known as the *exogenous variable error*.
- **Residual adjustment**. Although the estimated equations do not fit the data exactly, on average they should neither systematically overpredict nor systematically underpredict. If such a fault develops over time, then the equation should be re-estimated to remove the bias. This may not be possible, however, and in this case a 'residual' is added on to the equation in forecasting to take the systematic error into account. The *residual adjustment* consists of setting all of these judgmental and other adjustments back to zero.
- **Data revision**. This takes account of the revisions to the published data on both endogenous and exogenous variables which are frequently carried out in the period following the initial publication.

When these three sources of forecast error are taken into account we are left with:

- **Model error**. This is the error which remains because the equation is not a perfect explanation of the behaviour of the economy (for example, the behaviour of exports).

To summarise, one can distinguish between *forecast error* and *model error*. The forecast error will consist of extra components in addition to the model error itself. These additional components are exogenous variable error, residual adjustment error and data revision error. In principle, the total forecast error could be decomposed into these four constituent parts.

The results of such an exercise are illustrated in Table 15.4.

Removing the other sources of forecast error so as to arrive at pure model error is a time-consuming process which in practice it is seldom possible to carry out in the way that the NIESR team did. The forecasters at the Treasury took this view when they wrote:

Table 15.4 NIESR February 1979 forecast: decomposition of forecast error

		1	2	3	4	5	6	7
					Composed of effects from			
Variable	Units of measurement	Feb. '79 forecast values	Actual values	Total error	Exogenous variable error	Model error	Residual adjustment	Data revision
GDP (output method)	index 1975 = 10	110.2	110.2	—	−0.6	5.8	−5.6	0.3
GDP (expenditure method)	£m 1975 prices	103 482	102 563	−919	−138	220	−1328	328
Consumers' expenditure	£m 1975 prices	68 777	70 816	2039	805	1747	−898	384
Gross fixed investment	£m 1975 prices	20 835	20 506	−329	−496	−234	186	215
Stockbuilding	£m 1975 prices	11 390	11 610	220	94	680	−424	−130
General govt. consumption	£m 1975 prices	24 020	24 334	314	314	—	—	—
Exports	£m 1975 prices	33 713	32 896	−817	210	746	−1570	−203
Imports	£m 1975 prices	33 430	35 250	1820	965	1853	−891	−107
Employment	thousands	22 232	22 269	37	44	36	−115	71
Unemployment	thousands	1350	1243	−107	−97	9	86	−105
Consumer prices	1975 = 100	158.0	162.1	4.1	1.9	2.0	−1.4	1.6
Money supply (M3)	£m	57 497	59 411	1914	3863	42	−1360	−631
PSFS	£m	−7991	−8344	−353	−1322	1656	−3650	2963
Visible balance	£m	95	−3404	−3499	−2454	315	−1189	−171
Effective exchange rate	May 1971 = 10	63.5	68.7	5.2	5.2	—	—	—

Note: The total error to be explained (col. 3) is the difference between actual values (col. 2) and ex ante forecast values (col. 1). Apart from rounding errors, cols 4, 5, 6 and 7 sum to the total error in col. 3
Source: National Institute Economic Review, February 1981.

In principle, there are two ways (of assessing the accuracy of forecasting models). The first is to ask what would have been forecast if the correct assumptions on policy had been made: the answer is that nobody knows, because it is not possible to reassemble the people responsible for the original forecast, their technical apparatus and their state of mind at the time. The second way is to ask present day forecasters what the outcome would have been if the assumed policies (rather than the actual ones) had been carried out. With the aid of an econometric model, some kind of an answer can be provided.

Source: Economic Progress Report, June 1991, p.3.

In practice, this is the technique which is often used to assess the accuracy of forecasting models.

In addition – and in contrast – simple **forecasting accuracy** is often used to assess a model and the modellers who control it. The results of a recent assessment of the model at the National Institute for Economic and Social Research are shown in Table 15.5.

Note that these are forecasts made in November of each year. The forecasts for the 'current year' shown in columns 1 and 2 are therefore partly ex post forecasts. The forecasts for the 'year ahead' are ex ante forecasts of the future (and the errors are therefore larger). The error shown is the **average absolute error** – that is, the sign of the error (positive or negative) is ignored. If this were not done, positive errors could be cancelled out by negative ones, thereby giving the impression that the model is a better predictor than it in fact is.

15.12 Fine-tuning

Our analysis so far has neglected one important aspect of economic policy, namely that the operation of such policies is subject to **long and variable time lags**. The existence of these lags, which are difficult to judge precisely, could mean that a policy designed to stabilise the level of demand could end up by producing a destabilising effect on the economy.

Suppose, for illustrative purposes, that demand is subject to fluctuations over time, as in Fig. 15.4. In the real world these **cycles** in economic activity are irregular in both duration and in severity but, for the purpose of illustration, we have assumed that they are reasonably regular around a rising trend, which indicates the growth path of the economy.

In the absence of any attempt by the authorities at smoothing out fluctuations, the **peaks** of the cycle will be characterised by the economy 'overheating', leading to shortages of labour and capital and to inflation; and the **troughs** of the cycle will be characterised by rising unemployment, falling profits and falling output. Clearly, a successful demand management policy would *reduce* the level of demand during the peaks of the cycle (by engineering a budget surplus) and *increase* demand during the troughs (by a budget deficit). Figure 15.5 illustrates an ideal policy where both the **magnitude** and the **timing** of the policy are exactly correct.

Table 15.5 Average absolute errors, NIESR forecasts made in November of each year, 1982-94 (all figures are per cent except for current account and PSBR which are £bn and are shown in italics)

	Current year		Year ahead		
	Average error	Error range	Average error	Average error range	Outturn 1982-95
Real GDP growth	0.5	0.0–1.5	1.4	0.0–2.9	2.4
Domestic demand growth	0.7	0.0–2.5	1.6	0.0–4,4	2.6
Consumers' expenditure growth	0.9	0.0–1.9	1.9	0.1–4.2	2.8
Investment growth	2.3	0.8–6.4	3.8	0.2–10.1	3.2
Export volume growth	1.3	0.3–3.1	2.5	0.0–7.0	4.2
Import volume growth	1.6	0.3–2.8	2.8	0.1–11.1	5.2
Real personal disposable income growth	1.3	0.2–2.7	1.5	0.2–3.1	2.7
Current account (£bn)	*2.3*	*0.4–5.8*	*4.6*	*0.5–13.7*	*–6.2*
Public sector borrowing requirement (£bn)	*2.6*	*0.3–4.7*	*8.6*	*0.1–17.6*	*12.5*
Retail price inflation (Q4)	0.2	0.0–0.4	1.6	0.4–4.8	4.7

Note: all errors defined by subtracting the forecast from the outturns for 1982–94.
Source: derived from *National Institute Economic Review*, Q4 1996.

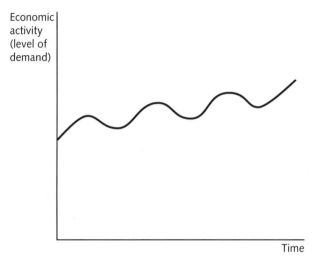

Figure 15.4 Fluctuations in activity

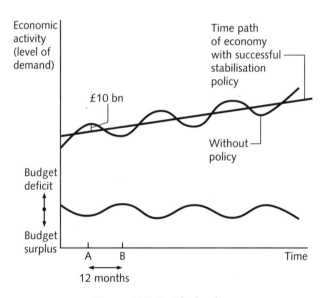

Figure 15.5 An ideal policy

For example, at the point in time labelled A, demand in the economy exceeds its ideal level by £10 bn. Note, however, that this does not imply that the budget surplus at that time should be £10 bn. The reason for this is two-fold. First, any action taken at A will not take effect immediately; it will be subject to time lags, so that a successful policy would need to have been implemented some months or even years earlier. Secondly, the budget surplus would not have to be exactly

£10 bn, because any fiscal policy would be subject to a multiplier effect, the exact size of which may be difficult to estimate. These problems emphasise the necessity of constructing forecasting models which accurately predict and reflect the way the economy works.

Suppose, however, that the policy is mis-timed even though its magnitude is correct. In the worst possible case, deflationary policies taken at A do not have their full effect on the economy until, say, twelve months later at point B. Here the boom has already passed and the economy is in the trough of a recession, so that further deflationary policies just make matters worse. In this extreme case, illustrated in Fig. 15.6, the fluctuations in economic activity are made worse by the ill-timed stabilisation policy of the government.

Because it is, in theory, possible that the existence of these long and variable time lags could make stabilisation policy operate in a perverse manner, some economists have argued that the government should not attempt to **fine-tune** the economy. Consider the analogy with a shower. Your objective, when standing in the shower, is to get the water temperature just right. There are two instruments available, a hot tap and a cold tap, both of which are subject to long and variable time lags. If the water is slightly too cold, you may be tempted to turn on the hot tap a little more, but when you do this, at first nothing seems to happen, so you turn it on a lot more. Then suddenly the shower is far too hot, so you turn off the hot tap and turn on the cold tap and this makes it much too cold. Your intervention has made matters worse rather than better because you did not fully appreciate the long and variable time lags involved in your actions.

In short, when the government tries to fine-tune the economy, there are difficult technical problems of timing and magnitude which may result in the policy having a destabilising rather than a stabilising effect on the economy. Monetarists

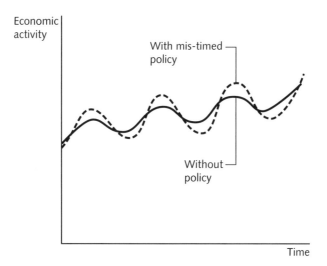

Figure 15.6 A mis-timed policy

generally argue that it is better for the government not to pursue **discretionary stabilisation policy**. Rather, it should rely on automatic **rules** or on what they see as the automatic, self-righting tendency of the economy. A market economy, they believe, is a self-equilibrating mechanism; that is, in the long run, given reasonably flexible wages and prices, the economy will tend towards the full-employment level of output. Thus, it is not *necessary* for the government in intervene in an attempt to stabilise the economy and it may be *undesirable* for it to do so, both for technical reasons (they may make matters worse) and for political ones (state intervention is bad *per se*).

This argument, however, ignores the fact that the government, whether it likes it or not, *does* influence the level of demand in the economy, through the expenditure it is committed to undertaking in the fields of health care, education, the environment and so on. It has a vastly greater influence than any other single agent because it is 'the last of the big spenders'. Moreover, it should be noted that the growth of state spending has in itself made the economy less susceptible to fluctuations in economic activity caused by random shocks to the system. Given the way in which public spending programmes are planned and executed, they fall much less readily in a recession than, for example, investment spending by private firms. This tends to reduce the magnitude of fluctuations. Some spending may even act in a **counter-cyclical** way, since social security and unemployment benefits, for example, tend to rise in a recession and fall in a boom, acting as a sort of **automatic stabiliser**. Britain in the 1990s, an economy with a large public sector, thus tends to be more robust than in the 1920s and 1930s.

However, given that, as we have seen, the government does exert a great influence on the level of economic activity, it follows that it is a powerful influence for good or evil. The idea that the economy is self-righting is quite untenable when one-third of economic activity (more or less depending upon how you define it) is controlled directly or indirectly by government. Thus, although one can admit the difficulties of fine-tuning and perhaps the undesirability of attempting to do so, ultimately the government cannot abrogate its responsibility for controlling the economy.

15.13 Forecasting and control

In the public imagination economic forecasters used to occupy the same sort of position as weather forecasters. No one believed them and their forecasts were treated with a sort of grim amusement. In recent years, however, photographs of weather systems taken by satellites and other improvements in technology have given meteorologists a perspective on their study which has enormously improved their forecasting and their knowledge about what determines the weather. Sadly, economic forecasters have still to find this perspective and, given the nature of their study, it is unlikely that they ever will.

In comparison with weather forecasters, economic forecasters suffer two major drawbacks. First, economists are dealing with a *social system*, the laws of which are subject to change, unlike the laws of nature that determine the weather and which are immutable. Secondly, weather forecasts do not in themselves affect the weather. If storms are predicted, this may cause people to take their umbrellas when they go out, but this in itself does not increase the probability of rain. In the economy, however, the outturn is not independent of the forecast, because forecasts affect people's behaviour. Thus, if high rates of inflation are predicted, this may cause individuals to reduce their stocks of money by purchasing goods and other assets, which in turn may affect their price. Similarly, business confidence and hence the level of corporate investment may be affected by the publication of surveys of companies' investment intentions. In short, forecasts can have an impact on events in the economy.

While this may be seen as a disadvantage which the economic forecaster has in comparison with the meteorologist, it also provides the most important reason for continuing to strive to understand the economy. For, if the economist understands the way the economy works, then he or she can *control* it. Meteorologists, no matter how good their understanding, can never affect the weather – they can never make the sun shine nor the rains come. But economists can, if they are successful, improve employment prospects, reduce inflation and improve living standards. They can, in short, make a better world. Or, if they are misguided or incompetent, a worse one.

Summary

Conflicts exist between the various objectives of economic policy. An economic policy consists of using a combination of instruments so as to achieve the best possible level of the target variables, taking into account the conflicts which exist between them. To this end, macroeconomic models are used. These are sets of equations which try to represent the behavioural relationships that exist in the real world. To assess how good a model is, one can compare actual versus predicted values of all the key variables. However, one must first of all strip out from the total forecast error the errors which are attributable not to the model itself but to other causes.

Discretionary intervention could in theory destabilise the economy rather than stabilise it, and for this reason some economists advocate a 'hands-off' approach to economic management.

Notes

1 *Economic Progress Report*, June 1981, p.2.
2 *Economic Progress Report*, June 1981, p.3.
3 Using Ordinary Least Square regression, this technique fits a line such that the sum of the squared differences between the actual export levels and predicted export levels is minimised.

Key terms

Review questions

15.1 Here is a list of variables which enter into most macroeconomic models. Classify them into:

Exogenous – instruments (controlled by policy-makers)
– pre-determined (not controlled by policy-makers)
Endogenous – targets
– other endogenous

But beware: controversy exists as to how certain of these variables should be classified.

(a) indirect tax rates;
(b) revenue from direct taxes;
(c) the exchange rate;
(d) the price index;
(e) import prices;
(f) world trade;
(g) interest rates;
(h) government spending;
(i) the labour supply;
(j) the money supply.

T his appendix is designed to provide an elementary understanding of the microeconomic theory of value, or what is usually known as demand and supply analysis. This forms part, undoubtedly the most basic part, of the economist's analytical apparatus – the 'bag of tools' used to interpret economic events taking place in the real world. Anyone who has successfully completed an introductory course in microeconomics will already be familiar with these concepts.

A.1 Demand

Consider the concept of a market. The 'market' that we are talking about here need not have any physical existence in space or time (although some markets such as the stock market did possess these attributes prior to deregulation). In general, however, the word **market** refers to the totality of buyers and sellers, both actual and potential, of a particular good or commodity. Thus, we could talk about the housing market, the market for cars, for shoes, for wine and so on. Suppose we illustrate the concepts of **demand** and **supply** in the context of the market for orange juice. Although it is obvious that there are different brands of orange juice, some brands being more expensive than others according to specification, we will make the simplifying assumption that they are all sufficiently similar to be treated as the same commodity. That is, we will assume that orange juice is a **homogeneous** commodity.

It seems intrinsically obvious that the demand for orange juice will be inversely related to the price – that is, the lower the price the more will people be willing to buy and, conversely, the higher the price the less will people want to buy. Other factors will also affect the demand for orange juice, such as the extent to which it is promoted by advertising, the price of other drinks, of fresh oranges and so on. For the moment suppose that all these other factors can be held constant – this is the so-called **ceteris paribus** assumption. We can then study the relationship between the demand for orange juice and its price in isolation. Such a relationship, if it were plotted on a graph, might look like that in Fig. A.1. If the selling price were very high, say £3 per carton, then few people would be prepared to buy it – so sales would be only 5000 cartons per week in our example. But, if the price were to drop to, say, £1, then sales would rise to, say, 20 000 cartons; and if the price were to fall further to 50p, then sales of 40 000 cartons a week would occur.

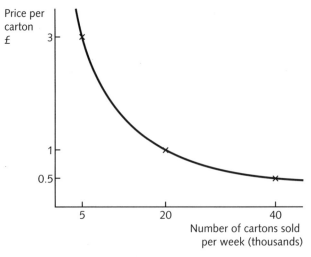

Figure A.1 The demand curve for orange juice

The demand curve (or demand schedule) shown in Fig. A.1 is, of course, only illustrative, but it demonstrates the fundamental axiom that, in the market for any commodity, if all other factors are held constant, then demand will be inversely related to price – the higher the price, the less will be demanded, and the lower the price, the more will be demanded.

A.2 Price elasticity of demand

We now consider the question: 'How sensitive is the demand for orange juice to changes in its price? For example, would a fall in the price of orange juice of, say, 10 per cent lead to an increase in demand of 5 per cent, 10 per cent or 20 per cent?

Economists use the term **elasticity** to describe the responsiveness of one variable (in this case demand) to another variable (in this case price). The **price elasticity of demand** is a numerical value which describes the degree of responsiveness of demand to changes in price. Price elasticity of demand (e_D) is defined as:

$$e_D = \frac{\% \text{ change in quantity demanded}}{\% \text{ change in price}}$$

This number will vary between zero and infinity. We can identify three ranges, as follows:

less than 1 – inelastic, that is, not very responsive to price changes.
equal to 1 – unit elasticity
greater than 1– elastic, that is, very responsive to price changes.

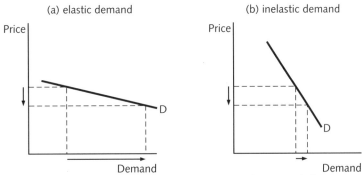

Figure A.2 The slope of the curve gives an indication of elasticity

For example, if a 10 per cent fall in price leads to a 20 per cent increase in demand, then the value of the elasticity coefficient is 2 (or strictly speaking, minus 2) and demand is said to be *elastic*. However, if a 10 per cent fall in price leads to a rise in demand of only 10 per cent then demand is of unit elasticity. And finally, if a 10 per cent fall in price leads to a rise in demand of a mere 3 per cent, then the value of the elasticity coefficient is 0.3 and demand is described as being very inelastic.

There is a relationship between the *slope* of the demand curve and its elasticity and it is sometimes convenient to represent the slope of the demand curve as an indication of elasticity (though it is not strictly correct to do so). For our purposes, however, we cay say that the *steeper* the slope of the demand curve, the more *inelastic* (insensitive) is demand. Figure A.2 illustrates this. The same fall in price produces a much greater increase in the amount demanded when the demand curve is elastic (as in diagram a) than when the demand is inelastic (as in diagram b).

A.3 Shifts in demand

Up to now we have been analysing the demand for orange juice as if the non-price factors affecting demand were constant (the *ceteris paribus* assumption). We now relax this assumption and consider the effect of changes in these other variables. The demand for orange juice can be expected to increase as a result of a successful advertising campaign by the manufacturers or retailers. We can show the effect of this by a *shift to the right* of the demand curve, indicating an increased willingness to purchase orange juice at each price.

In Fig. A.3 the effect of the advertising campaign is to shift the demand curve to D'. Thus, at a price of £1, demand increases from 20 000 cartons per week before the campaign to 28 000 cartons per week after the campaign.

A.4 Supply

We now turn to a consideration of those factors which influence the supply of a good. In the example chosen here, the market for orange juice, the supply

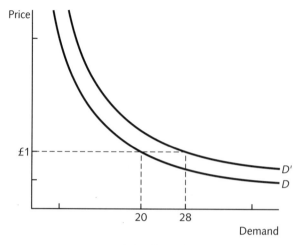

Figure A.3 A shift of the demand curve

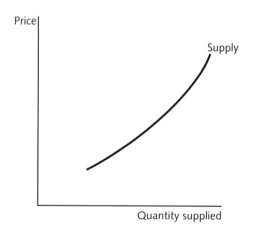

Figure A.4 The market supply curve

emanates from a large number of producers and manufacturers. These firms are interested in profit. Hence, the higher the price of orange juice the more they will be willing to supply, and the more new firms there will be who are attracted into the market for supplying orange juice. Thus, we could imagine a sort of market **supply curve** – in many ways the analogue of the market demand curve – such as that depicted in Fig. A.4. This market supply curve is drawn under the same *ceteris paribus* assumptions that we applied earlier to the demand curve – that is, all non-price factors which affect the supply of orange juice are assumed to be held constant. The positive slope of the supply curve illustrates the axiom that an increase in market price is associated with an increase in supply, and *vice versa*.

A.5 The elasticity of supply

In the same way that we talked earlier about the responsiveness of demand to price changes, so we can talk here about the responsiveness of supply to price changes. This is measured by the **elasticity of supply**. The price elasticity of supply (e_s) is defined as:

$$e_S = \frac{\%\ \text{change in quantity supplied}}{\%\ \text{change in price}}$$

This too will vary between 0 and infinity, a value near zero indicating that supply does not respond very readily to price changes, and a value substantially greater than one indicating that it requires only a small increase in price to bring forth a greatly increased supply. As before, the steepness of the slope of the supply curve gives a rough indication of its elasticity, a steep slope indicating an inelastic supply and *vice versa*.

A.6 Shifts in the supply curve

Moreover, in the same way that we talked earlier about changes in non-price factors causing shifts in the demand curve, so when we look at the supply curve it is clear that changes in certain non-price factors will affect supply. This will result in a shift to the right or to the left of the supply schedule. For example, late frosts which affect the orange blossoms will reduce the yield per hectare and as a result growers will supply less at every price than they did previously. This is illustrated in Fig. A.5.

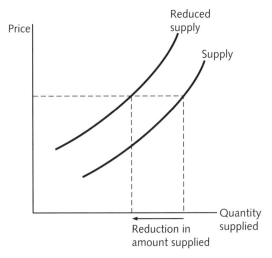

Figure A.5 A shift in supply

A.7 The determination of market price

We can now show how the price at which goods are sold is determined by the interaction of demand and supply. In Fig. A.6 we put both the demand curve and the supply curve together on the same diagram. At a price of £1.20 per carton, total market demand will be 18 000 cartons per week. Provided they receive £1.20 per carton for their product, sellers as a group are willing to supply 18 000 units. Thus £1.20 represents an **equilibrium price**, a price at which the demand is equated with the supply.

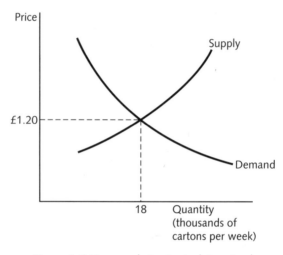

Figure A.6 How market price is determined

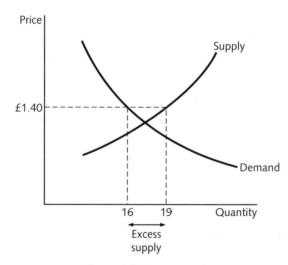

Figure A.7 Excess supply

To emphasise this point, consider what would happen at a price of £1.40, as in Fig. A.7. This is a disequilibrium situation because the increase in price from £1.20 to £1.40 chokes off some of the demand, which falls back from 18 000 cartons to 16 000 cartons per week. Because of the higher price, however, manufacturers will be persuaded to increase their output of orange juice to 19 000 cartons per week. Supply at 19 000 cartons thus outstrips demand at 16 000 cartons. This results in unsold stock in supermarkets and in the manufacturers' warehouses. Production is cut back in order to avoid an excessive build-up of unsold stock and retailers and consumers are offered 'discount' prices in an attempt to increase sales. As long as there is an excess supply this process will continue. Prices will fall until we reach the equilibrium price, at which point consumers are prepared to purchase all the output being produced.

It should be stressed that a market – whether it be the market for orange juice or any other market – is a self-equilibrating mechanism. No outside intervention is required in order to ensure that the equilibrium price and equilibrium quantity will eventually be arrived at since there are forces which arise automatically, which tend to push the market towards its equilibrium point. Thus, although the market may be out of equilibrium temporarily – and this disequilibrium situation may sometimes be rather prolonged – eventually producers and consumers will respond to the price signals which the market emits, and the amount supplied and demanded will come into equality.

Chapter 1

1.1 (a) spending on imported goods – withdrawal (leakage);
   (b) saving part of one's income – withdrawal;
   (c) government spending on defence – injection;
   (d) an increase in taxation – withdrawal;
   (e) an increase in export sales – injection;
   (f) building a Channel Tunnel – injection.
      In this simple model of the circular flow it makes no difference whether the Channel Tunnel is financed publicly or privately. Spending is spending no matter how it is financed.

1.2 There are two reasons why an increase in demand may not lead to an increase in output.
      First, some of the increased spending may go on imported goods and services, in which case domestic firms would not increase their sales.
      Secondly, one must distinguish between *real* output and the *money value* of output (sometimes called *nominal* output). An increase in demand (for domestically produced goods and services) will lead to an increase in output. But this increase in output may simply reflect the fact that the same *volume* of goods is being sold at higher prices than before. So an increase in demand may lead to inflation – without there being an increase in real output.

1.3 A cut in taxes will increase people's disposable income, so spending will rise. *Ceteris paribus* (other things being equal) this will result in increased output (real output) and there will be more people needed to produce this larger volume of goods and services. So employment will rise and unemployment will fall.

1.4 This will reduce the demand for UK-produced goods and services which, *ceteris paribus*, will lead to a fall in output and employment.

1.5 (a) Demand will increase. So will output, *ceteris paribus*.
   (b) This is equivalent to new investment. The fact that it is financed from Japan is irrelevant, as is the fact that the investment takes place in Wales rather than England. Investment is an injection, so demand and output rise.
   (c) Consumption spending is likely to increase, so demand and output rise.
   (d) This represents a reduction in an injection, so demand falls.

(e) Pensioners spend their incomes. Demand increases.

(f) Even though the action occurs outside the UK, the demand for UK-produced goods and services will rise (bullets, helicopters, army boots, ships). This represents increased defence spending by the government – an injection into the economy.

(g) This too represents increased government spending – an injection which, *ceteris paribus*, raises the overall level of demand and output.

1.6 Natural disasters, like wars, usually lead to an increase in spending. This will be the case particularly in an advanced society where some of the damage will be covered by insurance. Lloyds of London will pay out. The effect will be to boost spending, incomes and output in the Florida economy.

Of course, if the Florida economy was heavily dependent on tourism and the hurricane put off the tourists, then the reduction in exports of services would *cut* demand in the Florida economy.

1.7 Statement (c) is correct, as is (d). Statement (b) is definitely incorrect.

1.8 It does not matter what sort of output it is; if the National Accounts statistician can measure and record it then output is output and it all contributes to GNP. By definition black-market transactions are not recorded so these are the only ones which would not constitute an increase in GNP.

Chapter 2

2.1 (a) This would tend to *reduce* the demand for houses since it would become more expensive to borrow money for house purchase.

(b) This would tend to increase the cost of building new houses. Even though new houses represent only a small fraction of houses being offered for sale at any one time, it would, *ceteris paribus*, tend to increase house prices generally. This is a cost-push mechanism.

(c) Houses in Acton are substitutes for houses in Ealing. A fall in the price of a substitute will cause some switching on the part of buyers. The demand for houses in Ealing will fall.

(d) Increased availability of money for house purchase will lead to demand-pull type inflation in house prices.

(e) This too will increase the demand for houses, leading to an increase in prices.

2.2 Statements (a) and (b) are correct.

Note the meaning of the terms deflation, reflation, and inflation. Deflation/reflation refer to a reduction/increase in *demand*. Inflation refers to an increase in *prices*.

2.3 Statements (c) and (d) are correct.

(a) is incorrect because cost increases may be absorbed by producers in the form of lower profit margins, in which case prices will not increase.

(b) An increase in wages is not synonymous with an increase in *wage costs*. The increased wages may simply reflect higher productivity in which case wage costs – that is, costs per unit of output – need not rise.

2.4 The dramatic fall in oil prices in 1986 (from about $30 a barrel to less than $20 a barrel) was caused by a glut in the oil market. That is, a shortage of demand depressed prices. In 1974 OPEC raised the price of its oil – which for the oil companies was analogous to a cost-induced price increase. Note, however, that this high price eventually – in 1986 – proved unsustainable.

2.5 The statement implies that the fall in inflation was a result of the incomes policy. This may be true but, equally, other factors such as a fall in the cost of imports or a reduction in the money supply may have contributed in part or in whole to the reduction. *Post hoc non ergo propter hoc.* (because one event follows another in time it does not mean to say that the first event caused the second event)

2.6 $(30\% \times 0.3) + (45\% \times 0.6) + (10\% \times 0.1) = 37\%$.

Chapter 3

3.1 (a) This is an increase in government spending. If we assume that other areas of public spending stay the same – part of the *ceteris paribus* assumption – then the impact on the overall level of demand in the economy will be to raise it.
   (b) This will discourage consumption so demand will fall.
   (c) Investment by firms is likely to rise as a result of this survey. This is part of the overall level of demand which therefore rises.

3.2 (a) False. *Some* of the increased demand will leak out in the form of spending on imports but most will be passed back in the form of spending on domestically produced goods, so domestic firms do benefit.
   (b) False. Some of the increased income will be saved, but most will be spent (and most of this will be on domestically produced goods). So domestic firms do benefit.
   (c) and (d)
       By definition the increase in demand means that firms can sell more. Whether firms respond by running down stocks or, alternatively, by increasing production depends on whether they believe the increase in demand is likely to be sustained. If they believe that it is likely to be permanent, then they will increase production, probably taking on more labour. They are unlikely to do so, however, if they believe the increased demand is a purely temporary phenomenon.
   (e) False. Even for higher income earners the marginal rate of deduction through income tax is significantly less than 100 per cent. So post-tax incomes will rise, and so will spending.
   (f) Maybe. It will depend *inter alia* on their assessment of the price elasticity of demand for their product which in turn will be affected by how rival firms react to a price increase.

3.3 (a) This depends on what form the expenditure took. If the £50m represented spending on *imported* American missiles then the net effect on demand will be zero. To see this, consider the national accounts identity for E (total spending on domestically produced goods and services):

$$E = C + I + G + X - M$$

If both G and M fall by £50m, the net effect on E is zero.

Alternatively, if the £50m represented spending on submarine construction in Scotland (and there was no import content), the reduction in G would cause E to fall by £50m.

(b) Consumption will rise, initially by about £50m, because students have a very high propensity to spend (because their incomes are low).

(c) The net effect here is not zero because the rich would have saved a fairly high proportion of that £50m whereas the pensioners will spend almost all of it. The net effect, therefore, is to expand Aggregate Demand.

The smallest impact on demand will be produced by (c). If all the spending on Trident represents domestic expenditure (rather than imports), then this will have the largest impact. Only if the students spend 100 per cent of their extra income will this produce as large an impact on E.

3.4 In theory, the increased flow of loanable funds will result in lower interest rates. In practice, however, interest rates tend to be determined by the Chancellor of the Exchequer or (since May 1997) by the Monetary Policy Committee of the Bank of England. They use them as an instrument for manipulating the demand for sterling on foreign exchange markets, and for influencing the level of domestic demand.

Other things being equal, a fall in interest rates will indeed encourage more investment by firms but there is no reason to suppose that the additional saving will be matched by an *exactly equal* amount of additional investment.

The requirement for equilibrium is that *total* injections will equal *total* withdrawals, that is

$$I + X + G = S + M + T$$

There is no requirement for equality between the individual 'pairs' – X and M; G and T; S and I.

3.5 (b) and (c) are both correct. Statement (b) is a piece of economists' jargon which means that investment is insensitive to changes in interest rates.

Statement (a) is probably correct but does not explain investment behaviour. Firms with funds which are surplus to requirements will lend via banks to other firms, while firms requiring funds will borrow from banks. The crucial determinant is the firms' appraisal of the likely profitability of an investment which will depend on future sales prospects.

Statement (d) is not totally incorrect, but saving is rather insensitive to interest rates, both real and nominal. Moreover, the availability of funds will not be determined solely by the level of current domestic saving – though it will be influenced by it.

3.6 (a) This does constitute investment (fixed capital formation).

(b) This does not.

    (c) For a jeweller, gold is a raw material or a stock-in-trade. So this represents investment in stocks.

    (d) This is the acquisition of a capital asset which will increase the productive potential of the salesperson. It will therefore be treated as investment.

    (e) Same car, maybe, but only companies can invest. This is consumption expenditure.

3.7 (a) If net investment is negative, this means that the total level of investment spending is insufficient to replace that part of the capital stock that has been used up in the process of production.

    (b) It occurs because investment is a very volatile magnitude, being dependent upon expectations.

3.8 (a) In period 3 investment rises from 10 per period to 40 per period. This represents replacement investment of 10 plus new investment of 30. This new investment was induced by a rise in GNP of 10. Thus the accelerator coefficient must be 3.

    (b) In period 6 GNP falls back from 130 to 127. New investment will therefore by $3 \times (-3) = -9$. However, we have to add replacement investment of $+10$ to this so that net investment is $+1$. In period 7 there is no growth in GNP so no new investment. Replacement investment of 10 will continue however.

      Note the volatility of investment over this period, particularly that which occurs when the economy enters a recession in period 6.

3.9 (a) Initially the equilibrium level of income will be increased by £10m.

    (b) A further £8m will find its way back into the economy in round two (£2m leaks out in the form of saving). In round three a further £6.4m is passed back (0.8 × £8m). Income will therefore have risen to £624.4m (600 + 10 + 8 + 6.4).

    (c) With a larger marginal propensity to spend, the induced rise in income will be larger because less leaks out. After three rounds income will rise to £627.1m (600 + 10 + 9 + 8.1).

3.10 The policies involve giving an extra £10m to (a) ordinary employees (b) pensioners, (c) highly paid employees. Pensioners have the largest MPC so this policy will have the greatest expansionary impact.

    The rich have the smallest MPC so this will have the smallest impact.

3.11 Net National Product is the figure obtained when we subtract from Gross National Product an allowance for capital consumption – a notional figure representing that part of the capital stock used up in the process of production (analogous to 'replacement investment').

3.12 (a) and (b) will not affect measured GNP in any way.

    (c) and (d) are examples of transfer payments. They do not appear in the calculation of GNP because GNP is a measure of output. Pensioners and students produce no output.

    (e) The education sector has an output – education, just as the health care sector produces an output – health care. However, since you cannot measure this output directly in money terms, statisticians are forced to measure output by the *inputs* that go into the production process. Thus since lecturers are an input, the value of that input (their salaries) is part of measured GNP.

3.13   Consumers' expenditure   116
      Gross domestic fixed capital formation   34
      Value of physical increase in stocks   3
      Government spending on goods and services   <u>38</u>
        Total Domestic Expenditure   191
      Exports   56
      Imports   (54)
        GDP at market prices   193
      Net property income from abroad   <u>1</u>
        GNP at market prices   194
      less taxes on expenditure   (30)
      plus subsidies   <u>4</u>
        GNP at factor cost   168
      less Capital consumption   (22)
        Net National Product   146

3.14   (a) £12.30   (b) 6%   (c) 4.7% $(111 - 106) - 1$
      (d) 3.6%
      The completed table will look as follows:

	1986	1987	1988	1989	1990	1991	1992	1993	1994	1995	1996
RPI (index)	79	83	88	94	100	106	111	115	117	120	123
GNP in current prices	349	424	471	516	551	576	599	631	669	704	742
GNP in constant 1990 prices	442	511	535	549	551	543	537	549	572	587	603

Start by noting that in 1990 current price and constant price estimates of GNP must both be the same. In 1991 GNP had gone up to £576bn but prices had gone up 6 per cent, so in real terms (or inflation-adjusted terms) this was worth only:

$576/1.06 = 543$ when measured at 1990 prices

That is, we are using the RPI as a deflator. The larger the figure for the RPI, the larger will be the denominator in our calculation, and hence the smaller the resulting constant-price estimate.
(e) and (f)
    Note from the table the severity of the recession in the UK in 1990-92. Real GNP in 1991 was less than that in 1990. Only in 1993 did the level of output regain the level it had reached in 1989.

3.15   (a) Current price estimates should be used.
      (b) Since what is required is the growth of *real* output, constant price estimates should be used.
      (c) Current price.
      (d) Constant price.

Chapter 4

4.1 It is a medium of exchange, a unit of account and a store of value.

4.2 (a) Cigarettes are widely used in prisons as money. They have almost all of the desirable attributes of money – scarcity, acceptability, durability, portability, and divisibility.

(b) Anyone worth his salt knows that the word salary comes from the Latin word *salarium* meaning a soldiers' salt-money.

(c) Wampum is a shortened form of the N. American Indian (Algonquian) name for beads made from shells and used as money.

　　This is nothing to do with cowrie shells. I just thought you might be interested.

(d) Cattle have been used as money from ancient times. They suffer from being distinctly non-portable, non-durable and non-divisible, however. Hence the invention of tokens which consisted of round pieces of metal with a picture of a cow stamped on them. These became the first coins.

4.3 The two main measures of the money supply are M0 and M4. M0 is narrow money which consists mostly of cash. M4 consists of cash plus all accounts at banks and building societies. See Table 4.1 for exact definitions.

4.4 The PSBR is the public sector borrowing requirement. It is approximately equal to the excess of government spending over tax revenue. It therefore represents the amount of money which the government has to borrow to finance that part of spending which is not covered by tax receipts. The National Debt is the accumulated borrowing requirement. A borrowing requirement of £10 billion implies that the National Debt will increase by a similar amount.

4.5 (a) to (e) are all ways of financing a budget deficit. An IMF loan is not. The IMF would lend *foreign currencies* to the Bank of England to assist it in maintaining a fixed exchange rate parity.

(g) 'Ernie' is an acronym for 'Electronic Random Number Indicating Equipment' – the primitive computer first used to pick the winning numbers in the monthly Premium Bond draw. These Premium Bonds are, of course, Government debt.

4.6 M is the money stock, V is the velocity of circulation, P is the price level, and T the volume of transactions. V will depend upon institutional factors and upon people's willingness to hold money. In a hyperinflation V will tend to increase.

4.7 Other things being equal, an increase in the money supply will lead to a reduction in interest rates. This will encourage investment (investment will rise) and, since investment is itself a component of aggregate demand, this too will rise. However, other things may also influence interest rates. Indeed, these are often controlled by the policy-maker (the Chancellor of the Exchequer or latterly the Bank of England). Moreover, investment will also be affected by other things that are going on in the economy – things such as the rate of growth or the expected rate of growth.

4.8 Contemporary monetarists would talk about a process such as that described in (c) whereas contemporary Keynesians would restrict their attention to a narrower range of assets – essentially the process described in (d). Statement (a) would be a 'naive' Keynesian view.

Statement (b) is incorrect. An increase in the money supply does not mean that people have more income. Income is a flow; money is a stock.

4.9 (a) The individual will reduce those holdings of assets whose value is eroded by inflation. This will include cash and, probably, bonds.

(b) The individual will expect share prices to rise and may therefore buy shares now in the hope of making a capital gain.

(c) The individual may decide to hold more money in a current account so as to avoid the possibility of having to pay bank charges if they accidentally overdraw.

4.10 The bond pays £10 per year. If market interest rates are 15 per cent then no-one would be prepared to pay £100 for such a bond since it only yields a return of 10 per cent. Therefore its market price will drop until the yield is 15 per cent.

yield (15%) = £10/x, where x = market price, so x = 10/15 = £66.67.

4.11 They are both forms of government debt sold primarily in large denominations to institutions. Bills are debt instruments which mature (i.e. have to be redeemed by the borrower) after three months. Bonds are longer term debt.

4.12 'Unmeasurable' because one cannot agree on an appropriate definition of the money supply. 'Uncontrollable' because the ability of the Central Bank to control the multiple credit creating activities of banks (and other financial institutions) is questionable.

'Irrelevant' because they argue that what is important is the *flow* of spending, not the *stock* of money.

Chapter 5

5.1 Only part of the increased employment would have come from those previously unemployed. The remainder would have come from persons newly entering the labour market (such as school leavers) or perhaps re-entering the labour market (such as housewives who had not previously registered themselves as unemployed). Empirically, it seems that (very roughly) half of the increased employment would have come from those previously registered as unemployed.

5.2 The activity rate is defined as:

$$\frac{\text{total in employment plus registered unemployed}}{\text{total population of working age}}$$

Female activity rates have shown a significant rise in the last 30 years. Male activity rates have declined. This undoubtedly reflects a change in society's attitude towards the rôle of women – and of men – within marriage and within society generally. Gender rôles have become less distinct.

5.3 The official figures are based on the 'claimant count' – the number of people in receipt of the Jobseeker's Allowance (formerly known as Unemployment

Benefit). Some individuals who are genuinely seeking work may be unwilling or unable to claim this allowance, and to this extent the official count may underestimate the true extent of involuntary unemployment. In contrast, some people may be in receipt of benefit who are not genuinely seeking work – hence the official figures may overestimate the amount of involuntary unemployment. The rules for eligibility for receipt of the Jobseeker's Allowance are stricter than those for the Unemployment Benefit which it replaced and this may be partly responsible for the reduction in recorded unemployment levels.

The ILO (International Labour Organisation) and the OECD publish estimates of unemployment based on a standardised international definition. Such estimates are published for the UK and they are higher than those based on national definitions based on the claimant count.

5.4 (a) Prisoners are neither in employment nor available for work. They are therefore economically inactive.

(b) By choice these individuals are economically inactive.

(c) Full-time students are economically inactive. Many such students take on a small amount of part-time work to supplement their income. What problems does this give rise to for the statistician trying to place individuals into categories?

(d) The fact that the individual is a part-time student is irrelevant to the classification.

(e) Since the official retirement age for men is still 65, it would appear that such an individual would be classified as economically active yet unemployed. However, changes to definitions in the 1980s removed such people from the official estimates of unemployed (hence reducing recorded unemployment).

(f) This individual is past the normal retirement age for women and therefore not part of the labour force.

(g) and (h) Such a person would be defined as economically inactive, as also would the person who cares for them.

5.5 (a) Increased disposable income will encourage additional spending. Output and employment will increase.

(b) This is a leakage. Spending on domestically produced goods and services will fall. Output and employment therefore fall.

(c) The spending of the newly employed traffic wardens will create income for others. Spending, output and employment rise.

5.6 (a) Here we must distinguish between money wages and real wages. Employees, whether unionised or not, are not always successful in securing rises in money wages which exceed the rate of increase of prices. In 1990, for example, wages rose more slowly than prices.

Statement (b) corresponds very crudely to a Keynesian view and statement (c) to a monetarist view.

5.7 They are all correct.

(a) The concept of demand deficient unemployment does not fit easily with the concept of the natural rate of unemployment. It is always possible – even at the natural rate – to reduce unemployment, albeit temporarily, by expanding demand. But the unemployment which exists at the natural rate is due to supply-side rigidities.

(b) Friedman (a monetarist) argues that, if unemployment were made less attractive, fewer people would volunteer for it.

(c) The state aid available to such an individual is likely to be considerable, probably almost as much as the income that he could earn in employment. This is the essence of the 'poverty trap' whereby means-tested benefits are lost when income from employment rises, leaving the individual no better off – and perhaps even worse off as a result of becoming employed.

5.8 The level of unemployment necessary to prevent inflation rising was higher than it had been when the relationship between unemployment and inflation was first studied in the 1960s by the so-called Phillips curve (discussed in Chapter 6).

5.9 To paraphrase, this is the difference between the supply of labour and the demand for labour at the prevailing wage rate. This is a disequilibrium situation and it represents *involuntary unemployment* (response (c)).

5.10 Construct the following table:

Number of pickers	Value of tomato output	Extra output (marginal revenue)
1	60	60
2	110	50
3	135	25
4	154	19
5	164	10
6	169	5
7	170	1
8	170	0

The farmer should hire only three pickers because the fourth costs £20 but produces only an extra £19 worth of tomatoes.

If wages rise to £26, the third picker will no longer be hired, so statements (b) and (c) are correct. The number of pickers hired will depend on how much extra output the marginal picker can produce.

(a) is correct.

(b) is incorrect. The reverse is true. Suppose the market price of tomatoes doubled. All the figures in column 3 above would therefore have to be multiplied by two since they are measured in money terms (marginal *revenue* product). If pickers could be hired for £26 per day, four pickers would be hired (since the fifth adds £26 to costs and only £20 to revenue).

(c) is incorrect.

(d) is correct.

(e) This is incorrect. The analysis assumes that all other factors of production – such as the number of glasshouses, the number of plants, the number of packing trays and so on – are all fixed.

(f) Again, this is true.

5.11 (a) Regions such as the North West of England and Northern Ireland have traditionally had higher than average unemployment rates.

Paradoxically, however, in the 1990s the 'region' with the highest unemployment rate has been Greater London, though the rest of the South East has the lowest unemployment rate in the country.

(b) Many regions have suffered an increase in unemployment as a result of the decline of industries which had hitherto been large-scale employers of labour. In the 1990s South Wales suffered as a result of the further decline of coal mining and steel making, just as a decade earlier high unemployment in the West Midlands was attributable to the decline of the car industry there.

(c) The period 1979–82 was the most severe of the post-war recessions, but a decade later another policy-induced recession brought large increases in unemployment (see question 3.14 for evidence of the severity of that recession).

5.12 (a) For much of the period Northern Ireland has the highest unemployment rate, but by the mid-1990s the unemployment rate in London is higher. than elsewhere.

(b) 1989 was a year of low unemployment everywhere so the unemployment that existed in Northern Ireland at that time is more likely to be due to regional and structural factors than to an overall deficiency of demand.

(c) East Anglia is an area of low unemployment, yet in 1993 unemployment was 8.4 per cent. As can be seen, unemployment rates in all regions rose in 1993, so demand-deficient unemployment was to blame.

(d) Any expansionary policy would reduce unemployment, but such policies might cause wage inflation to be generated in the labour markets in other regions.

Chapter 6

6.1 *Autonomous* in this context means in the absence of an excess demand for labour.

6.2 (a) A wage freeze is the easiest policy to monitor and enforce – though still extremely difficult. It is, however, extremely inflexible and in a situation where prices are rising a wage freeze effectively enforces a cut in real wages, which voters may not accept.

(b) Enforcing a freeze on prices may be even more difficult. Some exception would have to be made for unavoidable price increases such as those brought about by a rise in the cost of imports.

(c) This policy would give larger proportionate increases to those on low pay, leading to a narrowing of differentials. Policy (a) would do the opposite.

(d) 'Special allowances' open up a loop-hole through which most employees would easily pass.

(e) Ostensibly this is sensible since an increase in wages which is matched by an increase in productivity does not represent an increase in *wage costs*. However, for many groups of workers, it is impossible to measure, let alone increase, productivity.

It is argued that productivity is raised most easily in manufacturing and that the long-term application of such a policy would lead to a shift in earnings away from those in the service sector and towards those in the manufacturing sector. This may be based on a false premise, however, since certain groups in the service sector have achieved major increases in productivity over the last ten years – most notably lecturers in higher education who have doubled or trebled their output per unit of input.

6.3   (a) If firms wish to pay higher wages to attract or retain staff they will find ways of circumventing controls. Common devices would be to re-grade the employee or employees in question, or to re-define the nature of the job or to shorten the working week, enabling more hours to be paid at an overtime rate.

     (b) In a similar way *product specifications* can be changed. When the price of Mars Bars is fixed, manufacturers can reduce the size. And the specification of a Ford Mondeo GLX can change (downwards), thus masking a price increase. More subtly a new range of perhaps 30 different variants will be introduced, making it impossible to compare the price of the new model with the old one.

6.4   (a) The earnings of computer programmers are determined by market forces, as indeed are the earnings of most groups with the exception of cabinet ministers and judges who determine their own wages.

     (b) Printing workers are an example of a group who formerly received high wages. The demand for their services was highly inelastic since the actions of a few printers could stop the newspaper presses, resulting in the loss of an entire night's production with consequent loss of revenue for the employer. The print unions also restricted entry into the profession by enforcing a closed shop, rendering the supply of labour very inelastic.

        The introduction of new electronic technology meant that the specialised skills of print workers were no longer required (reduction in demand for labour) and expanded the supply of suitable operators (the supply became more elastic as more people were capable of working the new electronic equipment). The earnings of printing workers declined.

     (c) The demand for teachers is not a market demand since the number of jobs available in state schools is determined by the Department of Education, (or in Grant Maintained schools by the schools themselves). Similarly, the salary of teachers is not market determined. Teacher shortages do not, by and large, result in the increase in teachers' salaries necessary to call forth an expanded supply of suitably qualified staff. All of the factors listed, with the exception of (d), may play some role in determining teachers' wages.

     (d) The earnings which footballers receive depend upon the willingness of spectators to pay to watch them. The demand for these players is a derived demand, derived from the demand by spectators to watch football. Market forces are paramount.

6.5   It is compatible with both, though Phillips put it forward originally as evidence in support of the demand-pull theory. It is also compatible with a cost-push interpretation because the level of unemployment is correlated, it is argued, with the level of union militancy – at low levels of unemployment unions became more militant. When unions became more militant (push harder), wage inflation was higher – which is consistent with the Phillips curve evidence.

6.6 Import prices rose very rapidly in the mid-1970s as a result of the oil price increase, swamping the Phillips curve effect. By the mid-1990s imported inflation was relatively insignificant so the Phillips relationship reappeared.

6.7 They did, in the sense that there was an excess demand for goods. This could not manifest itself in higher prices, however, since prices were controlled. The effect therefore was to create shortages, queues and waiting lists – and a black market.

Chapter 7

7.1 'An increase in foreign sales of Rover cars will *increase the demand* for pounds and *leave unchanged* the supply. This will tend to make the value of the pound float up.'

7.2 (a) This represents an appreciation in the value of the pound.
  The terms devaluation/revaluation are used to refer to a step change in a nominally fixed parity whereas depreciation/appreciation refer to a market-induced fall or rise in a floating rate.
  (b) 3.5DM = £1.
  (c) At DM3.0 = £1 there would be an excess demand for £s. The Central Bank (Bank of England) would therefore sell pounds (and buy foreign currencies, adding these to its reserves).

7.3 We assume (a) that the UK exports oil, and (b) that the demand for oil is inelastic.
  Because the demand for oil is inelastic, an increase in price will lead to a less than proportionate fall in the quantity demanded. UK oil exports will therefore increase (in money terms, though in terms of quantity they will fall). An increase in UK exports leads to an increase in the demand for pounds on foreign exchange markets which can be illustrated by a rightward shift of the demand for pounds. The pound will appreciate.
  Now assume that the UK is a net importer and that the elasticity of demand is equal to unity. A ten per cent increase in price leads to a ten per cent drop in demand, so spending in sterling on imported oil remains unchanged. The supply of pounds to foreign exchange markets is unchanged.

7.4 (a) This will add to the demand for pounds and will be shown on the current account.
  (b) Ford Fiesta cars are probably imported so this will add to the supply of pounds. Current account.
  (c) To purchase these bonds, non-residents will first need to acquire sterling so there will be an increase in the demand for pounds on foreign exchange markets. This is a capital account transaction.
  (d) To answer this question, you need to make it clear what you are assuming:
    (i) in what currency are embassy staff paid?
    (ii) what do they do with the money when they get it?

If they are paid in sterling and they send their salaries home to the UK then there is no foreign exchange market transaction involved. If, however, they convert part of their sterling income into marks for spending in Germany then this will add to the supply of pounds on foreign exchange markets.

7.5   Only (d) is correct.

7.6   Cars sold in France yield an income of £13 000 (that is 117 000 Fr divided by 9), so it is more profitable to sell in France. If the £ appreciates, exporting becomes less profitable.

7.7   (a) Raising interest rates will discourage consumers from purchasing goods on credit. Some of these goods would have been imports. This reduction in imports will improve the trade balance.

           There will also be a capital account effect (an increased demand for UK bonds) but this is not the Trade account and so is not strictly relevant to the question.

     (b) The NIC is equivalent to a tax on incomes. A tax cut will increase disposable income. Spending – including spending on imports – will increase and the trade deficit will worsen.

     (c) Students will spend part of their higher incomes on imports, worsening the trade deficit.

     (d) This will encourage invisible exports of tourism. The trade balance will improve.

     (e) This will discourage UK residents from converting sterling into other currencies, either as tourists or for other purposes. It will improve the trade balance. Note, however, that there have been no restrictions on sterling convertibility since 1979.

7.8   (a) The trade balance is a deficit of 10.

     (b) The plus sign on IPD implies that the flow of interest, profits and dividends into the UK was larger than the corresponding outward flow.

     (c) A deficit of 5 (since IPD is included in the current account but not in the trade account).

     (d) There is a surplus of 2 on the capital account (acquisitions of UK assets by foreigners exceeded acquisitions of foreign assets by UK residents).

     (e) Total credits = 180 but total debits = 183. Therefore the central bank would have to add to the demand for the currency (buy 3). The foreign exchange reserves would have fallen as a result.

7.9   (a) British exporters will benefit from the stronger pound. Untrue. It will be bad for exporters.

     (b) German companies selling in Britain will suffer as a result of the fall in the value of the mark. Untrue. They will benefit from it.

     (c) If British exporters increase their foreign currency prices in line with the rise in the value of sterling, then export receipts will fall. Maybe. It depends on the elasticity of demand for UK exports.

     (d) The demand for British exports is likely to be more price-sensitive in the longer run so that exporters who increase their prices in line with the rise in sterling will experience a fall in their export revenues. Probably true.

Chapter 8

8.1 Only (b) and (d) are correct.

The amount of foreign currency we earn from exporting will stay the same, hence (a) is incorrect. Our exports do become more competitive and volume does increase (by 10 per cent) but value – our foreign currency earnings – stays the same.

8.2 (c) is correct because a given amount of foreign currency is now worth more in terms of sterling. Since exporting is now more profitable, the UK producer may concentrate his efforts on overseas sales and thus sell more – so (b) might also result.

8.3 Suppose one barrel is produced and the world price of oil is $30 per barrel. At an exchange rate of £1 = $2 the sterling value of this oil will be £15 ($30 ÷ 2) so PRT will be levied on this amount. If sterling were to appreciate to £1 = $3 (choosing easy numbers for simplicity) the oil will now be worth only £10 ($30 ÷ 3). So revenue from PRT will go down.

8.4 Here we have three bilateral exchange rates which must of course be consistent.

	Initially		Now	
	£1 = $2			£1 = $2
	£1 = DM4			?
	$2 = DM4			$2 = DM3

If the DM rises *vis à vis* the dollar (to $2 = DM3) but the sterling-dollar rate remains unchanged the German tourist should use her marks to buy dollars first and then use those to buy sterling. She can buy £1 with two dollars which will cost her only three DMs – rather than four, as it would do if the sterling-DM rate remained unchanged. Foreign exchange dealers – and anybody else for that matter – can therefore make profits in this situation. Nobody in their right mind will buy sterling using DMs (because they will have to pay 4 per £ rather than 3 as they would do if they went via dollars). Since nobody is buying £s for DM the value of the pound *vis à vis* the mark will continue to fall until these profit possibilities have been eliminated (which will be at a rate of DM3 = £1). This process is known as arbitrage.

8.5 (a) Incorrect. The pound fell in comparison with the yen, dollar, franc and DM but rose against the lira.

(b) Correct.

(c) Incorrect.

(d), (e) and (f) may be correct, but we are not given sufficient information here. If costs have remained constant in all the economies – or risen at the same rate – then a fall in the exchange rate *does* represent an improvement in competitiveness. It is unlikely, however, that the rate of increase in costs has been the same in all these countries.

8.6 (a) Correct. The non-resident is not concerned with the domestic rate of inflation in the UK. So (b) is therefore incorrect.

(c) Correct. Because the non-resident will have to convert his sterling interest receipts into his own currency at some future date.

(d) Incorrect. The non-resident is not concerned with the domestic rate of inflation in the UK.

Chapter 9

9.1   If a country has a balance of payments deficit, there will be an excess supply of its currency on world markets. Hence that currency is available to be held as a reserve asset by central banks or simply to be held by the private sector. In contrast, Germany and Japan have normally had balance of trade (and balance of payments) surpluses – hence there was already an excess demand for these currencies and they were not available to be held as reserve assets by other central banks. If other central banks had purchased them the excess demand would have been even higher.

9.2   The word *fiduciary* means 'based on faith' – that is, not backed by anything. In the modern world all currencies are fiduciary, since they are not backed by gold or other precious metals. Hence the dollar is a fiduciary currency. Neither gold nor SDRs are currencies, strictly speaking. The SDR is, however, fiduciary in the sense that it is not 'backed' by anything, other than the international agreement of the members of the IMF.

9.3   The ECU is a unit of account and not a currency. The same applies to the SDR.

Chapter 10

10.1 The price of each of these three things will be influenced by demand pressures and supply pressures. However, we might expect that sellers of minerals, ores and metals would have less influence over prices than they would over the prices for food in the developed world or over the price of manufactures, and that therefore prices for minerals and metals would be more volatile than for these other things. In general, this is borne out by the data. Note, in particular, the rapid rise in commodity prices in 1988, followed by a gradual decline until 1993.

10.2 The distinction between tradeables and non-tradeables is conceptual rather than operational. Houses (and land) would appear to be non-tradeable, but what if British people buy holiday homes in France? Similarly, haircuts are an example of a local service and would therefore be classified as non-tradeable. However, it is possible for a rich London lady to travel to France to have her hair styled by a Parisian coiffeur, in which case this becomes a tradeable service. Take-away fast food like hamburgers are non-tradeable. You have to eat them at the point of sale. Holidays in the UK can be sold to foreigners – hence are tradeable. Clothes similarly are tradeable.

10.3 In theory, inflation in the tradeables sector will spread like a ripple throughout the rest of the economy. The workings of the labour market are an important part of this process. Workers are attracted to the tradeables sector by higher wages there. This causes labour shortages in the non-tradeables sector, and the excess demand for labour pushes up wages in that sector.

Chapter 11

11.1 It refers to an increase in Gross Product so statement (e) is correct. Advanced economies tend to have relatively stable population levels so an increase in Gross Product is equivalent to an increase in the standard of living. In many developing countries, however, the growth of population is quite rapid. The standard of living of the average citizen will rise only if the growth of Gross Product exceeds the growth of population. It may therefore make more sense to equate 'economic growth' with an increase in GDP per capita (response (b)).

11.2 (a) is correct.

(b) In terms of the national accounts identity:

$$C + I + G + X - M = E = Y$$

an increase in I will, *ceteris paribus*, increase E (spending on domestically produced goods and services) and therefore increase Y (the output of these goods and services). Therefore, if economic growth is defined as an increase in output the statement must be true, but only within a strict *ceteris paribus* sense.

(c) In terms of the national accounts identity increased investment is clearly not necessary – an increase in output can occur without it. There are, moreover, examples of labour-rich countries such as China achieving large increases in output without vast amounts of fixed capital formation. However, empirically, investment and growth do tend to be correlated.

11.3 An increase in UK interest rates will encourage people to 'invest' in financial assets such as bonds which will now be yielding a higher rate of return. Some of these people will be foreigners (i.e. non-residents) who have been attracted by the high interest rates in the UK. This portfolio investment should not, of course, be treated as investment in a macroeconomic sense – indeed, the word 'saving' may be more appropriate.

High interest rates will discourage companies from embarking on fixed capital formation such as the installation of new machines since the increased cost of finance will reduce the profitability of that investment. That is, direct investment will fall.

11.4 If production levels remain unchanged, the fall in sales will lead to a build-up of stocks of finished goods. In a sense firms are 'investing' in these stocks though they do so involuntarily. The fall in demand will engender pessimistic expectations of future sales, so firms are likely to delay or abandon any plans for increasing capacity. That is, they will cut their investment.

11.5 (a) This statement is wrong. It implies that there is insufficient demand, but the question talks about an increase in demand.

(b) is possible, as is (d).

(c) however, is incorrect.

11.6 (a) bicycles, wheat.

(b) local policing services, roads.

(c) the services of London Transport? (though foreign tourists also use it).

(d) By definition, something which cannot be sold (i.e. is non-marketable) cannot be sold overseas.

11.7 (a) Local Authority Sports Facilities.
NHS dental care (!)
   (b) All the charitable organisations such as Help the Aged or the NSPCA fall into this category. They are non-governmental organisations and hence, strictly speaking, in the private sector. They are not, however, commercial organisations in that they do not seek to maximise profits.

11.8 Crowding-out implies that the government spending multiplier is not greater than one. Increased public spending does not raise equilibrium output.

Chapter 12

12.1 No. Not even approximately correct, because the figures do not take account of the size of the population.

12.2 In 1995 the Czech Republic became a member of the OECD, and started producing national accounts according to the standardised system used by the OECD countries. Hungary and Poland joined in 1996. Russia, which has not yet joined, still produces accounts based on the concept of material product (that is, excluding services).

12.3 The scarcer a resource becomes, the higher the price of that resource. Suppose the price of hardwood went up. Products which contained hardwood would also rise in price and consumers would therefore reduce their consumption of such products, preferring instead to buy products which used a different material to perform the same function – materials such as plastic, aluminium and so on. This would tend to reduce the demand for hardwood. In addition, this substitution in consumption would be reinforced by substitution in production. Manufacturers would switch to other materials, motivated by the desire to keep costs down and hence sell at lower prices, to secure a bigger market share than their rivals.

12.4 Within the economy itself the supply of positional goods is fixed, regardless of the rate of growth. A high growth economy may be able to import positional goods from abroad, however.

Chapter 13

13.1 (a) The public sector had a surplus of £6.8 bn.
   (b) The overseas sector had a surplus of £19.1 bn.
   (c) The current account was in deficit by this amount (similarly in 1989 it was in deficit by £19.1 bn)

13.2 (a) correct.
   (b) not necessarily.
   (c) correct. This represents a net injection.
   (d) not necessarily. This is the crowding-out hypothesis which, as we saw, is not supported by the evidence.
   (e) not necessarily. It depends on the rate of growth of each of them.

13.3 (b) and (c) are correct.

Chapter 14

14.1 Only (b) is correct. The key phrase is that *on average* their expectations are correct.

14.2 (a) If tax revenue increases proportionately with the tax rate there is no apparent disincentive effect. But, if revenue increases less than proportionately to the increase in tax rates, this is evidence of a disincentive effect, so it is claimed. So (a) is correct.
　　(b) This would only be correct if the economy were being operated beyond point B in the diagram.
　　(c) Up to point B in the diagram this is true.

14.3 Income tax and Capital Gains tax are direct taxes. VAT and vehicle excise duty are indirect. The Council Tax is also an indirect tax.

14.4 Indirect taxes are the most regressive – the top 20 per cent of income earners pay a smaller proportion of their income in indirect taxes than the bottom 20 per cent.
　　As might be expected, cash benefits are the most progressive measure.

14.5 (a) Other things being equal, this is true. So (c) is true as well.
　　(b) This statement is equivalent to saying that the economy is already operating on the downward sloping part of the Laffer curve and, as we have seen, this is unsupported by any evidence.
　　(c) People are probably more aware of taxes on income than they are of sales taxes and some may resent paying them. It does not follow that they shouldn't pay them, however.

Chapter 15

15.1 (a) indirect tax rates. Exogenous instrument.
　　(b) revenue from direct taxes. Endogenous(depends on the level of income).
　　(c) the exchange rate. It depends. If the authorities are trying to operate a fixed exchange rate policy (as was the case up until 1992) then it should be regarded as an exogenous instrument. If the exchange rate is floating then it is an endogenous variable.
　　(d) the price index. Endogenous target.
　　(e) import prices. It depends in what currency they are being measured – foreign currency or sterling. If they are measured in foreign currency then they are exogenous. If they are measured in sterling then again it depends what sort of exchange rate policy is being pursued. If a fixed rate, then import prices in sterling are exogenous (since exogenous × exogenous = exogenous). But if the exchange rate is floating then import prices in sterling will have to be treated as endogenous (since exogenous × exogenous = exogenous).
　　(f) world trade. Exogenous.
　　(g) interest rates. An exogenous instrument – though according to some accounts it is determined in the money market by 'market forces' and hence should be regarded as endogenous.
　　(h) government spending. Exogenous.

(i) the labour supply. Exogenous. But the activity rate depends on what is happening in the economy, so in that sense it is endogenous.

(j) the money supply. It is an exogenous instrument if the monetary authorities can control it (there is some disagreement about how good they are at controlling it).

T his is a brief guide to those statistical sources which you will find most useful. Not all of them will of course be available in the library that you use, but some such as *Social Trends* and the *Monthly Digest* are usually available even in small public libraries.

Statistical sources can be divided into three types:

- Those relating to the UK only, most of which are published by the Office of National Statistics (ONS), formerly the Central Statistical Office (CSO).
- Statistics relating to European Union countries. These are the various Eurostat publications which come from the Statistical Office of the European Communities.
- International statistics covering not only the UK and Europe but also the rest of the world. These are published by the OECD (the Organisation for Economic Cooperation and Development) or by the IMF (the International Monetary Fund).

They are listed below in that order.

UK National Accounts (formerly known as *National Income and Expenditure*) but more normally referred to simply as the **Blue Book**. Published annually in August by the ONS it is the most important source of data for the UK economy. Most of the data presented are annual and the tables usually cover a twenty-year period. As with all ONS publications, recent editions have become more user-friendly.

UK Balance of Payments (known as the **Pink Book**). The sister publication to the Blue Book. Published at the same time as the Blue Book by the ONS.

Economic Trends is published monthly by the ONS. Most of the data are quarterly extending back over, perhaps, five years. It covers a range of areas including output, prices, employment and trade. The **Economic Trends Annual Supplement** is particularly useful for obtaining long series of both annual and quarterly data, some series going back to 1945.

Regional Trends is published annually by the ONS. It includes economic and social indicators, broken down by the various regions of the UK.

Social Trends, published annually by the ONS, is more like a 'coffee-table book'. It uses statistics to 'tell a story' about how people's lives in Britain are changing. *Social Trends* can genuinely be described as 'a good read'.

Annual Abstract of Statistics An amalgam of topics are covered. Annual data.

Monthly Digest of Statistics As the name implies, an amalgam of statistics published monthly. It covers a wide range of topics, including economic, social and demographic.

General Household Survey
Family Expenditure Survey The results of a sample survey of households are published annually in the GHS and FES. Economic and demographic aspects are covered.

Key Data A variety of official sources are drawn on for this compilation published annually by the ONS.

Employment Gazette A monthly publication covering labour market issues. Detailed information on wage rates, productivity, hours worked and so on for various sectors of the economy. It also includes articles about the labour market. It formerly contained information relating to the Retail Price Index (and other indices) but this is now contained in *Business Monitor* (see below).

Business Monitor MM23 The responsibility for the compilation of price indices has been removed from the Department of Employment and now rests with the ONS. Hence, this Business Monitor is now the source of detailed information on prices.

Financial Statistics Monthly publication of the ONS relating to financial indices such as interest rates, exchange rates and the money supply.

Bank of England Quarterly Bulletin Published by the Economics Division of the Bank of England, containing a number of articles and statistics about the money supply and the financial sector.

National Institute Economic Review Unlike all of the above this is *not* an official government publication. However, it does contain a statistical appendix which is a very useful compilation of UK and international data on a wide range of economic issues. Published quarterly by the National Institute of Economic and Social Research.

Eurostat Published monthly by the Statistical Office of the European Union this contains comparative data on various aspects of EU countries. There are also annual publications under the Eurostat heading covering specific issues.

OECD Main Economic Indicators Published monthly by the Organisation for Economic Cooperation and Development containing annual and quarterly data on OECD countries. Very useful for purposes of comparison. Some of the former Soviet bloc countries, such as the Czech Republic, are now members of the OECD.

International Financial Statistics Published monthly by the IMF, it covers a larger number of countries than *OECD Main Economic Indicators*. Statistics relating to all member countries of the International Monetary Fund (IMF) are included. The data are annual, quarterly and monthly where appropriate. The **IFS Yearbook**, published annually, has annual data going back over a longer period.

Index